m7/2

THE GENDER GAMES

ALSO BY JUNO DAWSON

Hollow Pike
Cruel Summer
Say Her Name
Under My Skin
All of the Above
Margot and Me
Being a Boy
Mind Your Head
This Book is Gay

Juno Dawson

THE GENDER GAMES

THE PROBLEM WITH MEN AND WOMEN... FROM SOMEONE WHO HAS BEEN BOTH

TWO
ROADS

www.tworoadsbooks.com

Some names, places and identifying features have been
changed in order to preserve anonymity.

First published in Great Britain in 2017 by Two Roads
An imprint of John Murray Press
An Hachette UK company

1

Copyright © 2017 Juno Dawson

The right of Juno Dawson to be identified as the
Author of the Work has been asserted by her in accordance
with the Copyright, Designs and Patents Act 1988.

A CIP catalogue record for this title is available from the British Library

Hardback ISBN 978-1-473-64858-6
Trade Paperback ISBN 978-1-473-64859-3
Ebook ISBN 978-1-473-64861-6
Audio Digital Download ISBN 978-1-473-66982-6

Typeset in Sabon MT and Avenir by
Palimpsest Book Production Ltd, Falkirk, Stirlingshire

Printed and bound by Clays Ltd, St Ives plc

Hodder & Stoughton policy is to use papers that are natural,
renewable and recyclable products and made from wood grown in
sustainable forests. The logging and manufacturing processes are expected
to conform to the environmental regulations of the country of origin.

Hodder & Stoughton Ltd
Carmelite House
50 Victoria Embankment
London EC4Y 0DZ

www.hodder.co.uk

To Charley

CONTENTS

PROLOGUE

It was a balmy, sticky night in mid-July, the type of weather Yorkshire calls 'close'. On the corner of Heath Street, the back door of the end terrace was wide open, to entice what little breeze there was across the concrete yard and into the narrow kitchen.

As Angela was washing up at the sink, quite without warning, a kitchen cabinet came detached from the wall and crashed to the floor. Plates and cups and glasses smashed and clattered over the lino. Ian – a man with a fashionable handlebar moustache – pelted in from the lounge to investigate the commotion and ensure his heavily pregnant wife was unhurt.

She was fine, but as she was cleaning up the mess, Angela realised she'd gone into labour. Her baby, the couple's first, wasn't due for another three and half weeks. The young couple rushed to Ian's Ford Escort and sped to Bradford Royal Infirmary.

The labour was relatively quick. In three short hours, a baby was placed in its mother's arms. The midwife, a red-faced woman with a sturdy Yorkshire bosom, took a cursory glance between the baby's legs and said,

'Congratulations, Mr and Mrs Dawson. You have a healthy baby boy.'

And that was where it all went wrong.

1.

THIRTY YEARS LATER . . .

AKA The Twist

~~Once upon a time there was a little girl.~~

No.

~~Once upon a time there was a little boy.~~

Also no. Any creative writing teacher worth their salt will tell you that a great story never starts at the beginning, it starts when something *changes*. On 6 August 2015, I told my mother that I was a woman.

Her reply was, 'Well, I can't say I'm surprised.'

It would be lovely if the story *did* start with 'Once upon a time there was a little girl . . .', but while that should have been the case, it wasn't nearly so simple. You see, to the rest of the world, Juno Dawson was born a boy. She looked like a boy, she had a boy's name, she had a boy's body.

But she was *never* a boy.

The problem was that maternity ward introduction to Gender. Gender, like so many imaginary friends, lied to me about the world. I was a child, so I believed him. For many, many years he was to feed me lies. He told me the world was made up of two types of people – men and women – and that these two distinct, dissonant groups, their sex set in stone, behaved, thought, dressed, *existed* in certain ways.

Gender, long before my arrival, had whispered the same story into the ears of my parents, my peers, my teachers, society and the media. Like Maleficent at Aurora's christening, he materialises at every birth, without invitation, and bestows his curse. He's silver-tongued, and has an admirable, global work ethic. His stories have been shared and recycled so often that, for most, they have become fact.

That is why *my* story – my change, my 'turning point' – began some thirty years after that baby was born.

Gender and I were *always* heading for a showdown. It was only a matter of time, and it's a battle not yet won.

Back to 6 August 2015. The day it all changed. Telling my mother I'm transgender was the hardest thing I've *ever* done. Harder than living through a divorce as a child; harder than being mugged for a *Buffy* VHS boxset outside Virgin Megastore in Bradford; harder than being a queer teenager in rural Yorkshire; harder than being a teacher in an Ofsted failing school; harder than getting my first novel published; harder than being unceremoniously dumped by the love of my life. Yes, even harder than telling Mum I was a gay man more than ten years earlier. That was, I know now, a personal misdiagnosis, for which the catalyst was what Gender had told me.

I struggled home to Bradford, navigating the London Underground with a wonky wheelie suitcase and my Chihuahua, Prince, with the sole purpose of telling her. I couldn't not. By that date, I'd reached deadlock – definitely a woman, always should have been a woman – and my transition couldn't properly start unless she knew.

I *wanted* her to be OK with it. But had she not been,

there's precisely nothing I could have done about it. I *needed* to transition. About a year earlier, I'd sought the advice of *Boy Meets Girl* actor Rebecca Root after we'd done a panel event together at the Australian Literary Festival at King's College, London. She had told me, 'I always say, if you can survive without transitioning, don't transition.' I'm starting to understand what she meant by that – it's not something to enter into lightly.

Wants and needs are different.

It was with heavy, sad feet that I boarded the Leeds train, knowing – or rather fearing – it could be the last pilgrimage I made.

You see, 'coming out' as LGBTQ comes with a profound fear of rejection. Yeah, we have our Ellens and Caitlyns and Eltons, but they all have their mothers and we have ours. My mum doesn't give two shits about Tom Daley, she cares about me and, as far as she was concerned, she had one son and one daughter. Not her fault, Gender's. One of Gender's most common refrains is that 'if it looks like a boy and it sounds like a boy, it's a boy.'

Peterborough, Grantham, Stevenage, Warrington Bank Quay, Wakefield Westgate and home. Two hours, twenty minutes.

The ideal scenario would have been hazy and soft-focused. She would embrace me and say, 'James, we've always known, but you know that whatever choices you make, we support and love you. It's what's on the inside that counts.' In that version of events, my mother would be portrayed by Susan Kennedy from *Neighbours* or Connie Britton's character in *Nashville*. I didn't know what my real mum's reaction would be, but I knew it wouldn't be that. We are not that kind of family.

Coming out as a gay man was a slow process for me. It was cowardly, but I let her work it out for herself, gradually distancing myself from her until it was down to her to reel me back in, like a fish on a hook. She initiated the final 'coming out' conversation as we took a stroll on Brighton seafront in the summer of 2004. I still remember the harbour boat sails chinking in the breeze as we walked over the pebbles. At the time, I sported a 'fashion mullet', with a blond stripe in both the front and back. For a visual, you may wish to google an image of the boyband Phixx. It was very on-trend, I assure you. If you want a visual of my mother, imagine me but much shorter and with a blonde bob. She's quite glamorous for a grandmother-of-two and certainly doesn't look like she's in her sixties.

My mum *really* likes a plan, and she wanted to know what our plans for the evening were. 'Well,' I said, 'we've got a restaurant booked for seven.'

'What about after that?'

I hadn't thought that far ahead, but my grandparents were back at the hotel and I guess you have to have contingencies in place. 'I don't know. Maybe we could get a drink.'

'Where?'

I despair. 'A pub?' Brighton has enough pubs to visit a different one every day of the year. They all serve the same drinks.

'What about that one we drove past by the pier?'

Ah. Now that pub had to be either R-Bar or Charles Street. 'Oh, that's a gay bar,' I told her.

Without skipping a beat, she said, 'Well, that's your life and we're fine with it.' No more was said.

But she assumed that was the end of it, as had I at the time. Not so. The irony was that, since that day by the seaside, our relationship had been stronger than ever. Fast forwarding to 2015, it seemed sad that I would now jeopardise everything we'd worked so hard for.

I decided to do it on the Saturday morning. I couldn't spend all weekend with it hanging over me like Damocles's sword. Mum was getting ready in her bedroom, putting on her make-up. It reminded me of watching her get ready on a Friday night in the 80s: the smell of nail polish, Elnett and Tendre Poison. Even back then, I would watch in awe, *Dynasty* on in the background, as she applied her make-up: sharpening her eyebrow pencil with a razorblade, blowing her pink fingernails to dry them. I was quietly learning, even then.

'Can we have a serious talk?' I asked her. In my family, we do not have serious talks. We talk about the weather and *Strictly Come Dancing*. Her face fell, presumably because she thought I'd gone and become HIV positive.

I began: 'For the last year I've been seeing a therapist about my gender.' Then babble mode kicked in. She didn't say anything, so I went into maximum overdrive. I honestly can't remember the exact speech, but it definitely mentioned that the time for talking was done and it was time to start doing. I told her that I was 70 per cent excited, 10 per cent scared and 20 per cent overwhelmed by how much there is to do.

(There is so much to do.)

My voice wobbled and quivered, wafer thin. Her eyes glazed over with tears but they did not fall. I told her that it'd be a slow process, that I was on a waiting list and hadn't even started my hormone therapy yet – the oestrogen that would *medically* turn me from James into Juno.

I was actually dying to get going. Now that I knew what I wanted and who I was supposed to be, the change couldn't come fast enough, but I also appreciated that I had to give my family warning and that the process is glacially slow. At that point, I had told only a handful of trusted friends and my publisher.

With a world-weary sigh, Mum told me how she so keenly remembered the younger me, the one who had not yet learned it was best to hide such quirks, pleading for dolls and dresses in the aisles of shops. All those years ago, she'd worried in silence, trying as best as she could to shield such behaviour from my father. When we agreed I was gay, her queries had been resolved. I had thought so too.

Typically of my family, there were no histrionics, no wailing, no screaming, no command to 'get out and never come back'. Only a quiet bedroom in a sunny, semi-detached home. I relaxed a little. I'd done it. I'd told her.

Her second concern: 'What will you do about relation-ships?' I swear I have Bridget Jones's mother sometimes. A perfectly valid worry nonetheless, and one I shared. I guess it's natural for parents to want to see their children settled, finished in bow-wrapped happy-ever-afters. It's ironic, as my mother never remarried after her divorce and seems quite satisfied in her singledom. Nevertheless, she wants me married off. I want me married off, but I want to marry as myself, the real me. In a gown and veil (or, preferably, a replica of Jennifer Connelly's ball gown in *Labyrinth*).

'To be honest,' I told her, 'my future relationships couldn't possibly be any more dysfunctional than the ones I've already had.' Even she had to smile at that. By this point I was lying face down on her bed with the dog sat in the curve of my spine. Deeply uncomfortable for me, but it seemed a shame to disturb him.

My love life and sexuality is something that continues to bewilder even my friends. *So are you a straight woman now?* I guess so, although a lot of people think I am neither of those things.

Mum then said, eyes now dry, that she hoped it would make me happy, although she wasn't sure it would. She said she thought I was making my life harder. Unnecessarily hard.

Two things as an aside: life was not always easy as a gay man. I *suspect* we'll talk about PRIVILEGE some more later, but regardless, as a gay man I've been spat at, bullied, discriminated against and mocked. These things weren't fun, but I haven't half developed a thick hide. Second, I don't think this step is a magic wand. Transitioning is not going to mystically solve all the worries in my life. I will still be skint. I will still get lonely sometimes. I will still be driven and overambitious. I'll still be jealous and competitive.

But I will be a woman.

I will be Juno.

I will be righted.

I will be me.

After we'd finished talking, we went into Leeds city centre to do some shopping and get something to eat. In Nando's, some monster hadn't screwed the lid onto a bottle of tomato ketchup. I accidentally shook the bottle over my head and that of the woman sat behind us. It looked like the prom scene in *Carrie* and Mum had to literally run to Topshop to buy me new clothes while I sponged myself off in the toilet. I was cotton-budding sauce out of my ear for days afterwards. I like to think that, in years to come, that's the bit of the day Mum will remember.

And so the story truly began. That was it. There was nothing left to stop me. I could become the woman I was always supposed to be. I didn't for one second think it was going to be easy, and I was so, so right.

2.

EVERYTHING YOU'VE BEEN TOLD IS A LIE

AKA The Mission Statement

I was a sickly baby. After my birth, I had to spend time in an incubator, but Gender soon followed me and my parents back to the house in Heath Street.

Gender is in every childhood photograph in the album. He's in the swords, guns and toy soldiers I opened on Christmas morning. He's in the colour of the clothes and shoes I wore. He's in the cub scout uniform, haircuts, pencil case and Mickey Mouse birthday cake.

He's in every last snapshot hiding in plain sight.

Before we get into the complicated, life-long relationship Gender and I have had, we need to break it down a little and define some terms, or the rest of this book isn't going to make a lot of sense. *Here comes the science part, so concentrate!*

SEX

If you believe the Bible and the Qur'an, God created man and woman – Adam and Eve (from one of Adam's spare ribs) – on the sixth day, and was so wowed by his creation that he took the next day off. If you favour science, humans

(and indeed all mammals) are divided into two sexes char-
acterised by XY (male) or XX (female) chromosomes.

This is 'sex'.

Sex determines sexual reproduction. Males produce male
gametes. In the case of human males, this means sperm-
atozoa (a middle name I briefly considered). Females produce
eggs. In humans, 'sex' usually refers to five characteristics.

1. The presence of an XX or XY chromosome.
2. Gonads (ovaries or testicles).
3. The prevalence and levels of sex hormones – oestrogen
   and testosterone.
4. Internal reproductive anatomy (i.e. uterus, prostate).
5. External genitalia (penis, scrotum or labia, clitoris).

Everything else we think of as 'sex' – body hair, size,
strength – is actually sexual dimorphism. Humans are *not*
the most striking example of sexual dimorphism in the
natural world. Some birds, insects and mammals have
marked and dramatic differences in appearance and physi-
ology between the sexes. In humans, males *tend* to be taller
and heavier, and have greater lung capacity. Anything else
is up for discussion, and the cause of much research and
controversy.*

Around 1 per cent of live births, depending on which

---

* Indeed, over a hundred years after Victorian scientists deemed women
inferior for their smaller skulls, it's thought females may actually
possess slightly more grey matter than males (Marner, Nyengaard,
Tang & Pakkenberg, 2003).

study you read, are in *some way* sexually ambiguous, intersex or – to use an outmoded term – hermaphroditic. Approximately 0.2 per cent of the population receive some form of medical intervention for this reason.* Such 'ambiguity' covers a multitude of variations, from physical 'abnormality' to genetic variations of XX and XY. So, even when it comes to *sex*, it's not *nearly* as simple as XX or XY.

Science and religion are not necessarily *lies*, but they are both widely open to interpretation. Science and religion offer us *nothing* in the way of gender.

Gender is not sex.

Gender is something else.

If that's all anyone takes away from this book, I've won.

Gender, as convincing as he is, is full of shit.

If you take *that* away from this book, even better.

GENDER

Gender, despite anything he might tell us to the contrary, is nothing but **characteristics *we* have *assigned* to the sexes.** Like a group of horny teenagers with a Ouija board, Gender was summoned into being by *us*. Gender has nothing to do with the five sex characteristics listed above. He is neither science nor God.

Let's unpack the sentence in bold.

We: Me, you, 'society', religion, doctors, the media, teachers, language, culture, your parents.

* Fausto-Sterling, 2000

Assign: Over time, what 'We' have attached to each gender has shifted, evolved and, frankly, flip-reversed so many times it's impossible to keep up. Some gender traits are more inflexible, but most are a question of taste, opinion and fashion.

Even the World Health Organization (WHO) defines gender as 'the result of **socially constructed** ideas about the behaviour, actions, and roles a particular sex performs.' Social constructions are key, as where you are, and the culture you grew up in, will set the norms for gender expectations. For example, some cultures have gone beyond two distinct notions of male and female – the hijra of Pakistan, Bangladesh and India; the kathoeys of Thailand; the māhū of Hawaii; the Native American notion of 'two spirit' people; the fa'afaine of Polynesia. Wherever you are in the world, there will be slightly (or sometimes hugely) different traits associated with gender binaries (man vs woman). Sometimes there are subtle differences; one person's 'man bun' is a Sikh man's rishi knot. Sometimes the differences are profound; in modern-day Kenya there is thought to be at least one matriarchal tribe consisting of only women.

Even the words 'man' and 'woman' move us away from sex and into gender ('man', initially, was a gender-neutral word until after the Norman conquest – see? Shit changes).

In any given place, in any given time, gender will have an impact on little things – clothes, hair, make-up – but also the biggies: rights, liberties, resources, access to healthcare. Ultimately, power. And in any given place, in any given time, society has *tended* to favour men.*

---

* Well, except that one tribe in Kenya, I guess.

Where gender gets interesting (and a lot more complex) is when we consider gender as an identity. If gender is a construct, a person identifying as 'man' or 'woman' is, in fact, aligning themselves with a fiction. Sex is sex – although as I am testament to, nothing is set in stone – but everything else regarding gender shifts like quicksand. **What it *means* to be a man or a woman, our perception of masculinity and femininity, is constantly in flux.**

It's worth saying that, for the purposes of this book, I've decided to use 'male' and 'female' to refer to biological sex and 'man' and 'woman' to refer to gender identity. Does that make sense? I choose *not* to wrap myself up in linguistic knots regarding labels. I know they are a sore spot for a lot of academics, transgender people, feminists and Twitter warriors, but this book would be a hot mess if I had to redefine male, female, man and woman every time they crop up.

Gender is the bogeyman under *all* our beds. Gender's constant demands and expectations are tedious, exhausting and downright dangerous. Men, stereotypically, are expected to be strong (physically and emotionally), to provide financially for a family, to be sexually capable and prolific. Women are expected to be sweet, caring, docile, compliant, sexually pristine figures. Dig a little deeper and we *also* expect modern men and women to be the polar opposites of all these things, creating a schism in what is considered acceptable.

With so much baggage attached to each end of the gender spectrum, it's no wonder some people are now calling bullshit to both 'man' and 'woman' and opting for 'gender-fluid', 'genderqueer', or 'non-binary'.*

Some people find it hard to see beyond sex. Believe me, I know. Some people, even some seemingly intelligent people, believe you should behave a certain way according to your sex. Attitudes linking sex and gender are very, very entrenched. Personally, I think it would be *awful* if about 50 per cent of the world behaved identically and so did the other 50 per cent. Surely no one really thinks that ALL women act and think a certain way and ALL men another?

Sex can change too. If we look at those five characteristics of sex, I'm in the process of adapting at least three. I sometimes wonder if people are so wary of transgender progress because we highlight how something we often consider carved in stone can be so easily manipulated. Indeed, non-trans (cisgender) people take the contraceptive pill, undergo hormone replacement therapy, are castrated in accidents, are circumcised and all manner of other things that in some way alter their 'sex' characteristics.

I am changing some elements of my sex because I feel much more attuned to the female *gender*. Perhaps this is folly when we've already agreed the things I'm buying into are a moveable feast, but it does feel right. The times we live in *are* gendered (whether I like it or not) and one of the genders (woman) feels to fit me much more than the binary alternative.

In a world without socially defined gender rules, maybe no one would need to transition, but I confess that I also

* There's a glossary at the back of the book.

want my body to possess female characteristics. I can't go back in time through a wormhole and be *born* female, but I want to get as close as I possibly can. This is how I have always felt. If life wasn't a motherfucker, I'd have been 'born that way'.

If you like, you may call *me* a 'transsexual' because (dictionary definition) I am changing *sex*, as of mid-2016. For the first eighteen months, in which I only really changed my hair and clothes, I was technically 'transgender'. That said, a lot of trans people really fucking hate the term transsexual, so best be careful with it.

I know a lot of people fret about what to call 'us'. I always think no one minds being politely asked, but *for now* transgender seems like the safest bet. It separates gender – how an individual identifies – from their bodily sex.

What about 'cisgender'? I'm going to use that throughout this book because I don't want to describe people who are satisfied with the gender they were given at birth as 'normal'. This wording automatically insinuates that trans people are 'abnormal', and few of us feel that's the case. Cis is Latin for 'on this side of', and has been used to describe gender since 1914. Some people don't like the term cisgender, but – for now – I'm not sure there's a better shorthand. So most people, if they're not trans or genderqueer, are cisgender. It's kind of the default.

No panel, no scientist, no politician, not the WHO, no one can tell me – or you – how it *feels* to be male or female. Perhaps, rather than a bogeyman, for most people Gender is more like the 'dæmons' of Philip Pullman's *His Dark Materials*. Everyone has a Gender, and for most it's a fluffy sidekick they carry on their shoulders, hardly aware of it for much of their lives. For others, it's more of an albatross. I'm quite sure most men and women carry Gender along with them through life with graceful ease, entirely relaxed or blissfully ignorant of gender expectations. For others, Gender is a constant sense of pressure or failure. Experience of gender is wholly individual.

For me, transitioning felt appropriate. Since starting my transition, I have absolute certainty that had everything gone according to plan in the first place, both my sex and gender would have been female.

And you can't say shit about it.

This is *my* book about gender. If you don't like it, I actively encourage you to write your own. I do not – in fact I definitely do not – want to speak 'on behalf of the trans community'. That would be a community many thousands strong and I've spoken to, like, a hundred of them. The trans voices you see in papers or on TV are not wholly representative and I am doubly wary of putting words in the mouths of trans people of colour or disabled trans people. There are many ways to be transgender. This is *my* transition, my story.

On that: We must also be mindful that the value of a trans person goes beyond stories about 'their journey'. Trans stories have often been limited to the inner world of the trans individual. While that's important, I am interested in how I interact with the world and how the world interacts with me. I'm a journalist and bestselling author, and I have more to offer society than a glorified makeover story.

But this is also not solely a book for trans or genderqueer people. Whatever your sex and however you view your gender, **you** have bought into, or at the very least been exposed to, a series of 'facts', 'truths', 'myths' or 'outright lies' about what it is to be a man or a woman. Where are these messages coming from? Who is perpetuating them? Are we all stuck in a cage of our own manufacture? Is Gender really making any of us happy? How much of our lives are determined by our sex and our gender?

MALE-ASSIGNED GENDER TRAITS	FEMALE-ASSIGNED GENDER TRAITS
Facial hair	Breasts
Body hair	Lack of body hair
Short hairstyles	Long hairstyles
Developed muscles	Make-up
Tallness	Skirts/dresses
Sexual promiscuity	Jewellery
Physical strength	'Broodiness'
Economic independence	Emotional literacy
Emotional resilience	Housework
DIY skills	Cookery skills
High alcohol consumption	High-heeled shoes
Fatherhood	'Slut'
Laid-back attitudes	Motherhood
	Dieting
	Hysteria

Hopefully, you recognise that everything in both of those columns is nonsense. None of those attributes apply solely to men or women, and yet they are keen *signifiers* of gender. A man or a woman dipping their toe in traits not assigned to their sex – see Jayden Smith – would probably (and depressingly) in some way have their masculinity, femininity or sexuality* challenged.

LET THE GENDER GAMES BEGIN!

Gender came to *your* birth too, and I doubt he's making you feel like you're winning. Yes you, dear reader, YOU. I'm not suggesting that I'm Tranny† the Gender Slayer, I'm instead suggesting that as a culture we might want to examine our tenuous links between sex and gender and what they're doing to us all. Are the limitations of gender making us happy? I doubt it. As with *The Hunger Games*, I'm not sure *anyone* truly gets out unscathed.

What I would wholeheartedly encourage you to do, as I walk you through my lifetime of interactions with Gender, is reflect on the ways in which Gender has given you a leg up or held you back.

That absolutely applies to men *and* women, cis *and* trans. By playing along with Gender, all of us can derive rewards. Likewise, all of us can feel his stranglehold. Maybe you haven't been aware of it, or maybe you have. Have you ever, ever said to yourself 'I probably shouldn't do that' or 'What will people say?' or 'I'll look a right dick if I wear that.' That's not you, that's Gender.

* A completely unrelated factor.
† I'm probably allowed to say that; you – if you're not trans – probably aren't. We'll talk more later.

There are big stakes to play for. Can you feel it? With my deadline looming, I'm frantically writing in a coffee shop as, sixty miles away, an anti-Trump Women's March is bringing London to a standstill. I dearly wish I was there. It feels like more than a march. It feels like the start of a rebellion. . . a *resistance*. Do you get the sense that, with apologies to House Stark, Feminism is Coming? Not since the 1970s and the 'Women's Lib' movement has gender been so on the agenda. People – women, men and non-binary people – on all ideological sides are fighting it out in the coliseum of the media. The prize is equality and better representation for women and LGBTQ people.

As with the misguided #AllLivesMatter brigade, it should be obvious that – when it comes to men and women – one of those houses is on fire (women's rights) and the other is not (men's rights). It's fairly clear that the fire-fighters should tackle the burning building first. I, as a feminist, want things to be *immediately* better for women and also for men *in the long term*, once the fire is extinguished on female inequality.

Women may appear to have been 'liberated' from the kitchen sink fifty years ago, but we are yet to achieve anything even vaguely resembling equality. However much individual men are suffering (and *of course* they are), societally and globally, women are still overwhelmingly getting the shitty end of the stick: Unpaid labour; the wage gap; rape and sexual assault; domestic violence; female genital mutilation; access to healthcare and education.

The vote and the contraceptive pill were not the be-all and end-all of feminism and women's rights. There is growing recognition that to make *real* gains in society, to truly tackle inequality, we must ALL come together for the concerns of women, and that those concerns will be varied. We must take into account the challenges of poverty, race, religion, sexual orientation, disability and, yes, transgender issues.

My credentials to speak on such issues have been challenged, but I think trans voices are uniquely positioned to discuss inequality. For thirty years, I was given access to the ultimate prize: white male privilege. As you'll learn, I never 'passed' as a straight man, so it's hard to say what power I ever really had at my disposal, but I have lived as both a man and a woman while at the same time never being accepted *wholly* as either. Like some mad soothsayer in mythology, I've lived slightly outside of gender my whole life – and I've seen both sides.

What if, by questioning the **entire notion of gender**, we could make things better for **everyone**? The world is currently embroiled in discussion over immigration and 'free movement' of people, and most of us on the liberal side would say that being able to live where you can be happy, safe and free from persecution is an important thing. But what about 'free movement' between traditional notions of gender? I'm not saying YOU have to start changing your hair and clothes, but I dare to dream of a world where people can dress, speak and behave how they want, free from mockery, derision, judgement, harassment and danger.

This is what I want. Who's with me?

3.

BEFORE

AKA What Gender Did First

With technicolour HD hindsight, it's clear my own struggles with Gender started the day I was born into a world he'd already done a real number on, so it is necessary to go back to the start.

Jesus knows, I didn't want to write a memoir. I think you should be over eighty before you are allowed to write a memoir. Unless . . .

1. You are a former Spice Girl or . . .
2. Have in some way shaped or changed history or society. Like the Spice Girls did.

I do not claim to be or have done any of these things. For me, in the middle of gender transition, transitioning is actually incredibly tedious. In fact, I'd give anything to have a day off, to be honest. That being said . . .

1. Childhood stories are relatable and I really want you to like me.
2. Gender is a total paedo. Gender fucks kids. I was fucked

by Gender as a kid. You were fucked by Gender, and this happened in childhood.

Therefore, grudgingly, I accept we might need to explore my childhood in order to better understand how I became the MOST BEAUTIFUL TRANSEXUAL IN HOVE. Or something.

'BORN IN THE WRONG BODY – A STORY OF SURVIVAL'

When I was little, every night I would lie in bed and make a deal with God. *If I'm good, tomorrow can I be a girl?* Gender slept at the foot of my bed, curled up in a ball like a contented cat.

It was a vivid goal. In the morning, I would reach up and see if there was thick chestnut Tiffany Amber Thiessen hair spilling across the pillow, only to be disappointed. I didn't get it – I'd been good. Mostly.

As a small child, I was the architect of an elaborate inner fantasy world. In the parallel universe, I'd have been born Katy Rebecca Dawson. This is the name I'd have been christened with had I been born biologically female. I did not like this name. I still don't like this name, hence Juno. Kate, as I'd have chosen if forced, had long blonde hair and dark eyebrows. I don't know who I based her on phys-ically, but there's just something about blondes, isn't there? We do treat them differently (just ask little girls who they prefer – Anna or Elsa). It's possible Kate was somewhat modelled on the cartoon character Tara, from *Attack of the Killer Tomatoes*.

Kate, in the dream, was never a little girl. Weirdly, even as a child I wasn't into childish things. I grew up on *Neighbours* and *Round the Twist* and *Byker Grove*. Children were crap, but teenagers were *cool*, and I wanted to be one. Kate Dawson was born aged fourteen.

I didn't think living this vivid alternate life was especially unusual.

I thought everybody longed to be somebody else.

I'm getting ahead of myself. Let's start at the very beginning, even *before* I was born. You might start to suspect that I'm hiding, shielding or protecting some aspects of my childhood. That would be because I'm hiding, shielding and protecting some parts of my childhood.

Since the 1990s and the phenomenal success of both reality TV and misery memoirs, we, as consumers, have come to expect limitless access into each other's lives. If I'm standing here, telling my story *for money*, I should be ready, willing and able to drag a knife across my belly and spill the entirety of my guts (with a smile on my face) because we know that this is how we get people to like us. We share *everything*.

A while back, I had a meeting with some TV producers who were interested in MY JOURNEY™. While most had honourable intentions, and one was very much on the same page as me in terms of my gender destruction quest, the general consensus was that we needed 'an angle'.

Very quickly, little needling fingers were prying into my childhood: Was I sad? Did I consider suicide? Was I abused?

What were my parents like? It felt like eels writhing around in oil. I came away from the meetings feeling decidedly grubby.

In every woman's life, I suppose, comes the moment when she must answer the question, 'How much of your soul are you prepared to sell to become rich and famous?' You can be one, the other, or both, but neither without a degree of sacrifice. I really believe that. Would I exploit my mother for an hour of droopy, emotionally manipulative television where Holly Willoughby or someone asks if it feels like 'James has died'? No, I won't be doing that.

I won't be doing it here, either. This is not a misery memoir because I am not miserable. I was not a miserable child. If you are in some way disappointed that my mother didn't burn me with cigarettes or attempt to sell me to a pimp for crack, I'd politely suggest you indulge in a spot of therapy.

BINGLEY

As mentioned, I was born to Angela and Ian Dawson of Bingley. Bingley is a small market town about ten miles from Bradford; home of excellent curries, Zayn Malik and Kimberley from Girls Aloud. Bingley is famous as the birthplace of the Damart thermal underwear empire and the historic Five Rise Locks – a feat of engineering so impressive, Wikipedia tells me, that up to THIRTY people still stand around to watch a barge pass through.

Now that you're back from purchasing your tickets to witness this forgotten wonder of the world, I'll continue.

Growing up in Bingley was shit. The town was racist

and small-minded. I understand you're not meant to slag off your home town lest you never earn the key to the city or whatever, but I couldn't care less. It was shit. Even as a small child I was aware of how shit it was.

Of course, not all the blame can be laid at the doors of the inhabitants. Like many northern towns, it's been left to rot by central government. Oh yes, I've lived in London and the North–South struggle is real, let me tell you. Poverty is felt far more keenly where our politicians can't see it.

Some cities, a chosen few like Leeds and Manchester, have been selected as 'second cities', and huge investment has been pumped into them. Because rent and property prices are so much lower Oop North, extra disposable income means shopping in Leeds (in particular) and Manchester is NEXT LEVEL. The last I checked, all of Leeds city centre now exists under a glass-domed shopping paradise, like some strange consumerist utopia.

Bradford, let alone its outlying suburbs, has *not* bene-fitted from urban renewal – or at least it hadn't in the 1990s. No – back then the city was famous for just one thing: riots.

The so-called 'Bradford Riots', first in 1995 and then 2001, reflected a very sad truth about a segregated city. To outsiders, Bradford is often held up as a shining beacon of diversity. It isn't. There were two warring communities: white-British and British-Pakistani. The actual rioting attracted disenfranchised young men on both sides of the race divide. To be truly diverse you'd surely expect the rioters to be a jolly mixture of white, black, brown, South

Asian, East Asian, LGBTQ and anyone else who wanted to party.

In my experience, Bradford was a forlorn place to grow up. Racism was so much a part of my childhood I wasn't even aware it was racism. There were white areas and brown areas of the city. Many of my primary school teachers used racially offensive terms to describe the Pakistani community. I thought, in a very innocent but ultimately quite stupid way, that corner shops were legitimately called 'Paki Shops'. That is what literally *all* the white people called them. I think back on that and cringe in horror.

At one point, my twee village school in Bingley was paired with a 'Brown School' from central Bradford. I'm not even kidding, that was what we were told was happening. Each white child was assigned a brown one like a pet, in the same way that Mildred Hubble got her kitten in *The Worst Witch*. Fuck knows how that was supposed to be a cultural exchange, when we all ate at the same fucking Little Chef* anyway.

Truth be told, I was well into my teens before I realised that a lot of the messages I was receiving were a) inaccurate and b) just awful. The picture I'm painting, I hope, is one in which *anyone* who wasn't white, straight or cisgender wouldn't feel, let's say, nurtured. Segregation was in the DNA of the city, and therefore its residents – or at least any of them who didn't *want* to know better or rise above it. Black/white, gay/straight, male/female: people were expected to stay in their boxes.

* 'Little *Thief* more like!' – My frugal father.

This brings me back to my parents. Both had been raised in this environment, although my dad had spent some time in Cyprus as a child. I believe firmly in the saying 'You Can't Be What You Can't See', and it's very much the case that my parents were *not* exposed to a wide and exciting cross-section of society. Both were kept firmly in the White British, straight, cisgender enclave that is Bingley. Their childhood narrative of the Pakistani community was the same one we now see about Eastern European immigrants: the story of the foreign 'invaders', coming for our jobs and women.

As such, I don't (and have never) especially blamed my parents for their relative lack of experience. Where were *their* role models? They weren't in Bingley, and vitally – as we'll explore later – they certainly weren't in the media.

This is probably for another book, but if, like me, you were born outside of London, or in the north, or in a country with fewer human rights than the UK, I'm sure you'll be all too familiar with that sense of limitation. A feeling of being held back and trapped by geography. I think so many of us have to work doubly hard to get half as far as those people, both men and women, who were born into money and privilege. Hell, I'd suggest those of us born outside of an easily commutable distance from London are disadvantaged before we even get going. Imagine being able to travel into London, work for internship money or, worse, do unpaid work experience, and then travel back to Esher with Daddy.

To this day, I'm oddly proud to come from the North. As both a gay man and a trans woman I have relied on the armadillo-thick skin I developed during those years. I'm going to need it for the rest of my life. That time was a survival boot camp I have sorely needed.

Where we're from, both the location and the environment we've stewed in, has a massive impact on the adults we become.

Before I was trans, before I was gay, I was from Bingley.

4.

JAMES MATTHEW

AKA Slugs and Snails

So, little baby me. I was pretty poorly *and* a first-born son, so I imagine I was pretty goddamn special in a Ross Gellar 'I was a MEDICAL MARVEL' sort of way. My parents certainly weren't rich, but neither my sister nor I ever went without.

I'll skip to the good bit. My earliest memories are filled with a sense of 'getting it wrong'. Simply put, like a giraffe masquerading as a rhinoceros, I wasn't very good at being a boy.

Some scattered memories:

- Being told to stop skipping everywhere. I had a joyful skip to my step! I couldn't help it!
- Being obsessed with the women on the 1980s covers of Mum's ultra-glam Jilly Cooper books like *Imogen* and *Prudence*
- Repurposing a tatty Barbie into a 'Penelope Pitstop' doll, only for her legs to snap off in our fireguard

Attempts were made to boy me up. I can't tell you how horrified I was when my dad returned from a work trip to America and I was gifted a TOOL KIT. I was bought bikes and skateboards (I really wanted disco-style roller boots), I was taken to Bradford City football matches (before the catastrophic stadium fire put my mother right off that idea), I had guns and footballs and skulls.

Gender, ever present, kept telling me what I *should* like, what I *should* be doing. I did make half-arsed efforts – I would, once in a while, give football a go – and even these scant attempts were disproportionately reinforced. GOOD BOY JAMES, my parents and teachers would say, GOOD BOY. Playing with traditionally female toys was met with concerned glances and screaming silence. How often, when we tell children they are 'being good', do we mean they are blindly conforming?

But, as Mum pointed out when I told her I was trans, I was a girl long before I conceived Kate. I was always girly. Moreover, I was *stereotypically* girly.

SUGAR AND SPICE

From a very young age, despite Gender's best efforts to steer me right, I displayed no interest whatsoever in *traditionally* male clothes, things and pursuits, and a keen interest in *traditionally* female ones. It'll take someone with much more theoretical knowledge than I have to dissect *why* I was so attracted to archetypally female things. Is it innate or is it learned behaviour?

As a teacher, and later as an aunt, I have witnessed infant girls make a frenzied beeline for pink clothes and toys. Is it simply a joyous and uplifting hue?

To be honest, I don't really care. It just *was* that way for me. Looking at it now, and only being able to speak for myself, the key draw seems to have been *glamour*.

Let me explain. When I was little, baby dolls, kitchens and Sylvanian Families held no appeal. Motherhood *still* holds no appeal. However, Barbie, Girls World styling heads and My Little Ponies were my catnip. They had names like Applejack, Bowtie and Cotton Candy! They had hair I could brush and braid. They were pastel candy-coloured and lovely. They were, to me, aesthetically pleasing.

Like any child, I loved going to our local toyshop, Toymaster in Keighley. Don't get me wrong – I would head straight for the action figure section because that was 'OK', but would then skulk backwards to sneak a look at the eye-blisteringly pink girls' section. How I wished I could legitimately explore Barbie's vacuum-packed fashions – her magenta off-the-shoulder lycra dresses and fur-lined Christmas capes.

Instead, I made do. As a 'boy', society allowed me action figures, not dolls, so I got my doll fix by getting that one sad female figure in any range: the April O'Neil, the Janine from Ghostbusters, Teela from He-Man (She-Ra was considered too girly, and thus forbidden), Cheetara from Thundercats. Through them, I had my doll collection. I even went so far as to write a letter to Hasbro to find out why I couldn't purchase a Jenny the Psychic Cat from crap 1990s cartoon *Bucky O' Hare*.*

---

* This is why it makes me really angry that you can't readily buy Black Widow or Scarlet Witch action figures. Nowadays, toy makers just don't bother with the female characters. There are tiny trans girls out there who need society-approved doll substitutes in their lives! Also, why wouldn't little boys want female characters, and little girls want dolls that kick ass?

But the toys were not *really* what I wanted. Even if I had been given all the Barbies in the world, I don't think they'd have been enough. What I wanted was to *be* a girl.

'Let Toys Be Toys' has become the cry of excellent parents reluctant to impose gender norms on their children by way of the toy industry. In the name of research, I schlepped to market leader Toys R Us, who had committed to making their stores less gender divided. In 2015, the company declared – to much praise from parents – that it would be removing the separate Boys' and Girls' sections. You can imagine my surprise, then, when I walked into a room the size of an airport hangar and to my left there was a sea of nuclear pink, while to my right was the rest of the colour spectrum.

No signposts needed.

Pink, today, is a *very* gendered colour.

It's fairly clear which way the 'girls' stuff' was, and I can't imagine a young child who's been told they're a boy is going to feel particularly welcome on the pink side of the shop. They might as well run an electrified barbed wire fence down the centre of the store.

A closer inspection was no less depressing. The pink section contained a lot of dolls and babies. These puppets stimulate creative, nurturing, role-playing games. Excluding boys from this style of play, I think, has far-reaching consequences. Don't we want boys to become fathers? To hold and cuddle and nurture their infants? Don't we want boys to learn that fifty per cent of parenting is their responsibility? Do we not also think that, by not exposing little boys to dolls, we are perpetuating the myth that only women look after children?

This myth, of course, is also establishing a clear destiny for *all* little girls, whether they like it or not. If you're a girl, you're meant to want babies. They are for *you*.

No dolls or babies on the non-pink side. Lots and lots of masked superheroes and soldiers, but they are for killing each other, not caring for. I accept those toys also encourage creative role play, but certainly not with nurture in mind.

The flipside is also true. Although every *other* colour is male by default, I wonder how welcome supposed girls would feel on the non-pink side of the shop. The set-up of the store screams 'stay in your lane'. In more positive news, DC Comics now do a range of female superheroes – Wonder Woman, Batgirl and Supergirl. However, these bug-eyed figures are definitely dolls. They are separate from the action figure range produced by the same company. It's not a case of being able to pick between Batman, Superman and Harley Quinn; it's action figure, action figure and doll. (After public pressure, you *can* now buy Marvel's Black Widow and Rey from *Star Wars* figures, so that's a start.)

Even family favourite Lego has succumbed to Gender. In the non-pink section you can buy a Lego airport for £69. In the pink section you can buy a Lego Friends airport for £79. The only difference, you've guessed it, is that the Lego Friends airport is pink. IT IS AN AIRPORT.* It was at that point, regrettably, I burned the store to the ground.

---

* These days, as a woman, I only ever fly from pink airports while shaving my legs with pink razors and writing with pink Bic pens. I actually am typing this on the pink MacBook, so maybe I'm part of the problem.

Even more sinister was the fact that any toy that wasn't a baby or a doll was on the non-pink side; home experiment kits, puzzles and arts and crafts (of the non 'Glitter-Jewel-Princess' variety) were out of reach. The message was very simple: little girls (or fans of pink at a stretch) should be thinking about fashion dolls or babies, not experimenting, building, tactics games, or creating. Of course there's nothing wrong with dolls and babies if that's what you're into. But what if you're not?

Moreover, despite another headline-grabbing move from Barbie-makers Mattel that Barbie would now be more realistic in terms of her height and weight, I saw no evidence of those dolls on the high street. It was still shelf after shelf of stick-thin blonde boob. Dressed in pink.

Don't even get me started on the makers of Monster High dolls, who decided having flesh was just being too fat and made their girls ACTUAL SKELETONS.

Children's clothing is also the topic of much debate. Again, many children's clothes stores have clear gender divides; predictably, pink dominates one half of the shop. Worse, girls' tops – even those designed with five- or six-year-olds in mind – are 'skinny fit' or figure-hugging. They display captions (and these are all from a leading supermarket's clothing line) such as 'Cute Lil Sister', 'Princess' or 'Babe'. Boys' alternatives are 'Champ' and 'Legend'. There's a boys' T-shirt with 'PLAY FOR 1ST PLACE' on it. Not even kidding. I wish I were.

I have no doubt what Toys R Us will say: that they can only stock the toys that manufacturers are making. The manufacturers will say they only make what is selling. But who actually *buys* toys? Children have no money; it's adults who buy toys and adults who are pushing gender norms onto unsuspecting children.

Children will nag for toys – and will let adults know exactly what it is they want – but I suspect most children aren't very old when they learn which toys it's 'OK' to ask for and which it isn't. When I was a teacher, I saw children aged five and six playing happily with any sort of toy, but seven- or eight-year-old children knew to 'stick' to gender-typed toys or face mockery from their classmates. I stopped asking for a Barbie at around the same age, switching my focus to those 'acceptable' female action figures.

It takes a phenomenally brave child to continually defy Gender's wishes. It also takes brave parents.

5.

THE ACT

AKA Walk Like a Man

To this day, I recall the transformation of Plain Jane Superbrain in *Neighbours*, in which she pulled off her glasses* and put on some lippy for the first time so that she could seduce Guy Pearce. She was gorgeous, and it was *so* glamorous. I'm not saying that glamour is what separates men and women, but it transported me, as a child, well outside the boundaries of 'societal norms'. Ah societal norms, so claustrophobic, so suffocating.

Of all my childhood memories, and I don't know why this one hasn't decayed, one of the strongest is of walking through Bingley with Mum one time, gleefully excited because she'd just bought a pair of white stilettos. What? It was the late 1980s. On our way home, we ran into a friend of Mum's and I was so thrilled with my mother's purchase that I made her unbox the shoes *on the street* to show her friend, and further proceeded to model the sound they made by shoving the shoes on my hands and clip-clopping them along the pavement. I still remember both my mother's bemusement and the bewilderment on

* God forbid a woman look 'brainy'!

the face of her friend. This behaviour, clearly, is not very 'boy'.

It's not the 1940s any more. Men are allowed to be glamorous, clearly. Look at Kanye, Jidenna or David Beckham. I also think it's fair to say that a number of gay men are drawn into outwardly glamorous industries – hair, fashion and make-up. You can see how I'd be convinced I was a gay man, but my fascination went deeper than that.

I didn't just *like* girls, I wanted to be one.

When I was about four, we moved from the poky terraced house on Heath Street to a more middle-class suburban house with a big back garden. There were plenty of other children to play with. As a child, much of my time was dedicated to role play, in which I was *always* a female character. If we played *Doctor Who* in our cul-de-sac, I was Bonnie Langford's Mel; if we played *Terminator* I was Sarah Connor. I loved redheads – Sheila from *Dungeons & Dragons* and Daphne from *Scooby Doo*. In fact, me, my sister and the little boys across the road used to play a game called 'Boys and Girls' in which I was a girl. I *ached* to be a girl. If other playmates wouldn't let me be a girl, it was a real slap in the face: 'But you're a boy.'

No, no I wasn't. To me it was SO OBVIOUS, like everyone was arguing the sky was green and I was the only one who could see it was blue.

When I was about six, we were lined up to go into the dining hall, which was in a big Victorian building across the road from the main primary schoolhouse. I vividly remember a conversation with a childhood friend in which we both expressed profound frustration – hers at being a girl, mine at being a boy. Even then, as infants, we were aware of how stupid it was that we couldn't just 'swap'. I often wonder if that little girl, now an adult, is going through the same process that I am.

I even had little proto-relationships. When role-playing, I'd be Charlene (obviously) and my school friend John would be Scott. We wouldn't kiss as far as I can remember – although we may have – we more used to just cuddle and sort of wrestle each other under a duvet. We'd have been maybe six or seven years old. It wasn't a gay thing; I was just being a girl and he was being a boy, emulating what we'd seen on the TV.

I knew it was 'wrong'. I knew it must be kept a secret. Once, Matthew, the little boy from across the road, grassed my Charlene activities to my mum. I got a clip around the earhole and told to never, *ever* do that again.

It's interesting. Girls are praised for being girly. When they *look* sugar and spice, compliments are heaped on them, often to the detriment of anything they have done or achieved. Girls are actively encouraged to perform, do ballet, sing and make pretty things. Boys, less so. In fact, if boys are stereotypically girly, they are mocked. I speak from personal experience. Like I said, the few times I 'got it right', praise was lavished on me to reinforce my conformity.

Societally, girls rejecting feminine gender norms are tarred with 'tomboy', which isn't in itself derogatory, but nor is their traditionally masculine behaviour reinforced; 'tomboy' is said more with resignation, when little girls won't conform. Little girls who don't toe the line are often met with low-key shaming along the lines of 'you'd look so pretty if you wore make-up' and such like.

Moreover, culturally celebrating tomboys (Scout in *To Kill a Mockingbird*, Katniss Everdeen in *The Hunger Games*, Arya Stark in *Game of Thrones* etc) for adopting traditionally masculine pastimes and behaviour goes some way to shame or criticise traditionally female or 'girly' behaviour. We're setting up the myth that masculinity is somehow better than femininity. This is damaging for *all* children.

Boys, on the other hand, get 'sissy', 'gayboy' or the misogynist chorus of 'you run/throw/walk/talk like a girl'. That's not something I've ever heard used as a compliment. It speaks of centuries-old sexism. Traditionally female behaviour is sneered at while girls emulating male behaviour are better tolerated. After all, who wouldn't want to be a man, right?

Little children are androgynous creatures to begin with. Yes, I was quite small, sweet and avoided football, but I didn't otherwise stand out – not if you didn't examine my behaviour too closely. Once at middle school and on the cusp of puberty, I learned that any feminine traits I was displaying were best concealed. My voice was mocked, my walk, my face.

I learned, very quickly, that I was doing it all wrong.

There followed a dark few years of trying to fit in. I kept my head down. I was still fascinated by girls, and many of my early 'girlfriends' were simply female friends I idolised. I just wanted to be one of them. My mum (as I think many mums do) managed my childhood friendship circle – always with other boys – but I had little in common with them.

My clandestine obsession continued. I would steal my sister's copies of *Sugar* and *More* magazine to learn the secrets from the inner sorority sanctum. I knew precisely how to deal with period pains I would never get. I knew how to make boys fall for me and how to be a good best friend.

At thirteen (and still very tiny) I left the relative safety of middle school and started at Bingley Grammar School. A grammar school in name only – it wasn't selective – it was a sprawling Victorian redbrick with endless corridors and high ceilings. It had the feel of an asylum. My mother had attended the same school thirty years earlier and, as far as I could tell, little had changed. It seemed that whatever I did, I just couldn't blend in. I was now a very small fish in a very, very big pond.

PE lessons are especially traumatic for anyone who won't go along with what Gender is telling them to do. First, you're brutally segregated based on sex alone. Then you're herded into sweaty, foot-odoured rooms and told to get naked. From there you'll be asked to dress in ill-fitting skimpy gymwear. Swimwear and gym shorts actively accentuate body parts you're not altogether comfortable with. Then, even if you're five foot nothing and weigh about seven stone soaking wet, you'll be asked – being a boy – to play rugby.

Needless to say, much of my childhood trauma stems from PE lessons. Let me be clear, not *fitness* or *sport*. I like keeping fit and I like the sports I like. Unfortunately, Gender had beaten me to the PE department and, at Bingley Grammar School, boys – all boys – did rugby, football and weightlifting. Gender had comprehensively informed routines and practices, and I was at their mercy. As a tiny, delicate little sparrow I was laughed at, piled on, mocked.

And it wasn't just me: penises and pubes were measured and compared. Biceps were flexed. Size mattered. Over in the girls' changing room, I have it on good authority, discussion was focused on cup size, periods and who was or wasn't in a bra. Puberty got to me late. As time ticked on, I was still a little thing, with a little boy body, in a changing room full of hairy, hulking young men. I was so deeply ashamed of how I looked.

One time, after I 'grassed' on a fellow student for something I can't even remember, he and his friends scooped up handfuls of mud and started to hurl them at me. I was beaten down and covered head-to-toe in thick brown dirt. It was almost a shot-by-shot soily re-enactment of the shower scene at the start of *Carrie*.

The teacher rescued me and I broke down on him. When he asked me who was responsible, I could only answer 'all of them', because it was true. I cried. That was the one and only time they got the tears they wanted.

In the end, a chance examination during a period of bad back pain revealed I have a condition called scoliosis – a slight curve in my spinal column ('Hahahahaha Dawson's bent' etc). I seized on the opportunity and used the pain to sit out PE for the last two years of school. The pain subsided after a few weeks, but I certainly wasn't going to tell anyone that. It's funny; the sad little reception area where they put kids who couldn't do PE was largely occupied by nerds and people who turned out to be LGBT. WHO COULD HAVE PREDICTED THAT?

#ProtectYoungPeople. Reform PE now.

Worse still, in the 1990s, boys and girls were still segregated for sex education (a practice, unbelievably, that still takes place in some schools). On the most basic selection criteria – our genitals – we were herded off into different rooms for different videos. It did not feel right. Our sex education at that time featured no mention of LGBT people, as we were being educated under Margaret Thatcher's poisonous 'Section 28', which forbade 'the teaching in any maintained school of the acceptability of homosexuality as a pretended family relationship'. LGBT+ people of my generation are so clearly covered in the shiny silver scars of that piece of legislation.

I can't remember the exact point I realised I wasn't going to mystically transform into golden girl Kate as I slept, but I imagine the dream died so slowly I wasn't even conscious of it. For now, Gender had won and I was in submission.

6.

WON'T SOMEONE THINK OF THE CHILDREN?

AKA Thoughts on Babies Today

What does it all mean? Am I the result of a repressed Yorkshire childhood? Had I just been allowed a fucking My Little Pony in 1987 could all this have been avoided?

Clearly not. In spite of Gender screaming at me every chance he got, I was still irreversibly drawn to cross-gender toys and clothes. My gender preferences were pronounced *long* before the media or socialisation had a chance to fuck with my head. If nothing else, I was an innocent, sheltered child, one who was granted a blissfully long childhood. I'm glad I didn't grow up too fast; I really wrung every drop out of being young.

It's pretty clear to adult Juno that infant James had exactly the right idea. He knew he was meant to be a girl. It's just a shame the world he was born into wasn't *quite* ready for her. God, pronouns galore.

In modern times, there isn't really an excuse. Unless parents are actively *shielding* children from the world (which does sadly happen), there shouldn't be too many children who won't grow up with visible LGBT role models. We only need look at the number of under-eighteens referred to Gender Identity Clinics (GICs) to know that more young people than ever before are identifying as transgender.*

You'll have no doubt seen the *Daily Mail*'s reportage of 'furious parents' up in arms about CBBC's 2016 *Just A Girl* drama. 'Sex Change Show for Kids', the newspaper stirred, suggesting – as have various other outlets – that a powerful trans lobby is prowling towns and villages like the Childcatcher in *Chitty Chitty Bang Bang* to steer gender-confused children into operating theatres. The sentiment was echoed in BBC Two's 2017 documentary *Transgender Children: Who Knows Best*.

What utter rot. 1) I was about three or four when I first knew I wanted to be a girl. I'm living proof it happens and it happens young. 2) No children are having 'sex changes', you morons. They might be prescribed hormone blockers. This (temporarily) puts puberty on hold while they take some time to *think about* transitioning as adults. Delaying the onset of puberty means your body will transition more smoothly *if* an individual chooses to take that step later. Otherwise, they simply stop taking the blockers and go through puberty late. I'm glad we could clear that up. Again, contrary to what the *Daily Mail* et al would have you believe, this is not a new-fangled regime. The practice was first trialled at the Tavistock Clinic as far back as 1992.

I don't regret spending my twenties as a gay man, but NOW I'd have been able to get my hands on those pills in

* Referrals to the Tavistock – the UK's only under-eighteens' gender clinic – have doubled in the last twelve months.

my teens and prevent my body from going through boy-puberty. I'd have never had this chin or these shoulders.

Shoulda, woulda, coulda.

Psychologists have shown – although it should be obvious really – that a child's earliest exposure to what it means to be male or female comes from parents.* From the time their children are babies, parents treat sons and daughters differently, dressing infants in gender-specific colours, giving 'boys' toys' or 'girls' toys' and expecting 'appropriate behaviour' from boys and girls.† One study indicates that parents have different expectations for sons and daughters as early as twenty-four hours after birth.‡

Children are born into a world already decimated by gender expectations. Sure, we've outwardly done away with the 1950s model of stay-at-home mums and breadwinning dads, but even with many mums working, they often return home to 'the second shift'.§ Mothers *still* spend more time with children than fathers, even in homes with two (mixed-sex) parents and even if the mother works full-time.¶

Don't shoot me! I'm just the messenger! Although fathers say they want to spend more time with their kids,** mothers still spend two to three times more time with their children††

* Lauer & Lauer, 1994
† Thorne, 1993
‡ Rubin, Provenzano, & Luria, 1974
§ Hothschild, 2003
¶ Craig, 2006
** Milkie et al, 2004
†† Baxter, 2002

and fathers' interactions with them are often limited to play rather than nurture or instruction.*

What does this all mean? It means an ongoing cycle of gender expectations – for both child and parent. Parents behave according to their gender and then pass this on to the next generation. The first people a baby sees and interacts with (usually) are their parents. And from day one, they're learning that there is a fundamental difference between men and women. This is what mummies do, this is what daddies do. Once gender is set, for most of us, it is set for life. The tapestry of your life is pre-woven, ahead of time. This is what men do, this is what women do.

A 2017 study by the journal *Science* showed that, by the age of six, little girls think 'brilliance' and 'smartness' are words that mostly apply to boys. Children aged five think the words are equally applicable to both. What lesson is learned – and from where – at this critical time?

Parenting is tough. How people survive both being parents and the constant flow of information in the media and online telling them how wrong they're doing it is beyond me. I think all parents, since the dawn of time, are singing from the same song sheet: how do we not kill or fuck up our kid?

Too many boundaries, you fuck a kid up. Too few boundaries? Yep, just as fucked up. Since *This Book is Gay* came out in 2014, I get dozens and dozens of letters from parents asking how they should broach the gender or sex and sexuality topic with their teens.

* Craig, 2006

First, I'd say that it's too late by the time they're teens. The trick is in getting them young. How can it be 'inappropriate' to talk about something as pervasive as gender with children? By the time I was a teenager, the damage was already done. I felt almost entirely like I'd failed at being human. It's no wonder I did so bloody well at school and college – hello, compensating much?

How would I have wanted things to be different? I would *not* have wanted my mum to sit me down in front of a computer, aged four, and show me YouTube videos of gender reassignment surgeries (I know some parents who have done this and that is utter fucking madness). I guess I'd have just wanted to be reassured that I wasn't doing anything wrong.

There's a difference between stifling a child and having boundaries. I think boundaries are good and we might as well get used to them because life is jam-packed with boundaries, but gender needn't be one. Acknowledging that gender isn't rigid or binary is pretty much a piece of piss, I'd have thought. It's as important for all children to learn their gender shouldn't and doesn't inform or limit *any* of their life choices.

Listen to children, for they are wise in their innocence. Children haven't learned it's sometimes best to lie, so for god's sake, *listen* to them. I wonder if I ever asked my mum why I wasn't a girl. I've asked her now and she can't remember. On the day I came out as trans in a Buzzfeed interview, I got many, many lovely letters and emails, but one really stood out. It was an email from a woman I was at school with. It went like this:

Hey James,

Looking at all the support you've received you certainly don't need any from little old me. But genuinely I'm so proud to say I know you. Private messaging as I too shared that awful secondary school experience. It was such a fine line to walk, and I realise I had much less to worry about than you did. My four-year-old son tells me he wants to be a lady like me when he grows up and I tell him that's fine! He can be whatever he wants to be to be happy in his own skin. So good luck James and sending love from the town I haven't quite managed to get away from.

If every mother and father shared her attitude, just think how much lovelier the world would be.

Many of my friends are now parents, and they are working so hard to be the protective barrier between their child and Gender. They are struggling against a tsunami of pastel pink and baby blue in shops and on TV, and still, *still* battling against random strangers on buses criticising their gender-neutral clothing and toys. Seriously, my friend's daughter is constantly misgendered because she favours clothes with dinosaurs on. EVERYONE KNOWS ALL DINOSAURS WERE BOYS AND THAT'S WHY THEY'RE NOW EXTINCT.

I'm guilty of it too. Even while a baby is a bump, I've asked 'do you know if it's a boy or a girl?' The answer, regardless of scans you've had or information a nurse has given you, is *always* 'I don't know', whether you like it or not. I know that's a biggy for expectant parents, but it's the truth. You might well have an idea as to the baby's *sex*, but you don't have a clue about their *gender*. That's why it's so important to not push gender onto a baby from the day they're born. They might not like it.

Instead, rebel against the tyranny of pink and blue. There's a whole fucking spectrum of other colours to choose from. Shops only sell that pink and blue shit because people buy it. Buy other colours and they'll make more stuff like that.

I mean, I'm not saying go full Whole Foods and start calling your kids 'Omega' or 'Concept', but the best parents are the ones who *listen* to their children and allow them to express themselves. Statistically speaking, the vast, vast majority of children aren't going to be gender-variant and even fewer will actually be trans, but allowing a child to choose cross-gendered clothes or toys is a kindness. It will make them feel at ease, give a sense of comfort, a sense that the things they like, their choices, are perfectly harmless.

I think this sets a precedent for the rest of their lives: 'your sex isn't your destiny.'

You might *think* you're protecting your child by making them conform. You might worry that schoolyard bullies will target your child if they're allowed to dress and act how they like. Well, guess what? Kids are fucking vile to each other every day *regardless* of how they dress and act. I honestly don't think the bullying I received at school would have been any worse had I been wearing a dress.

At the time of writing, comedian Russell Brand is taking flack for telling the press he won't gender his newborn child. Speaking on *The Jonathan Ross Show*, he said, 'We don't know the gender. I may not even ever impose a gender upon it, let the child grow up and be whatever the hell it is, never tell it there is such a concept.' He has been widely mocked, accused of being a hippy and/or having a messiah complex. Gender owns the collective consciousness too, seemingly.

Beyond the 'playground teasing' issue, which I get as a concern, the only other reason to panic about children expressing their true gender is the impact it will have on *you*. WHAT WILL THE NEIGHBOURS SAY? Who gives a shimmering shit what the neighbours say? People are going to talk shit whatever you do. Who cares what the basics at mother and toddler groups say? Answer me this: What's more important – your public image or your child's happiness?

Parenthood is the ultimate step off the edge of a cliff. You have no idea what's waiting on the other side: illness, disability, addiction, behavioural problems. A child being LGBT is actually pretty small potatoes compared to some developments. As ever, parents adapt, fuelled by unconditional love. I'm so glad I continue to evolve alongside my parents, and they've never once given up on me or counted me out.

So what *should* you do? I am not a parent (my Chihuahua baby probably doesn't count) so the last thing I want to do is teach a grandma to suck eggs.* The odds are (ever in your favour) a baby *won't* be trans or intersex, but a great many are. How does *any* parent prepare for the infinite complexities of raising a human life without fucking it up?

* What a fucking foul phrase *that* is.

Or do we just accept we probably *will* fuck up our kids to an extent, even if we try really hard not to?

I think some things expectant parents, or parents of infants, could do are:

1. At the scan, don't ask for a sex. I *know*, that's a BIG request. Why? Because you'll start gendering the poor fucker. *A girl will be like this/a boy will be like that.* If you don't (I can understand wanting to wrestle some control out of a situation in which parents can feel like they're in free fall, but beyond that, the only concrete reason to know is what colour shit to buy it and thinking of a name), other people will. If you're thinking 'well I'd rather know', the point I'm making is I AM EVIDENCE YOU MIGHT NOT KNOW. Even the smartest parents I know made certain presumptions about their unborn children based on what sex they were assigned. I heard many of them say, 'Dave would prefer a girl.' Why? What is 'a girl' like and why would he prefer that? Not knowing will better prepare you, I think, for all eventual-ities, *including* a child who is in some way gender-incongruent. Going into parenthood simply expecting a baby – an *individual who is not defined by ONE WORD a midwife told you* – is a very wise move, I think.

2. Know your enemy. It sounds nuts but perhaps, given that all parents *will* be told a sex sooner or later, the best thing we can do for a baby is to understand the environ-ment, the world, the culture, the climate it's being born into. Understand, as best we can, the privileges and disadvantages of both sexes. Acknowledge and

overcome the pressures your child will face if confined within their given – or chosen – gender. So read about it, and engage with people who are talking about it.

3. When people ask if you're having a boy or a girl, *even if you know*, reply 'it doesn't matter', 'we're not telling people the sex' or even 'I'm having a baby'.

4. Don't buy surprise gifts for humans that can talk, especially gifts based on assumptions about 'what boys/girls like'. Should be obvious, but a lot of people bought me a lot of boy shit I really didn't want. I soon felt too scared to ask for the things I wanted. For humans that can't talk, I suspect it probably doesn't matter too much, they'll just slobber on it regardless.

5. Be mindful of parent bias. There are a slew of studies on gender bias in interactions with infants. Mothers talk to babies more than fathers, and respond faster to infant vocalisations.* Mothers use more supportive and positive language with children than fathers, while both parents use more supportive language with daughters than sons.† Mothers tend to underestimate their daughter's physical capabilities.‡ Parents tend to ignore baby boys' pained expressions and attend to those of girls.§ It seems likely that parents are bringing gender assumptions to the table. How can this not go on to influence how the child views itself? I'd argue many parents create

---

* Johnson, Caskey et al, 2014
† Leaper, Anderson & Sanders, 1998
‡ Mondschein, Adolph & Tamis-LeMonda, 2000
§ Malatesta & Haviland, 1982

a self-fulfilling prophecy of gendered behaviour. I can attest that if a child cannot live up to gender expectations, it feels like a failure.

6. Be mindful of language. Already there's increasing awareness of emptily praising children. It's thought that giving 'process praise' – e.g. 'You worked so hard!' or 'How did you do that?' – that reinforces a child's effort and thought-process is a better approach than 'person praise' – e.g. 'you're so clever' – because *clever*, *smart*, *pretty* or *brave* are inflexible traits, which a child can't do much about.* I would suggest 'good girl' or 'good boy' is the ultimate 'person praise'. What is a child supposed to take away from 'good boy' or 'good girl' other than a reinforcement of gender stereotypes? In fact, in other European languages, 'good boy/girl' are rarely used, and it's thought the terms are a bit of a hangover from English Puritanism.†

7. Do as I say, not as I do: Research by Craig (2006) indicated mothers are still doing the lion's share of parenting. There's not a lot of good in trying to explicitly parent in a gender-neutral way when there's nothing implicitly gender-neutral about the parenting.

8. Check out schools. A great question to ask of prospective nurseries and schools is 'do you group by gender?' When I was teaching, it was considered very poor practice to divide on the basis of boy/girl. Yet some teachers still say 'Girls line up by the door please!' or 'Boys go to

* Zentall & Morris, 2010
† Wierzbicka, 2004

lunch first today!' Worse still is segregating boys and girls for PSHE (Personal, Social and Health Education) and Sex Ed. I think this mystifies gender on both sides and is hugely counter-productive.

The late actor Alexis Arquette, in their later years, referred to themselves as 'Gender Suspicious', and I think that's healthy. As I said, you can only shelter children from Gender for so long – he will get to them sooner or later – but do *you*, your baby's parents, want to be the source of something they'll very much come to resent? Whether your child turns out to be male, female, gay, straight, trans or cis, what I'm aiming to do with this tome is demonstrate that *all* the kids will in some way suffer from exposure to rigid gender binaries. Babies born now are probably the first to grow up in a more *aware* society. This society, our future, occasionally looks very frightening indeed. Let's see if we can make Gender a bit less scary.

7.

FRIENDSHIP NEVER ENDS

AKA Finding Your Tribe

My parents divorced when I was seven. *Oh, is that it?* I hear you cry. *Is that what messed her up?* The answer is a resounding NO. For most of my childhood, my father worked away from home. *Oh, THAT'S it then? Absent male role models?* Also NO.

As my sister and I were primarily raised by my mother (again, Gender made sure our house ran according to the rules), we didn't see that much of my dad. He was out winning bread. So, when my sister and I got the 'I'll still see you on weekends' speech, it was dimly exciting, because I assumed I'd probably see *more* of my father. We'd go to see the butterflies at Tropical World in Leeds or the taxidermy wonders of Cliffe Castle in Keighley, we'd eat ice-cream, we'd go to the Little Thief. It was fairly standard.

Our parents teach us two sorts of lessons. The first are the explicit ones: don't play with matches, don't stick your hand in that crocodile's mouth. The second, more important sort are the ones we just learn by watching.

From my father, I learned a strict work ethic and respect for women and my elders, but I'm nothing like him. We've very different temperaments – and that has nothing to do with my gender (my sister is more like my dad than I am). From my mother, I learned two super-important lessons:

1. Being single is not a bad thing.
2. Your friendships are more important than your relationships.

Every other Friday, my mum would go on a Girls' Night Out. While she was the first of her friends to get divorced, she certainly wasn't the last. Soon they were a regular #Squad: Mum, Gill, Linda, Lindsey, Denise, Julie. She'd known some of them since school and they'd all had kids at about the same time.

Mum would get ready as I described before: painting her nails on the settee, Braun hot-brushing her hair to be more like Princess Diana's. My grandma would come over to babysit. Before bed, we were allowed to watch re-runs of *Doctor Who* and *Some Mothers Do 'Ave 'Em*. My mum would prepare grandma a supper of salmon paste sandwiches and Hula Hoops.

I've known my mother's friends all my life. I've seen all of them marry, divorce, remarry and date various men, but *they* have stayed consistent in each other's lives for fifty years or more. Men may well come and go, and it can be heartbreaking, but I learned, implicitly, that girlfriends will always be there, will always have your back.

As a small child, all my friends were little boys, because that's what Gender said was normal. I wasn't very good at being a boy, so my friendships did little to inspire me. Stereotypically boyish pursuits such as bike rides, football matches and super-masc computer games held little appeal.

Attempts to socialise me with boys didn't end well. The less said about Cub Scouts the better. I did *want* to go along, because I thought the uniform was cute, and I did like the idea of collecting little badges for stuff, but from even the first session (in which we had to make omelettes – masc) I knew that an all-boy environment was utterly alien to me.

To make matters worse, within weeks of joining I was sent on 'Cub Camp'. Three bad things happened.

1. David Grant, who was in the year above me at primary school, farted in my mouth. No really. We stayed up super late one night and he told me to close my eyes and open my mouth on his bunk bed. I did so (what?) and he proceeded to guff in my mouth. *This*, girls, is the type of *banter* you're missing out on.

2. I was sort of sexually molested. After overnight rain, the outdoor assault course was slippery. I lost my footing and slipped off a wooden beam, skinning my back. I was sent for first aid to a man, who – in hindsight – looked exactly like how you'd draw a sexual predator. He dabbed my back with antiseptic before also asking to 'check' my genitals. At the time, I thought that was a perfectly reasonable request and allowed him to ensure they were still in one piece. I'm very grateful (and lucky) that it went no further than that. In fact, it was only quite recently that I even clicked that that was some prime dirty-old-pervert behaviour.

3. I had my first panic attack. During 'orienteering' (which is little more than fancy talk for 'getting lost'), Baloo decided it would be funny to run off and leave thirty pre-pubescent boys to fend for themselves in dense woodland. This was, evidently, a time before Risk Assessment culture took hold. While trying to sprint our way out of the forest, a full-blown panic attack started. I couldn't breathe. I couldn't move. It was horrific. One of the other boys managed to track down Baloo, who returned and asked if I had asthma. I didn't. He told me, helpfully, to 'stop being a girl'. More, much more, on Gender's ideas about strength later.

I stopped attending cubs about a week and half after Mum had forked out for the uniform. She accurately observed that I 'didn't like it'.

Out of primary school, where I drifted between friendship groups (the way some children do), I went to middle school, where there was more pressure on 'who I'd play with'. Initially I was adopted by a girl in her final year, Jane, who sort of kept me as a pet. It was a bit odd.

Jane moved on to high school and I struck up a turbulent friendship with a girl called Carly. The only acceptable way for a ten-year-old 'boy' to spend so much time with a girl is to be their boyfriend, and so that's what we did. We sometimes had a clandestine playground kiss, but it was all terribly innocent. We were more like best girlfriends. We bickered, we stole trolls, pencils and scented rubbers from each other's Head pencil cases, we took out social hits on other girls we didn't like. Looking back, we were a right pair of little cunts, actually. Our slightly intense friendship endured for most of middle school. It ended because I told her I thought *Dirty Dancing*, her favourite film, should actually be called 'Clean Dancing'. Oooh, burn.

My mum eventually intervened, as it was felt I should be playing with boys, because that's what boys do. By this stage I was clearly never going to be one of the popular, sporty, play-football-every-break-time boys, so I was matched with the swotty, nerdy kids – at least two of whom were also destined for the LGBTQ community.

However, in moving to an all-male friendship group, I sort of ended up with my first boyfriend. Sam and I formed the least-closeted gay asexual coupling Bingley had ever seen. To all intents and purposes, we were a couple. We just didn't know it. I was surrounded by boys, but my behaviour was still stereotypically girly. I would seethe with jealousy if Sam attempted to form other friendships; I would scheme to bring down 'rivals'; I wanted Sam all to myself. Not exclusively female motivations obviously, but not quite the norm for a pubescent boy and his male friend, perhaps. Also, again, what a little cunt I was.

I went through secondary school mostly trying to keep my head down. The aforementioned 'mud-slinging' incident was the worst single episode of bullying, but there was a steady drip-drip-drip of verbal abuse, most of it homophobic. Teachers were either unaware of it, or unable to act, under Section 28. One PE teacher called me 'Dolly Dawson', which I briefly considered reclaiming post-transition. I certainly hope *he* didn't die in great pain. Oh no, wait, I do.

At school, I continued to hide behind a herd of nerds on the central quad – there's safety in numbers – and on weekends I mostly stayed home. I grew my VHS collection of *Doctor Who* episodes (I was – and remain – more interested in the companions than I ever was the Doctor). I read books. I started to write. Nowadays we'd call it 'fanfiction', but at the time I was just writing my own *Doctor Who* stories or ones about 'Professor Holmes' – my thinly veiled rip-off of *Doctor Who* about a university lecturer who time-travelled in a kitted-out Transit van.

By the time my nerdy tribe wanted to start sneaking into Bingley's pubs – the White Horse, the Brown Cow, and other coloured animals – I looked way younger than my sixteen years. I was left behind. If they invited me along they'd all get ID'd. To be honest, I wasn't especially bothered. I thought most of them were insufferable.

The change came when I moved into the Sixth Form after my GCSEs and the four 'houses' of the school were combined. This meant I had new subjects with new classmates. After quickly realising I was going to fail A Level Chemistry (I basically can't count, let alone do molar equations), I switched to the much easier Sociology, where I was in a class with Kerry, Phyllis and Beth.

I'd known Phyllis for the longest. We'd actually been at primary school together, although we didn't mix too much. Even then, she was hugely gifted and singled out as a child prodigy. Her parents were bohemian and her clothes a hodgepodge of colourful cast-offs. Snotty suburban parents disapproved and she was often accused of having lice in her flowing ginger hair. As a teenager, she retained her beatnik spirit and grandiose vocabulary, wearing velvet dresses and bindis (this was before 'cultural appropriation' became a thing).

Kerry had evolved from nerdy computer-gamer and *Quantum Leap* fangirl in middle school to Tank Girl at Bingley Grammar. At six feet tall, Kerry stood out, however much she tried to fade into the background and, in the end, had little choice but to go Dark Willow. She dyed her hair jet black with purple or pink stripes and her ears were lined with safety pins. She regularly dragged boys down corridors by their hair. I think, knowing what I know now, the boys quite enjoyed it.

Finally, Beth had moved from North Wales in Year 9 and struggled to fit in. She was conventionally beautiful and petite, but despite this – or possibly because of it – she put the Pretty Popular Girls' noses out of joint. Through her English lessons she became good friends with Phyllis and Kerry, who were, for a brief time, a couple.

So I already knew all three girls, but we weren't friends as such. I sat with them in Sociology and slowly started to get to know them. I can't tell you *what* drew me to them, but magnetically drawn I was. Almost immediately, I knew, on a very instinctual level, I'd found my people. Luckily, Kerry was quite used to adopting the school's waifs and strays, and I was accepted into the fold.

Looking back, I think our *difference* bonded us. We were all somehow *other*. It's that moment – a moment you can't teach – where we each chose to celebrate our weirdness, embraced it instead of running from it. Kerry once said, 'I realised people were going to talk about us whatever we did, so I thought we might as well give them something to talk about.' That exact quote found its way into *Hollow Pike*, my debut novel, in 2012.

There's one evening we spent together at Beth's that remains my favourite memory. Beth's bedroom was in a converted attic and she had her own VHS player. That night, we watched *Night of the Demons 2: Angela's Revenge*, a truly, truly awful slasher horror movie, and ate popcorn. I thought it'd be funny to try Beth's wetsuit on. Beth is five foot one, I am five foot eight. With my lanky, skinny body, I looked like a strange frog alien. God, we laughed and laughed until we couldn't breathe.

It was more than just hanging out together because there's safety in numbers, instead it was more like *Captain Planet* – each Planeteer combined to become one stronger entity. All of a sudden, school didn't seem so bad. I looked forward to going in to see my new friends. Kerry taught me about cool music and fashion designers. Phyllis took me on adventures to Leeds and Manchester. Beth and I shared books and she let me do her make-up because I wasn't brave enough to do it on my own face. I made that poor girl look like JonBenét Ramsey. Of course there was drama – what group of teenage girls *doesn't* have fallouts? – but I found myself living in West Yorkshire's answer to *Dawson's Creek*.

It didn't make the bullying or abuse disappear, but with Kerry, Phyllis and Beth by my side, it stopped bothering me. I came to believe that most of my tormentors were fucking basic bitches who'd never amount to very much while we, as creative, clever, experimental weirdos, were the future.

I was right.

Flash forward twenty years and all four of us are doing exactly what we set out to achieve. Each of us is where we wanted to be – even if we didn't know it at the time. Kerry is a highly sought-after programmer; Phyllis acts as an agent for circus performers (seriously); Beth is a successful HR manager but, as a single mum, her real drive is raising her daughter. Without wanting to sound like a massive cock, I'm probably the most successful person in my graduating year. Definitely not in financial terms, but in terms of . . . well, notoriety, if nothing else. I'm Sandy Frank in *Romy and Michelle*, arriving at the high school reunion in a helicopter. I'm not bitter about school. In fact, I took all that pain and turned it into ambition. Maybe I had something to prove, and I proved it.

I wanted to share that – not *just* to brag, but because there's probably some young, weird, geeky, trans, queer kids reading this right now and having a pretty shitty time at school. To you, I say, *You're going to be fine. You're going to be **more** than fine, you're going to be a fucking supernova. Hang in there.*

The four of us are still friends today, although we're spread out by geography. Kerry and I are still neighbours in Brighton. Since school, I've never underestimated or undervalued the importance of female friendship in my life. While I was living as a gay man, I did make some gay friends, but it makes sense that I would feel most at home among women. Just as my mother still has her Friday nights out with her #Squad, now I have mine too.

Throughout my teens and twenties, I was phenomenally lucky to have some friends who stuck by me through a plethora of terrible haircuts and ill-advised fashion choices: Mullets! Gilets! Fake tans! Flares! Cowboy shirts! I think, on a very subconscious level, I envied them. I always felt like the gay sidekick. All I ever really wanted to be was one of them.

When I announced my transition, it was essentially banging on a previously ajar door. As a gay man I'd glimpsed the sorority house, but hadn't *quite* been inside. What trans people are doing is asking to come in out of the cold. I think the friends who have flung open the doors to welcome me in are truly going to be my friends in fifty years' time, just like my mother and Linda, Lindsey, Gill, Denise and Julie.

8.

SEX AND SEXUALITY

AKA Ticking the Wrong Box

It was during this time boy-puberty kicked me with all its hormones and my mind turned to sex. Except it isn't your mind, is it? Desire comes from that space between your belly button and genitals. As has been well documented, my sexual awakening first started with Billy Warlock as Eddie in *Baywatch*, and then Dean Cain's *Superman*. So clear now, but that fire I felt in my veins was a cocktail of lust *and* searing jealousy towards Shaunie and Lois respectively. Like all boys in the 1990s, I had a poster of a soggy Pamela Anderson on my wall, but I also had a poster of Lois and Clark, and that was my favourite.

After a couple of years, I identified that urge in my gut as sex, only by this time I was wise enough to know I wasn't going to magically morph into Teri Hatcher if I wished hard enough. That *must* mean I'm gay, I eventually deduced when I was about fifteen.

See, I knew what a gay man was. I'd heard of them, I'd seen a couple of them on TV and I'd certainly been called one at school enough times. Like a boy acting/throwing/running like a girl, I had also been assured, both explicitly by bullies and implicitly by the media and school, that this was a bad and different thing. Gay people get AIDS and die. Gay people bury their fathers under the patio (*Brookside*). Gay people spend Christmas day sad and alone (*EastEnders*).

Even so, my initial reaction to the revelation I fancied men was oddly calming. I slotted comfortably into the pigeonhole and found it a snug fit. All of a sudden, I made sense, and it's human nature to want to make sense.

Up until that point I'd assumed I was going to marry a nice, if beige, girl called Helen or Sarah or Ruth and we'd live a Barratt Home with a conservatory and have two children. That thought hadn't filled me with terror, but it also failed to excite me. My new imagined future with Dean Cain was infinitely more appealing. The fantasy involved Dean and me living somewhere near a lake with a swimming pool and hot tub. Such simple goals.

But like I said, the realisation you have a secret identity comes with terrible fear, and I was scared too: scared I'd be rejected, scared I'd be homeless, scared I'd get AIDS. These fears, though, were less than the excitement; I was champing at the bit to arrive at my future as a gay man.

Even back then there were fatal flaws with the portrait I'd painted of myself. I'd rushed gung-ho into the art supply shop, bought an easel and canvas and all too quickly committed my identity to the page. Yes, I'd correctly identified the gender of the humans I wanted to have sex with, but that's ALL I'd done. What I hadn't done, what I hadn't even started to do, was consider myself and my role in that future.

Sexuality and gender are two completely distinct notions.

I'd argue that they don't even interact. It's not so much a Venn as a Carroll diagram:

	STRAIGHT	NOT-STRAIGHT
MALE	A	B
FEMALE	C	D

Of course, that sort of diagram only works for people with very defined, **binary** ideals of both sexuality and gender.

I'll walk you through it slowly and assume you don't spend up to five hours a day on Twitter screaming self-righteous abuse at people who get this sort of thing wrong.

The above diagram may make it seem like both gender and sexuality are inflexible. We can see, even just by looking at me, that this is far from true:

James aged 0–15: Box A
James aged 15–30: Box B
Juno aged 30: Box C

Over the course of my life, my *identity* has changed even if I remained fundamentally the same at my core. Furthermore, the boxes presented above don't work for everyone. Many people would describe their gender or sexual identity as **fluid**. Other people still like the term bisexual (which would fall under 'not-straight', I guess).

People identifying as genderfluid or gender non-binary may do so for lots of different reasons: they are unhappy with abiding by society's still ridiculously limited notions of gender; they feel neither male nor female; they simply believe there is no such thing as male and female and they are outmoded terms; they aren't comfortable with the term transgender.

I'm a huge fan of the writer Kate Bornstein who, after escaping the Church of Scientology in the seventies, embarked on gender transition in the eighties. 'I was assigned male at birth,' said Bornstein in a 2015 interview. 'It never really worked for me, but I tried really hard to be a guy, to be a man. It just felt like I was lying. This was in the 1980s. So I went through a gender transition and they told me I was a woman. So I said "OK! I am woman, hear me roar!" For about six months, I tried and I tried and it also felt like a lie. Woman didn't work for me any better than man had. So I finally said "goodbye to being a man, goodbye to being a woman". I am simply neither.'

I almost envy anyone who is able to, in the words of performance artist David Hoyle, 'transcend gender'. The crux of the problem is this: none of us know how it 'feels to be a man' or how it 'feels to be a woman'. We have only a unique, personalised experience of how it FEELS TO BE US. The absolute, very best we can aspire to is vague comfort in our own skin.

I feel secure now in my identity as a straight trans woman, but that's not to say it won't change in the future. Having been through two coming-out processes, I'm now firmly in the 'never say never' camp. But I am also a dichotic character. I was always 100 per cent men in the boudoir and 100 per cent female psychologically. For some people, it's just not so simple.

The way I see it, the only person who gets to pass

judgement on a person's identity is them. Does someone identifying as non-binary in any way impact on my decision to transition? Hell no! Does someone deciding to transition in any way impact on what it means to 'be a woman'? I think not.

Another goal of this book is to encourage you – yes you – to dwell on your *desires*.

Desires and identities have been weirdly linked. In the next chapter, we'll look at the powerful influence of Gender in the media and the media's powerful influence on us. At the time of writing, a well-known politician was just set up by a newspaper 'cavorting' with male prostitutes. I was especially interested in commentators' use of the term 'gay sex'.

WTF is 'gay sex'?

It's just sex. No gay or bi couple ever said to each other, 'Darling, let us tonight enjoy gay sex!'

If a straight man and woman partake in anal sex, is that 'gay sex'?

No? So if two men or two women get it on, even though *they* would never call it 'gay sex', is it 'gay sex'?

Sex is sex: two (or more) people trying super hard to make each other orgasm. Gay is a sexual identity. The two are not linked.

Labels are like clothes. As a teenager, I took a whole armful into the changing room and tried them on for size. I wore 'bi' for a bit, and then I thought 'gay' was a much better fit, but only because the label store wasn't, at that time, stocking 'trans'.

Desire is a fancy word for want. What do you want? Who do you want to have sex with? Not who you *think* you want to have sex with, what's the bit below your tum telling you? What do you want to wear? How would you like to look?

Next question: if acting on any of the above – your sex life, your clothes – had no impact on your *identity*, on what people called you, would you act on them? I suspect a lot more people would. It's a shame though, because going forward and doing exactly what I wanted to do – transitioning – has broadly made me very happy. I think a lot of people don't fuck who they wanna fuck because they worry that it will define them.

If there is no such thing as 'gay sex', it can't.

9.

SPICE UP YOUR LIFE

AKA You Can't Be What You Can't See

My true female awakening came in 1996 with the advent of the Spice Girls. Bear with me, I really mean it.

If you weren't a teen in the 1990s, you're never going to get this, in the same way that I don't really 'get' vlogging. Skip this whole section. To outsiders, the Spice Girls look like fluff, like cotton candy and E numbers, but to those of us inside that bubble, they were beyond influential.

Even global megastar Adele acknowledges the impact of the Spice Girls. Speaking on James Corden's *Late Late Show* she said, 'It was a huge moment in my life. Five ordinary girls who did so well and *got out*. I was like: I wanna get out. I don't know what I wanna get out of, but I wanna get out.'

Up until the Spice Girls, I had sought some refuge in 'acceptable alternatives'. I definitely wasn't a 'boy's boy' but it was *acceptable* for boys to like Blur, Placebo or Pulp. There are *always* 'acceptable alternatives'.

I first saw the Spice Girls on *Top of the Pops* in 1996. The group were off on a promotional visit to Japan and were filmed lip-synching for their lives from some ornamental temple garden thing. Instantly I was hooked: the colour, the high-kicks, each girl's individual look. The cameraman clearly had ADHD – I only glimpsed each band member for long enough to know there was one with an afro, one with bright red hair, a blonde, one in a Liverpool kit and . . . another one. The fact that there was a band with five women was arresting enough. Sure, we'd had Eternal and En Vogue, but they weren't quite bubblegum pop enough for my taste.

Because I was outwardly a boy, I had to pretend I didn't like the Spice Girls except as masturbation material. I shunned them in the same way I shunned Take That and Boyzone. 'I mean "zig-a-zig-ah", that's so stupid,' I would lie shamelessly. 'What does it even *mean*?'

But over the summer of 1996, I just gave in to them. I couldn't resist. I started buying *Smash Hits* and *We Love Pop* magazine. Everyone agreed that 'Wannabe' was catchy, but the follow-up, 'Say You'll Be There', sealed the deal. I was a fully fledged Spice Girl/Boy. Initially my heart belonged to Geri, but I was oddly spellbound by 'Midnight Miss Suki' and my love for Posh soon developed into deranged pointing and pouting in front of my mirror.

It was *not* OK for a boy to like the Spice Girls as much as I did, but I couldn't keep it in. About this time, I'd met Kerry, Phyllis and Beth and stopped giving a shit what people thought about me anyway. I was forced, for want of a better phrase, to shit or get off the pot and pick an identity.

In fact, the day I first told *anyone* I thought I was gay was the day I bought the CD single of 'Stop' in 1998 (cruelly denied a number one by Run DMC vs Jason Nevins). That afternoon, having baked a treacle tart in our 'Enrichment Class' (a Wednesday afternoon activity designed to strengthen our university applications. Everyone knows how Oxbridge are ALWAYS on the lookout for a skilled treacle tart baker, right?), I was walking home with Kerry. Vastly more cosmopolitan than I, Kerry often caught the National Express to Manchester to hang out with her boyfriend. There, she told me, she would hang out in queer spaces with actual homosexuals. By the Leeds–Liverpool canal, I broke down. 'I think I might be gay,' I said, the last word barely audible.

'Oh, OK,' said Kerry. 'Well, you know I'm bi, right?'

And that was that. She came back to mine to make sure I was OK and we watched that day's episode of *Sunset Beach* so I could show her Father Antonio, with whom I was in love.

It's only now I see how hugely *important* the Spice Girls were to me. Never were the Spice Girls there for men. They were as unkempt as an underage hen-do being thrown out of Yates's. Men, to them, seemed an afterthought. Men rarely featured as a motif in their videos, and if they did, they were as disposable sexual playthings: tied to the roof of a truck in 'Say You'll Be There' or in the 'fantasy rooms' of 'Holler'.

Whether it was branding or not didn't matter to me, a teenage secret-girl. Feminist academics lampooning their male Svengali didn't matter one jot. What mattered was their very simple message: friendship – and in particular female friendship – never ends.

Their 'branding' (if it was) translated. There had been other 'girl squads' but this one was idiotproof: were you the cute one, the sophisticated one, the loudmouth, the tomboy or the pseudo-intellectual? I longed, *longed* to be a Spice Girl. It was a good few years until I realised I already was. The sixth, trans one.

Culture and society are a two-way mirror. Ropey and clichéd, but life does imitate art as much as art imitates life. 'The media is the message *and* the messenger,' said Pat Mitchell, former CEO of PBS, in the fantastic 2011 documentary *Miss Representation*.

Neither women nor men are passive receptacles of media messages, but the **instructions** about our identity and behaviour are far from subliminal. In a constant barrage of images and noises, it's hard to filter for 'the truth' or the reality of manhood or womanhood. What I can do, however, is identify the messages that were received loud and clear by me, a trans woman, as I was growing up. As I was unable to talk about myself (because I had no trans points of reference), all I could do was absorb these messages and make my own mosaic of womanhood from those I picked up on.

I found myself listening to both the messages I was *supposed* to receive (those for boys) and the ones I was genuinely interested in (those for girls). In short, with no real human 'teaching' me how to be a girl, I had to learn from the media. I think lots of other girls do too, and this is troublesome, given that some corners of our media actively loathe women and want them to suffer.

STORY TIME

The earliest messages about gender I got – and you probably got too – were through children's books and oral storytelling. Our culture, our *lives*, are built on a foundation of storytelling. When we gossip over lattes with our friends, we are – in fact – doing the same thing our ancestors did around fires hundreds of years ago: telling stories. We start with a framing device: ''You'll never guess what Jackie did last night . . .'; establish the scene, 'So we were in the chicken shop after we'd come out of the club'; build to a twist or reveal, 'She did! She sucked him off RIGHT THERE and THEN ATE POPCORN CHICKEN'; before a moral ending, 'and now she has herpes.'

Stories are so much a part of our lives, we don't even notice that they're the most fundamental way we communicate.

I was told stories from birth. Most children are. I was read to and learned to read young. As an incognito little girl, I was most interested in female characters. As mentioned, no one was *telling* me this is what little girls do – because they thought I was a boy – but I was able to glean much about what it is girls *are*.

- **Snow White:** Domestic servant to seven dwarves. Swallows after giving in to temptation. Is saved from temptation by a man who engages in sexual activity with her while she's unconscious. Her chief rival is solely obsessed with her looks and punishes Snow for being physically attractive.

- **Sleeping Beauty:** A woman is again saved by a man who engages in sexual activity with her while she sleeps.
- **Cinderella:** Domestic servant to women who envy her kindness and physical attractiveness. Although given a leg-up by a supportive female elder, is ultimately rescued from domestic servitude by a man's wealth.
- **Beauty and the Beast:** Belle is forced into domestic servitude by her father in a business arrangement. Develops Stockholm Syndrome with her abusive captor.
- **Rapunzel:** Rapunzel is trapped inside a phallus, her physical attractiveness her only hope of escape. She does so by consenting to let a man inside her prison. She is punished for this moral lapse by having her beauty impaired.
- **The Little Mermaid:** For the love of a man unable to recognise her face, a young mermaid rejects her entire culture and family.

As you can see, traditional tales do not serve women well. In some versions of 'Little Red Riding Hood', Red waits to be rescued from the Big Bad Wolf by a hunky woodcutter. I hope people don't still tell that version. That said, a girl who can't recognise a fucking wolf in a nightie probably isn't the best role model to begin with.

Pictures in books and Disney representations reinforce that princesses are thin, feminine, pretty and white. I was into my teens before Pocahontas repped for women of colour. Black Tiana in *The Princess and the Frog* is green for three quarters of the film.

The television I was watching wasn't *much* better,

although the 1980s did see *some* steps forward for children's TV. Remember, characters like Ellen Ripley (*Alien*, 1979) are great but, because of film certificates, often come along about eighteen years too late to influence the way a little girl sees herself.

There was She-Ra, *Thundercats'* Cheetara, Sheila and Diana in *Dungeons & Dragons* and *He-Man's* Teela, all of whom had some talent or agency with a weapon. Barbie was allowed a career (or twenty) while *Jem and the Holograms* was truly outrageous. All, to some degree, were heralded as beautiful. All were thin, most were white. As I got older, I had the cast of *Neighbours*, *Beverly Hills 90210* and *Saved by the Bell* to aspire to. Even *90210's* geeky Andrea underwent a makeover and cast off her glasses and perm. Kelly (pretty!), Jessie (smart!) and Lisa (sassy!) of *Saved by the Bell* were there solely as love interests and foils for the male characters.

I saw nothing problematic with these messages. When we played on the street, I wanted to be Bonnie Langford's Mel character from *Doctor Who* – a one-dimensional nightmare who screamed and ran away from monsters while wearing stilettos. None of those things mattered because she was a girl and I wanted to be one too. I would pretend to be Mel and Matthew-From-Over-the-Road would rescue me as The Doctor.

By the time Sophie Aldred took over in *Who* as tough, streetwise Ace, I wasn't interested because she didn't have nice clothes or hair. I'd been brainwashed by Gender. She wasn't 'girly' enough for me to be interested.

I did *see* male role models – the ones I was supposed to idolise – but I just wasn't interested. Heroes were even less diverse than their girlfriends. Lion-O, He-Man, Captain Planet: heroes through and through. Strong, physically and morally, honest, honourable and righteous. While Brenda and Kelly in *90210* bickered over boys, relaxed brotherhood was paramount for Brandon and Dylan.

Like I said, Gender is a ho and will fuck literally anyone. I don't think little boys are getting especially healthy messages from the media either. Paul Gascoigne was widely mocked for crying during the 1991 World Cup, men are *still* being mocked for crying at the 2016 Rio Olympics. More on that later.

As I moved into adolescence, my pool of exclusively female role models was becoming more interesting (Michelle Pfeiffer's Catwoman, Seven of Nine or Captain Janeway in *Voyager*, Buffy the Vampire Slayer, Dana Scully) but it was *music* that started to inspire and inform my identity more.

POP, POP, POP MUSIC

Where were you when you heard David Bowie had died? I had recently moved back to Brighton having finished a four-year stint in London. I'd been kept up for much of the night by my noisy neighbours (again), I trudged into the lounge and flicked *BBC Breakfast* on. It was breaking news: David Bowie: The Thin White Duke, Ziggy Stardust, Aladdin Sane and, most importantly, Jareth the Goblin King, was dead.

I flopped down on the settee, a little bit heartbroken. Carrie Brownstein said it better than I could: 'It feels like we lost something elemental, as if an entire colour is gone.'

I'm gonna square with you. I'm about twenty years too young to have experienced the peak Bowie excellence of 1972's *The Rise and Fall of Ziggy Stardust and the Spiders from Mars*. In fact, *my* Bowie moment truly came with 1986's *Labyrinth* – a wonderful yet much maligned chapter in his creative history.

Although I was only five when the film came out, I remember my dad refusing to take me to see *Labyrinth* at the cinema because he'd heard it was too scary. Instead we went to see *Basil the Great Mouse Detective*, which is also fucking terrifying. I must have seen *Labyrinth* first on VHS or on TV and it remains my favourite to this day.

Why is *Labyrinth* so overlooked by Bowie fans? Well first, I can attest as a children's author that anything made with children in mind is met with snobbery. It's not proper if it's not designed for middle-aged, middle-class broadsheet journalists. Well, let me tell you, my generation is now rapidly becoming the middle-aged, middle-class broadsheet journalists and *Labyrinth* is a fucking masterpiece.

God, I could talk about that film forever, but that's a whole other book. Suffice to say, a film about a Delevingne-browed girl on the cusp of a sexual awakening forced to question her firmly held childish beliefs and ultimately cast them aside was *dimly* influential. Bowie is awesome in that film. To say he's so much older than Jennifer Connelly but doesn't really come across like a skanky predator speaks very highly of his performance.*

---

* And yes, I am aware it is alleged Bowie engaged in sexual activity with underage fans, which, if true, is absolutely skanky and also illegal.

Just as those people who said Ziggy Stardust was a weird freak were wrong, so are people who said David Bowie jigging around in leggings with Muppets was naff. So there.

Anyway, I digress. Bowie's death prompted an 'outpouring of public grief' on both social media and the streets – Brixton hosted an impromptu street party in his honour (although the death of Margaret Thatcher also achieved this). As sure as day follows night, the public mourning was met by the Death Police telling us how we should appropriately grieve a celebrity: 'It's not like you're his family, have some respect for Iman' etc. Oh, social media, what have you done to us?*

But Bowie was more than a celebrity, he was a cultural icon and an especially important one for the LGBT/non-binary community. Actually, important to anyone, *ever*, who didn't conform. OK, his early music is well respected by indie darlings, but it was as Ziggy that Bowie captured the world's attention. No one – certainly not anyone in Bingley – had seen anything like it, and I use 'it' quite deliberately, as the gender lines were so intentionally blurred.

There had been queer icons before Bowie (April Ashley was outed as a trans woman by the *Sunday People* in 1961), but think about televisions. By the late 1960s, *most* homes had a TV. The stage was set. David Bowie, somehow neither male or female, and yet both, was able to infiltrate the semis and bungalows, the suburbs and cul-de-sacs.

People had defied Gender and his manifesto before, but

* 'Opinions are like assholes, everyone's got one.' Kennedy Davenport, *RuPaul's Drag Race*, 2015

few had done so on television. What's more, Bowie defied Gender *and* made it look cool.

Because his tunes were unquestionable bops, he was welcomed into hearts and homes. Glam rock was all about the clothes, the hair, the make-up and, importantly, an escape route out of the norm. Pop music has always had its subversive pied pipers, its socially acceptable rebels, and nearly always there's an element of theatrical transgenderism: Bowie, Madonna, Annie Lennox, Boy George, Pete Burns, Grace Jones, Prince, Marilyn Manson, Lady Gaga – all have subverted the 'norms' of male and female. Across the decades they offered hope, an alternative, an escape, a Narnia closet to those most in need: teenagers pushing at the edges of the cookie cutters.

Teenagers like me.

Bowie's androgynous beauty – how many dads found themselves with a curious stiffy while watching Bowie as his own backing singers in the 'Boys Keep Swinging' video in 1979 – added a new playful dimension to cross-dressing, something traditionally seen as sexually deviant or perverted. Simply put, Bowie got hold of Gender and made fun of him.

Moreover, and bear in mind this was the 1970s, Bowie was refreshingly open when discussing his sexuality. Right out the gate in 1972, Bowie told *Melody Maker* he was gay, later revising this to bisexual in an interview with *Playboy* in 1976: 'It's true – I am a bisexual. But I can't deny that I've used that fact very well. I suppose it's the best thing that ever happened to me.' Although he eventually came out as a 'closeted heterosexual' (1983), there's no denying Bowie had brought both sexuality and gender into the mainstream like no musician before.

Not only did Bowie change the landscape of music, art, gender and sex, but his success (regardless) gave tacit permission for subsequent performers to rebel (rebel) with sex and gender.

Bowie's legacy, the loosening of moral strings, was important for all women – cis and trans. Bowie's heyday in the 1970s was both cause and effect of a sea change of how sex and gender were portrayed in the media. The media evolved because of Bowie and Bowie existed because the media let him.

MADONNA

Madonna, by her own admission following Bowie's death, would be nowhere without him. She said, on stage, 'If you haven't heard about David Bowie, then look him up, mother-fuckers. He was one of the geniuses in the music industry, one of the greatest singer-songwriters of the twentieth century, and he changed my life when I went to see him in concert in Detroit. He showed me that it was OK to be different.'

Which is certainly true. If nothing else (musically they exist in different spaces) Madonna adopted Bowie's love of reinvention, if stopping short of creating discrete characters. Madonna, whatever she wears, is Madonna.

Madonna has been 'active' as a celeb presence my whole life, although I didn't become a fully-fledged obsessive until

1997's *Ray Of Light* – surely the greatest reinvention of them all.

There are so many ways in which I looked to Madonna for clues to womanhood. Debbie Harry, Chrissie Hynde and Kate Bush arrived before her, but there's something about Madonna's tenacity and work ethic that singles her out. Pitting women against each other is patriarchal sport if ever there was one, so that's not the point of this chapter. I love all of those women as artists. I also adore Kylie Minogue (*Kylie* was my first album, and at the time Kylie and Charlene Ramsay were inseparable in my mind), Cyndi Lauper, The Bangles, Belinda Carlisle, Siouxie and the Banshees, Cher and many other female artists who happily coexisted alongside Madonna in the 1980s and 1990s.

A little like Bowie, Madonna didn't *truly* get going until her second coming, 1984's *Like A Virgin*. All of a sudden, it got interesting. There she was: a previously generic pop-tart writhing around in a wedding dress (with all its societal connotations) begging the listener to fuck her like she's never been fucked before. You know, like she's never had sex before even though she definitely has (because she says so).

Ironically, I only paid attention later, and at the age at which you really 'get into' music, with *Like A Prayer*. By that point, Madonna was a bona fide megastar, and so my first experience of a woman in the public eye was a woman who was in every way as famous and powerful as her closest male contemporary (Michael Jackson). I didn't really see why people were so outraged at her 'black Jesus' motif. Like, why not?

As we headed into the 1990s, Madonna, like Bowie,

was able to discuss her sexuality in a way that women simply hadn't been allowed to. Madonna was so powerful that no one dared question her right to record the under-rated *Erotica* and release the *Sex* book. She wasn't without her detractors, and I clearly remember the general vibe among boys at school being 'she's a slapper'. One charming young man in our vinegar-soaked school canteen (Jamie Oliver hadn't by that stage banned the humble chip) said 'Imagine how many dicks she's had up her', and I quite clearly recall wondering why, exactly, that would be a bad thing.

But this was AIDS o'clock and people, especially Americans, were experiencing a new puritanism. Still, Madonna being Madonna, she addressed this head on with 'Human Nature' ('whoops, I didn't know I couldn't talk about sex') in 1995.

If Madonna was testing the sexy waters in the 1980s, then the 1990s decided it was a pool party. Perhaps AIDS *necessitated* discussion about sex, but soon it was every-where: in music ('Let's Talk About Sex', 'Waterfalls', 'I Wanna Sex You Up'); film (*Basic Instinct*, *Fatal Attraction* – which is basically AIDS: The Movie – *Showgirls*, *Sliver*) and on TV (Kathy Beale being raped on *EastEnders* just after tea). Madonna 'got away with it', therefore so could the media at large. Vitally, Madonna (unlike some of her pretenders, including Britney and Christina, I'd argue) didn't look remotely like she was coerced into her overt sexuality by a male management team as a sales tool.

But perhaps the most important lesson from Madonna

came at the end of the 1990s, when she audaciously proved she didn't need or want you to want to fuck her anyway. Arriving back on the scene for *Frozen* in a big black sheet, every inch the 'crone' women are supposed to run from, never mind embrace, Madonna truly earned her icon status: she outlasted all the others and, crucially, remained relevant in a way that, say, Sting, had not. By this stage, Michael Jackson was a Halloween nightmare, she'd outlived the naffness of New Kids on the Block and Vanilla Ice, and even icons of the 1980s like Prince had vanished in a blur of name-changing symbol weirdness.

And she was still, unquestionably, all woman.

In the video for 'The Power of Good-Bye', Madonna was apparently dissatisfied at how beautiful she looked so asked for her image to be digitally distorted in post-production. She evolved beyond simply being an image. The listener was forced to listen.

Arguably, the double header of *Ray of Light* and *Music* marked Madonna's last two truly excellent albums (although there are arguments to be made for both *American Life* and *Confessions on a Dancefloor*) and her musical output has tailed off, but they're not the end of the lessons I learned from Madonna.

Much is made of Madonna's stubborn refusal to grow old – her leotard-clad crotch-thrusting in 'Hung Up', cougaring Justin Timberlake in '4 Minutes' (in a way that male artists often perve on young women, but you know, patriarchy), her rumoured cosmetic surgeries and provocative style. I think we can interpret the media's mockery of Madonna in two ways:

1. Madonna, you are almost sixty! Please do what we expect of sixty-year-old women! We don't want to fuck you anymore because you are sixty. It is gross. Please die or become June Whitfield.
2. Madonna, you scare us because despite our many attempts to bring you down over the last thirty years, you, a woman, cannot be beaten.

I think women who mock and criticise Madonna, and especially her appearance, are the by-product of patriarchal brainwashing. What I've learned from Madonna is that, as a woman, I can do whatever the fuck I like for as long as I fucking like AND if I still have legs like that when I'M sixty, you can bet your arse I'll be getting them out. Even if I *don't* have legs like Madonna, she has shown that I can still get them out if I so choose.

Whether you like her music or not, Madonna has given zero fucks for the best part of forty years. Bow down.

SO I GOT TO THINKING . . .

Who knows if Darren Star and Michael Patrick King were inspired by the Spice Girls when they optioned the novel *Sex and the City*. Like the Spice Girls, there was a ginger one, a scary one, a posh one and a big baby. Oh, that's overly harsh, but the show was written to a formula – rarely would four friends have such clearly defined character boundaries – but it was another Girl Squad I soon wanted to join.

Initially, I didn't like *Sex and the City*. I was besotted

with another US, female-fronted show, *Ally McBeal*. Ally has *not* aged well: a phenomenally successful lawyer crippled by neurotic obsessions over men and thus unable to enjoy any other element of her life wouldn't fly now. *Ally McBeal* was written, largely, by a heterosexual, cisgender man – David E. Kelley. We can only be grateful we never had to endure his *Wonder Woman* reboot, which reduced the most powerful woman in the world to stressing about Facebook posts and boyfriends.

Sex and the City – which by episode five featured Charlotte's 'lovely cunt' – was startling to sixteen-year-old me, to say the least. Yes, it has oft been said the gay man writing the show made the women 'talk like gay men' (OK, let's go with that . . .) but if that means they spoke openly about their bodies and sex, how is that a bad thing?

As the show rolled on, my friends and I adopted the same attitude. Talking about sex, and indeed actually having it, was no longer seen as slutty; it was actually aspirational behaviour.

As a culture, we are getting savvier about intersectional feminism – a term first formally coined in the 1980s by civil rights advocate Kimberlé Crenshaw – and it's all too easy to take pot shots at *Sex and the City*: it was overwhelmingly white; they had extraordinary privilege; they were never sexually harassed or assaulted. Accepting these faults, perhaps King's MO was to present life as it *could* be for women, not *how it was or is*. This was a show about women who had careers, made life decisions, had casual sex, used condoms, had sexual health checks, spent disposable income the way men do, bought property independently, had kids and DIDN'T have kids. Let's not throw the baby out with the Check Your Privilege bathwater.*

In 1999, I decided I was going to be Carrie Bradshaw. Like me, she already prioritised her friendships over relationships (I still do), and she lived a seemingly impossible life of parties, lunches and glamour on a freelancer's budget. Somehow, with considerably fewer designer clothes and shoes, I have managed the same feat.

Learning how to be a woman from a TV show was stupid. It was no substitute for learning from actual women, but what I *didn't* learn was the struggle. We never saw Carrie's life as a dirt-poor intern, the years where she lived in a flatshare with nineteen other girls, sleeping in shifts (if she lived in Manhattan now . . . well she probably wouldn't be able to so now, she'd be in Hoboken). Thus, I never perceived obstacles to me becoming her. Perhaps this is lingering male privilege – I was never told I couldn't be exactly what I wanted to be, and I wanted to be Carrie. Like Carrie, I certainly never wasted time worrying about being single as my thirtieth birthday loomed.

When I got my first book deal in 2011 for *Hollow Pike*, I saw my chance and seized it with both hands. Was this impulsivity a traditionally 'male' thing to do? I had no children, no dependants – I threw away a stable career in teaching for the uncertain life of a freelance writer. With

---

* Yes, absolutely *Sex and the City 2* is one of the worst movies of all time and I could weep because I can't deny it exists. I mean Carrie MOCKS A MUSLIM WOMAN for EATING A CHIP. Fuck off. Fuck all the way off.

society not telling me – a supposed man – I had to worry about my 'biological clock' (more on that later), it was a no-brainer. TV said it was OK.

Although I didn't at that stage acknowledge I was a woman, this was my shot to be Carrie Bradshaw. I now understand how she lived a life of endless parties and lunches: credit card debt and Arts Council grants. Much like Carrie I also became a neurotic wreck – but that's just being self-employed all over.

ROLE MODELS TODAY

In my battle against Gender, I turned to the media for clues on how to be a woman. Are things better or worse now than they were in the 1990s?

Children's television is a strange space for a childless, thirty-something trans woman to occupy. But in the name of research, I sat down for a few hours of CBeebies, CBBC and CITV.

Paw Patrol: a plucky squad of rescue dogs features one bitch and she flies a pink helicopter. In *Ben and Holly*, Ben wears blue while Holly wears pink and fairy wings. Peppa Pig wears a pinky-red dress, her brother wears blue. The Pink Power Ranger is a girl. Resistance leaders like She-Ra and Princess Leia are nowhere to be seen.

Tween and teenage output is a mixed bag. I worry for the teenage girls of today. It's not all bad: they are free to curate their own role models online. Pre-internet, it's unlikely (although not impossible) that role models like

Tyler Oakley or Zoella would have been singled out by TV execs. Yet what we learn through this online self-selection of role models is that millions of teen girls are still drawn to Disney princesses. Regardless of their content, the most-subscribed *female* YouTubers are traditionally pretty, slim and predominantly white. It is heartening, however, that LGBTQ personalities (Jazz Jennings, Joey Graceffa, Troye Sivan, Hannah Hart and many more) seem able to flourish in online 'safe spaces'.

YouTube, Twitter and Instagram have democratised fame. No longer do we need middle-men (and it so often was men) to tell us who we should aspire to be. If you want trans women of colour (Janet Mock, Laverne Cox, Munroe Bergdorf and many more), you can so easily find them and build a fandom.

However, there is a clear divide between internet fame and the mainstream. My mum – even my sister – wouldn't be able to pick Zoella out of a line-up. TV, movie and music stars are still presenting depressingly limited instructions on masculinity and femininity to the masses.

Hollywood is the worst of all. Caught in a self-made cycle of cautiousness, fewer films are being made and those that are are 'tent poles' that must succeed. In a panic to ensure films 'play' globally, and for the masses, studios take few chances. The last ten years have revolved around WMC (White Man in a Cape) movies: Batman, Superman, the Marvel Universe. Despite the phenomenal success of *Twilight* and *The Hunger Games*, few gains have been made in terms of female representation. Indeed, it seems the only lesson learned from *The Hunger Games* was to cast Jennifer Lawrence more often.

Worryingly, the relative failure of the *Divergent* or *Mortal Instruments* series may well have convinced Hollywood that *The Hunger Games* was a fluke, and one never to be repeated. That said, Katniss Everdeen should not be underestimated. The success of the character *did* alert studios to a hunger (soz) for 'strong female characters'.* Without Katniss, I doubt we'd have seen *Frozen* dominate the box office. I doubt Disney execs would have greenlit a script about sisters – and let's not forget the gendered original title, *The Snow Queen*, was dropped so as not to alienate little boys.

Frozen deserves singling out. It is a bold film and one which will define a generation of girls (and a lot of boys too). Yes, the main characters are all skinny and white with freakish bug eyes. Yes, Elsa has a sexy dress. BUT, Anna and Elsa (and their developed inner lives) propel the entire film forwards. Elsa doesn't get a boyfriend or love interest at any stage. She makes terrible, if understandable, choices and later redeems herself without being a 'wicked witch' (in an earlier version of the script, she was an outright villain).

The vast majority of kids' and teen films (including Marvel Universe) still portray women as secondary characters. The

---

* The problem I have with 'strong female characters' – Ripley, Arya Stark, Katniss, Sarah Connor etc – is that we only include *physically* strong characters in think-pieces. I'd like to see discussions about 'strong female characters' also include flawed, multi-faceted ones who overcome weakness, addiction, bad relationships, abuse, leave shitty jobs, have abortions, stick with shitty jobs out of necessity and raise kids adequately to little or no fanfare. Only praising athletic super-women is just another stick to clobber most of us with.

implicit message to girls is this: *You* are secondary to the men in *your* life. However kick-ass Black Widow is, her story is a *Captain America* subplot. Efforts to address such imbalance (the *Ghostbusters* reboot, *Wonder Woman*) are very current and have been met with mixed reviews. Depending on what sources you read, *Ghostbusters* was either a barnstorming feminist triumph or simply mediocre (with box-office returns to match).

Undoubtedly signifying some sort of progress, *Ghostbusters* earnestly depicts professional women being professional. But that's pretty much *all* it does. Some questionable editing seems to have rendered anything *stereotypically* female unworthy of screen time. The friendships between the characters are thin and there are only hints to female sexuality. Once again, it seems the best way to be a 'strong female character' is to basically be a man. The project felt slightly like a pandering attempt to get male viewers to 'swallow' women. I actually thought Paul Feig's earlier *Bridesmaids* was a much more compelling, nuanced story about women.

One film can't be everything to everyone. The answer, of course, is that we need many, many more films about all different types of women.

TV fares better. With less budget at stake, young adult viewers today have far more TV role models than I had: *Jessica Jones* (who almost single-handedly makes up for piss-poor female characters on the Marvel big screen), *Orange is the New Black*, *How to Get Away with Murder*, *Scandal*, *The 100*, *Pretty Little Liars*, *Stranger Things* and many more female-fronted shows – especially diverse, post-*Hannah Montana* Disney Channel originals. Note: all of this programming is American. UK schedulers only make TV for white people in their forties, having seemingly admitted defeat to YouTube in creating content for young adults. At the time of writing, only the BBC's *Wolf Blood* and *Class*, E4's *Crazyhead* and soap *Hollyoaks* exist as dedicated teen drama content.

My biggest pet hate is pop music. WHERE ARE MY SPICE GIRLS NOW? I'm sure every generation laments the passing of its pop icons, and certainly Madonna was sexualised, but girls are witness to a deluge of misogyny on Smash Hits TV.

Sure, there's Adele (and thank God for Adele), but we're seeing a stark difference in male and female popstars. I've never seen Ed Sheeran's naked body. I've never seen Sam Smith's ass cheeks twerk. I've never seen Justin Timberlake tongue other boys in the name of coy faux-lesbianism. Even Beyoncé, the most powerful woman in music, even with her outwardly feminist statements, still wriggles around in her pants while her husband potters alongside in jeans and a baggy T-shirt. A recent Taylor Swift and ZAYN video collaboration sees him in a suit and her in a bra.

This is not to 'slut shame' Beyoncé, Ariana Grande, Rihanna, Nicki Minaj, Katy Perry, Taylor Swift or Miley Cyrus (for all of whom undressing is a feature of their videos). The problem is the fact that men don't *have* to dress that way, and also that these women wouldn't get very far if they insisted on wearing jeans and baggy T-shirt. In 2017, part of being a female popstar is near-nudity and highly sexualised performance in a way that IT IS NOT

FOR MALE POPSTARS – thus propagating deeply embedded sexism. In place of 'friendship never ends', we have Ariana Grande telling us how having a massive cock in her loo-loo has her walking side to side.

The message could not be clearer for modern girls: *What you look like, your body and your sexual availability are the most important things about you. Your body is your currency.*

There are beacons of hope. Sia goes as far as hiding her body and face entirely, letting her music and lyrics do all the talking. Adele has made a career of having precisely zero fucks to give about what anyone thinks of her. Anohni, Solange Knowles, Emeli Sandé, Robyn and Héloïse Letissier of Christine and the Queens manage to keep their kit on. Lady Gaga took her body and subverted sexuality, her provocative nudity more in line with performance art than sex. Tove Lo's masturbation scene in her 'Fairy Dust' video is designed to shock, not arouse – although it may well do both.

I am so ready for the spirit of the Spice Girls to return. After a decade of drippy male teen idols, reality show flotsam, highly sexualised Disney moppets and bed-wetters, I would kill for some girls singing songs about being girls.

INSTAGRAM FAMOUS

Of the top twenty-five most followed Instagram accounts, five belong to the female offspring of Kris Jenner, formerly Kardashian, amassing approximately 230 million followers combined. That is more than the population of Brazil.

I only recently discovered that the dynasty rose to prominence via the OJ Simpson trial, which eventually led to a reality TV show. With the exception of young Kendall – who is a highly sought-after fashion model – it's hard to define what the Kardashian/Jenner children *do*. Let's call them 'entrepreneurs', because they have attached their name to products both explicitly (clothes, perfumes etc) and implicitly (product placement on their social media channels).

It's unfair to single out the Kardashians. They were not the first reality TV stars and they won't be the last, but role models no longer need a discernable 'talent' in order to succeed and be hugely visible to both girls and boys. *Why study?* this career path whispers, *You can be rich and famous for nothing*.

Once again, flesh is currency. Instagram is awash with 'fitness models' or 'Instamodels'; people who wouldn't usually trouble a modelling agency's books but have garnered millions of followers and lucrative sponsorship deals. Let's be quite clear, regardless of any profession listed in the bio (fitness instructor, lifestyle coach, diet guru) most of these people are glamour models. They've sounded the death knell of *FHM*, *Nuts* and *Zoo*; you can now get all the tits and ass you need, for free, on Instagram. What started life as a twee way to photograph your cupcake is now a hotbed of spandex-clad softcore pornography. It's equal opportunities too – there are as many naked male hustlers on there as there are women. Agencies have woken up to this trend and now have 'Special Bookings' or 'Digital' lists.

Is it sex work? I'd say no more and no less than the models in *FHM* of old. I think the difference is, again, that we've removed gatekeepers who would historically 'select' which naked bodies were displayed in print media. Now, anyone with a smartphone can legitimately claim to be a model.

The success of scantily clad Instagram stars tells children that displaying a lot of flesh is a sure-fire way to make money. Male or female, your appearance is the most important thing about you. Whether you're skinny, plus-size, black or white, your value is based on your body. You are a visual commodity. Why bother learning anything in school? Why bother studying for that degree? You don't need an opinion or the ability to speak in coherent sentences. You'll make cash faster if you get your ass down the gym, inject a shitload of fillers in your lips and pout into direct sunlight while resting a box of Tummy Tamer Tea on your cleavage.

It's about role models, and the lack of diversity we see both in the mainstream media and online. If I was a teenage girl *now*, listening to Gender via the loudspeaker of media to try to learn how to be a woman, I basically think I'd be fucked.

10.

THE GREAT ESCAPE

AKA The College Years

Looking back now, it's fairly clear that my teenage years were underpinned by a tinnitus-like thrum of moderate, constant anxiety. When I was about twelve, on a holiday in Majorca, I had a huge panic attack one evening when we couldn't find our way back to our hotel. Even though I was with my mum and some family friends, we were lost, lost in Spain, and no one but me seemed to care.

Anxiety often starts with a traumatic experience. A sufferer starts to fear the trauma will be repeated, this impacts on their day-to-day choices and before you know it, the anxiety has generalised to a low-level worry about *everything*. Mine centred around getting lost and going to new places. This, in hindsight, did impact on my social life. How could it not?

It had peaks and troughs. Notably on Year 9 camp, away from home and very much lost, I broke down. I was a shivering mess despite the July heat, hiding in a tent. I was unable to eat, shower or take part in the activities. Part of the issue was the fear of getting lost – 'orienteering' was again on the menu – but also a *new* terror of being naked around my classmates in the communal showers. Another all-male environment where I felt naked *beyond* skin-deep. There was no way I was getting nude in front of my male tormentors. In the end, on the day of my fourteenth birthday, a kindly Physics teacher had to drive me home with 'sunstroke'. It wasn't sunstroke, it was pure terror.

A couple of years later, now hanging out with Phyllis, Kerry and Beth, my life *had* become more interesting. We went to the cinema,* we skived lessons to go shopping in Leeds, we had the odd trip to Manchester. Still, when the time came, I felt too young to leave home. I was *very* anxious about university. Every once in a while, I'd think about leaving the safety of boring old Bingley and I'd just feel *sick* with nerves.

I really, truly, 100 per cent think that had I moved to London, Brighton or Manchester I might very well be dead. Drugs or sex would have somehow killed me. As it was, I opted to study in Bangor, North Wales, so those vices weren't really a concern.

Bangor, famous for being the university of choice for Bridget Jones, is a small college city. About half the residents are students and it's nestled between Snowdonia and the Menai Straits. The view, with the mountains and the sea, is quite stunning – think *Lord of the Rings*. It was exactly what I needed at the time: I was forced to leave the nest but it also felt like a very safe place where I wouldn't get lost. Although I'd initially put down Bangor as an

---

* Including a memorable outing to see *The Wishmaster* with Phyllis. There were four of us in Shipley's now demolished Unit 4 cinema and the other couple had noisy sex while Phyllis and I giggled.

'insurance' choice in case I didn't get into Nottingham, I changed it to my first choice once I'd been for a visit. I won't lie – the fact the halls of residence were en suite was a huge incentive. No shared showers, no anxiety. The fact half the town were also teenagers created a *Dawson's Creek* environment in which I could thrive.

The best thing about university is the opportunity to reinvent and start afresh. As soon as I got to halls of residence, no one was to know that I'd been a MASSIVE LOSER at school and nor was being (seemingly) gay a bad thing. In fact, it was quite trendy. I was quickly accepted into a lovely clique. For the first time *ever*, I was popular. I liked it.

Freshers' Week became a casting extravaganza as I looked to make NEW FRIENDS. A good way to make friends, I'd hazard, is not to concoct a fictional story and take it on *The Trisha Show*. If you're unfamiliar, *Trisha* was a less carnivorous version of *The Jeremy Kyle Show* with fewer interventions and paternity tests.

During the second day of university, I happened to run into Lola, a girl who lived on the same corridor as some random girl I'd met on the first night. We hit it off instantly and became fast friends. It was only about two days later that we decided it would be fun to go on *Trisha*. As you do. I'd seen a trailer asking for participants for an episode called 'STOP YOUR WILD WAYS'. Lola, as someone who had had sex with THREE DIFFERENT MEN and liked a glass of wine, was – in my sheltered book – fairly wild. I suggested, kidding, that we should go on, but Lola thought this was a hoot. See? I told you she was wild.

We called the hotline and a researcher called us back right away. Luckily, we had our cover story all mapped out. Although, in truth, we'd known each other for a week, we told the researcher, Hannah (researchers are *always* called Hannah) that we actually knew each other really well from the 'gig circuit'. Fact: I had been to one 'gig' at this point and it was the Spice Girls at Sheffield Don Valley Stadium. We were booked for filming and summoned to Norwich a week later with Bethany, another friend.

However, shady Hannah called me *while we were on the train* to say the episode had been renamed 'YOU'RE SO GREEN WITH ENVY'. The shade of it all – the new story would insinuate that I was jealous of Lola's wild ways. *I did not sign up for this shit*, I thought.

It all went a little more *Jeremy Kyle* than we'd intended. Lola burst on stage in a pink wig, white PVC hooker boots and orange hot pants to Geri Halliwell's 'Look at Me', and was met by hissing and booing from the Norwich audience. She was, as we would now call it, slut shamed. One woman went so far as to stand up and tell her 'I'm twice your age love, and I've only had sex with one man.'

That's nice poppet. Sit down. Shush.

Rapidly, Bethany and I desperately tried to defend Lola, but the audience were baying for blood. In the end, Lola was taken to the show's counsellor, who made her beat her wig with a foam bat in some sort of metaphorical gesture. No, I'm not sure either.

A couple of weeks later, the show's producer called to ask if we wanted to take part in a televised teen debate on Sky 1. We both said NO THANKS.

Back in Bangor, away from the watchful gaze of my parents, this was the first time I could exist openly and properly out of the closet. I also felt confident enough to start challenging the messages Gender had instilled in me. University, we are told, is for experimentation and, inspired by Carrie Bradshaw, I started to buy my clothes in vintage shops. I would happily wear a mix of men's clothes and women's. I was hilariously Britpop-thin at the time, so was able to fit into skinny flares and belly tops with ease.

I'm not saying it was a *good* look, I'm saying it was a look.

Being surrounded mostly by students, no one particularly seemed to care. Inspired by Brett Anderson and Brian Molko – both of whom had clearly had their own words with Gender – I started to wear black kohl and nail varnish for nights out. That said, this did fall under the umbrella of the 'acceptable alternative' of the era.

At Bangor, in 2000, there were no trans students that I knew of. The LGB society was basically five gay men in an empty bar.

It makes sense, therefore, that I fell in love with my straight housemate. Yes, I properly fell in love for the first time. It was brilliantly teenage. I would lie in bed listening to 'Secretly' by Skunk Anansie or 'You Look So Fine' by Garbage ALL NIGHT and cry. Oh, all gay people need an unrequited crush on a straight person at least once, it's a rite of passage.

Let's call him Joe. Joe was on my course (Psychology, fact fans) and in first year was dating a friend of my best friend, Olivia. They all lived on the same corridor in halls and we all lived together for second and third year. This was the *90210* friendship group I'd always aspired to. Like many college friends, we bonded quickly and unhealthily. We spent about seven hours a day in each other's company. It was like *Friends* with less coffee.

I suppose it's natural I'd fall for him. He was kind and gorgeous. He was certainly open-minded enough to flirt with me. The crush did nothing for my Gender issues, however. Instead of thinking Joe might be up for a snog after a few drinks (most guys are tbh), I developed an even keener notion of the parallel life in which I was a girl.

'Kate' would have handled the situation very differently. She'd have plotted against Jenny, Joe's girlfriend, and moved in for the kill. She would have made a play for Joe, regardless of the cost. I know; not very sisterly at *all*. I didn't think it was actually going to happen, but a very vivid fantasy world started to exist alongside my real life. A lot of time was lost to fantasising about the parallel world in which Kate and Joe would have secret trysts.

Kate would wear this, *Kate* would have her hair like this, *Kate* would do this. Kate – possibly inspired by Annie Douglas from *Sunset Beach* – was a bit of a scheming cow. It's no wonder I didn't want to be her in the end.

In real life, Joe and Jenny broke up at the end of second year. Joe and James had a near miss on the last day of summer term. Drunk on cheap white wine Olivia had been given by an old lady she visited once a week, we all staggered down to Bangor pier. In that classic teen rite of passage, we vowed to stay up long enough to see the sunrise.

Olivia and Andrea – another friend – went off together,

leaving Joe and me to talk on a bench. We talked a lot about boys and girls. Joe wondered aloud if kissing boys is different to kissing girls. *That*, that right there, was my moment to say 'I'll show you.' I see now it was an invitation – his own experimentation – but I didn't seize it. I wasn't bold or brave enough. Yet.

I have so few regrets. *That* is one of them.

In awe, we all watched the sun rise out of the sea, watched the sky change colour. It was very beautiful. Everyone should do that at least once in their life.

The next day, we all went home for the summer break. All summer I thought about the kiss that never was. Strangely, back in Bingley, Jenny and I grew close, speaking on the phone frequently. Now he was single, I had decided – in third year – it would all happen between Joe and me.

We moved into a new house in Bangor in September, and I was *ready* to tell Joe how I really felt. When he arrived, he asked me to take him on a tour around the house. *This was it*. We were alone, up in my room.

He told me he'd got a new girl pregnant over the break. Cue intro credits.

Thus started the third season of our self-made teen drama. I never did get my moment with Joe. I half-arsedly tried it on one last time about six months later, but that year Jenny and I had grown even closer and I wouldn't have betrayed her like that. In fact, she and Joe were still off-and-on until Joe told *Andrea* he secretly loved her, but she was a Christian and was waiting for marriage.

It was all such, such fun. God, I miss those days a lot.

11.

THE FAME JAMES

AKA The Lost Boy

Despite the negative experience on *Trisha*, it was during university that I decided I definitely wanted to be famous. I wasn't sure what I wanted to be famous *for*, but it looked like a lot of fun.

In the olden days, to be famous you had to come from privilege, because most famous people attended very expensive stage schools. My parents certainly couldn't afford to send me to one of them. When I was fourteen, my English teacher, Miss Walker, saw a spark of acting talent and I was offered free membership to a local youth drama group. Unfortunately, as one of the mean bitches who made my life hell at school was also in the group, I dropped out after one session.

During college, I read (and reread) Geri Halliwell's seminal *If Only*. Again, if you underestimated the impact of the Spice Girls on my overall development, you're dead wrong. It became clear that, like me, Geri came from a working-class background, but she had gone on to achieve huge fame via an open audition.

Despite *If Only* essentially being a story of how Geri, by her own admission, struggled with mental health issues and loneliness *because* of fame, I *still* thought I'd really like to be famous. And so started my 'auditioning period', or a series of near misses with reality TV.

I am not here to slag off reality TV. Yes, it (momentarily) led to the death of quality drama output (I believe TV execs have since retreated from basing their schedules around reality since the advent of *Downton*, *Doctor Who*, *Game of Thrones* etc), but it also did wonders in terms of diversity in the media.

Let's face it, prior to *Big Brother* (2000) how many Irish lesbian former nuns did we see on television? Very few indeed. In scripted shows there might have been – if you were lucky – a sassy black or gay best friend, but with the notable exceptions of *Ellen*, *Will & Grace* and *Queer As Folk*, there were precious few LGB characters on screens in the 1990s and even fewer trans ones.

Right from the off, with reality TV casting directors were tripping over themselves to (perhaps in a tokenistic way) present minority communities. In those early days, the LGBTQ community was represented by Anna Nolan, Brian Dowling and Will Young, and it's worth noting that two trans people (Nadia Almada and Luke Anderson) have won *Big Brother* with public support from viewers.

Scripted TV drama is expensive. Reality TV is relatively cheap. With more riding on drama, execs take fewer risks. They play it safe with (white, straight, cis) docs and cops. I don't think the LGBTQ community would have come, in terms of rights, as far as we have without the normalising effects of reality TV. After the AIDS pandemic in the 1980s/1990s, Brian Dowling and Will Young were the young, *healthy* faces of gay men. It rehumanised us outside of the confines of the 'scene'. I don't think the societal impact of reality TV should be played down, whether you enjoy it or not.

Without a stage school background, and living outside of London, I thought reality TV was my fastest route to fame. In my late teens and early twenties I auditioned for *Big Brother* series two, *Pop Idol*, *Big Brother* series four (I got down to the last hundred apparently), *Hollyoaks* (they held an open audition as a publicity stunt) and *The X Factor*.

Pop Idol, ironically, wanted me to be more trans. I'd sold myself as the new Bowie or Brian Molko, but they found me a little too vanilla in real life. And yes, producers promised me a free ticket through to the televised audition stage if I amped up the freak factor. As I'm an average singer at best, I bottled it ahead of the audition.

The *Big Brother* auditions were especially gruelling and involved playing team games in soulless hotel conference rooms. You had to be a team player while simultaneously showing how quirky and characterful you were. Not easy. I remember one woman saying, 'Aren't you a bit too thin?' What are you even meant to say to that? I replied that I was anorexic (I wasn't) just to make her feel bad. Anyway, everyone knows that for fame, you can *never* be too thin.

If you could successfully build a life raft out of cereal boxes or whatever – while being charmingly sassy – you progressed to another round of taped interviews where producers quite clearly spelled out that being a *Big Brother* contestant was *no* guarantee of fame or fortune.

They repeated the doomy warning time and time again,

but it fell on hundreds of deaf ears. Deaf ears all searching for a way out. Like Adele said, I didn't even know what I wanted, but I wanted *something else*.

Of course, it's pretty clear to me now what the *something else* was. I was living in the wrong gender, and what I wanted was a way out of my body, as nuts as that sounds. I think fame-seekers (and I absolutely include myself in this) are a very particular type of person. I mean, think about it: fame is the faceless, unquestioning, *unconditional* adoration of strangers. An entirely one-way street in which the recipient never has to reciprocate affection.

What kind of person craves that sort of love? I think a lot of people, perhaps, who feel the love in their lives *is* conditional. The gay, lesbian and bi people who feel the love of their parents will only remain if they play it straight; the trans people who feel they'll be rejected at home and by society if they live authentically. When we (as LGBTQ) people 'come out' we know – to some extent – we're playing Russian roulette with the love in our life. Better perhaps to seek a much safer form of love, one which we don't really have to engage with on a personal level. Blind adoration, screaming crowds, devoted fans, 'followers'.

There will be people (PEOPLE IN DENIAL) reading this and saying, 'Hun, I'm not interested at all in fame. To me it's really all about the music/writing/my craft/the medium/my art/performing (delete as appropriate).' Don't delude yourselves! Yes, I am always seeking to be the best possible writer I can be. I hate the bit where a manuscript is prised from my grasp and I'm not allowed to edit it further because it absolutely *has* to go to press.

However, I can want to be the best writer I can be and *also* want to be famous. It's not either/or. Being famous (or in my case, fame-adjacent) has delicious perks. I get sent hundreds of free books; parties with extravagant goody bags; I'm invited to film premieres and award ceremonies; I get food, drinks and five-star hotels paid for by publishers and festivals. You also get to be pleasingly brain-dead – someone (usually a very hardworking publicist) organises your time and transport so you get pretty much carried, like semi-precious zombie cargo, from one event to the next. On tour, I've gone whole days without thinking.

It's addictive too. With recognition, too much is never enough. People who complain about press intrusion would be the first to throw themselves off a cliff (or go on *I'm A Celebrity Get Me Out of Here*) on the day it went away. It's not so much the *fame* (a nebulous entity at best) as much as it is the flattery, the attention, the *love* of it all. It is a pleasing sun to bathe under.

'I aimed for a career on TV,' says Dawn O' Porter, my friend who also happens to be off the telly, 'and by getting it, it meant that I had achieved my goal. So I found huge joy and pride with being on TV because of that. It was all really nice, I was on TV but I wasn't '"famous".'

I tell her that if my mum knows who she is, she's definitely famous. 'I wasn't doing red carpets or being given any fancy treatment. It was just a job. When I met Chris [*Bridesmaids* actor O' Dowd] I suppose I entered into "fame". It wasn't really because of me, so I found it uncomfortable at times, but then I rose above it and used any profile I had for my own gain or a cause I cared about.

Fame, to me, gives me opportunities. It's very manageable and not something I can't control. I feel very lucky with my level of notoriety. I'm not bothered or harassed and I have all the benefits of being able to make things happen. And so it makes me very happy.' Dawn notably organised a phenomenally successful clothing drive for refugees living in the Calais 'Jungle'.

'If it turned into the kind of fame where I couldn't live my normal life then it probably wouldn't. But I'd like to think I have enough control to stop that happening. Also, I don't do anything or work in a way where that would happen. So for me my fame is success, the ability to get my work seen, rather than a massive ego massage or being in the papers or anything like that. And yes, it makes me very happy to have even a tiny bit of power to Make Things Happen, have my voice heard and get word of my books out there.'

My goals – I *think* – are the same as Dawn's, but to this day I have to be very careful with Fame. Fame, like Gender, often whispers sweet nothings in your ear and they are just that . . . nothing. Very often, when I meet *actually* famous people they are either workaholics, entirely lack self-awareness or are utterly miserable – the sort of miserable that can only come from being dragged around the world, paraded in front of cameras and stretched as thin as beef carpaccio. Sure, *some* celebs have a coke problem or anorexia, but the vast majority mean it when they say they're suffering from exhaustion. Imagine not going home for about a year, living out of a suitcase and only eating plane food. It'd be shit. But they don't and can't stop. They are fame *junkies*.

We *know* this about Fame, and yet I *still* find myself thinking that if I was just a little bit better known, I'd be happier. If I sold a few more books, went on some more TV shows, earned some more money, all the troubles in my life would melt away. I think all this *despite* spending time with people who have fame and money and still seem thoroughly at odds with the world and, more vitally, themselves.

But how do you go from parties and freebies and *attention* to working nine to five again? The first generation of reality TV, YouTube and Instagram stars are about to find out. Nadia Almada is now a hairstylist. Look at her Instagram. She seems happy.

Fame is Diet Love. It tastes like love and looks like love, but there's zero per cent real love in it.

12.

THE BRIGHTON YEARS: PART 1

AKA I Need a Job I Suppose

While I was studying in Bangor, Kerry had moved south to Brighton with her then boyfriend. I had visited a few times, so when the time came to leave Bangor, I knew Brighton was a fun, nurturing, exciting city to live in. Bigger than Bangor, but not too big.

The last few months in Wales saw me living in a squat trying to 'make it as an actor' with a bunch of other graduates from the theatre society. Another grasp for fame, but after one Edinburgh Fringe disaster (in which I *very* convincingly played the straight, male, American romantic lead) I knew the life of a jobbing actor was *definitely* not for me.

I knew – at twenty-one – my fame window was closing. Also, if I couldn't be a Spice Girl, what was the point? I think, on a subconscious level, that I mostly wanted to be a famous *woman*. Fame and Gender were very much knotted together and I couldn't identify what it was I really wanted.

I shifted my ambitions and decided to be Carrie Bradshaw instead. I wanted my own hipster flat and, vitally, financial independence. To do that, I'd need a steady job. So, perhaps in desperation, I embarked on a post-grad teacher-training course. It *was* a compromise. I knew I didn't want a corporate cocksucker job. I'd spent my childhood watching my dad get stressed about how many bags of Jelly Babies supermarkets were stocking. I didn't want to care about that. Instead, I saw teaching as a helpful job that served the greater good and gave me room to be creative. I looked forward to using music and drama and art every day.

Sadly, my plans for a trendy Carrie-style Manhattan crash pad with a walk-in closet were a tad ambitious. My first flat was a 'studio' (see also, 'bedsit') near Brighton station. Kerry and I painted it a fresh, minty shade of green and filled it with Ikea furniture, but it was still a shithole. I mean that almost literally. A scary man, not dissimilar in appearance to Captain Caveman or the thing that lives behind Wendy's in *Mulholland Drive*, lived down the hallway and, one day, he (I assume) curled out a turd in the middle of the communal bathroom floor.

I promptly moved in with a friend instead.

You'll notice there now follows about ten years where Gender slid to the back of the closet. Don't get me wrong, he was still very much present in my life but, as for many white men, his presence wasn't felt quite so keenly as it is for other parts of society. At this time, stepping out into adulthood, I definitely reaped some benefits because I looked, outwardly, like a white man.*

Moreover, for the first time in my life I was *busy*, too busy to spend a lot of time dwelling on Gender. Teacher training

---

* I believe I was only accepted onto the PGCE course as there was a supposed shortage of male primary school teachers. Despite my first-class degree, I had *very* little relevant experience.

is tough – way tougher than being an actual teacher. You do the whole course in a single year, squashing in both study and practical experience in schools. That being said, I enjoyed that year greatly, and much of the seven years that followed.

Here's the thing with teaching, it *should* be the best job in the world, but it just isn't.

I did love working with kids and have a million different anecdotes from those years. . .

Keystage 2 science exam: *Name a life process that adults can do that infants cannot.* Child's answer: *drive.*

Having twenty six-year-olds dress as mummies and dance to 'Walk Like an Egyptian' in a Christmas production.

Staging a student fashion show better than some LFW shows I've seen.

Telling ghost stories on the Year 6 residential, not to mention doing some very masc things I thought I'd never do – abseiling (finally overcoming the Year 9 camp horror); quad biking; potholing, zip-wiring. It's amazing what you'll do when you don't want to look like a twat in front of eleven-year-olds.

One year, as part of our project on the Antarctic, I made my Year 5 class apply to go on Shackleton's expedition. We built the necessary skills by having a survival expert come to school and show us how to erect tents and light fires, but the pupils still weren't prepared for the day when I said 'Right, we're off to the South Pole!' I'd chartered a boat from Brighton Marina especially and, by the time the coach dropped us there, some kids had started panicking that we really were setting sail to Antarctica. As it was, we just did a couple of laps around the pier and back to school, but I like to think it was an experience they won't forget.

Some stories were sadder. The first school I taught at was in the middle of a fairly forlorn council estate in East Sussex. While most of the kids came from supportive, loving families, on my first day I was handed a child protection folder as thick as my wrist for various children under my supervision. One of my colleagues once left her cosy home on Christmas Day to drive around the estate and make sure one of her pupils wasn't roaming the streets by himself.

The school failed its Ofsted inspection. Our *teaching* was responsible for poor exam results, you see, *not* the fact that the kids were roaming the streets by themselves on Christmas Day.

And this is why teaching is *not* the best job on earth – the bureaucracy. I'll never forget a meeting with our inspection team. Being an ambitious young *man*, I was quickly promoted to Keystage leader, long before I was actually qualified to be one. Primary teaching is one of the few professions where there are more women than men, but men disproportionately hold positions of power.* Publishing is another.

In the meeting, the council supervisor told me there was NO REASON why a particular child shouldn't achieve a Level 4 in his SATs tests. I told them: 'Well, his dad *has* just gone to jail for being a paedophile.'

---

* That said, I was once on a hiring panel led by a female headteacher who wouldn't hire a deputy head as the candidate had recently got married and was a maternity leave 'risk'.

'No,' she replied, leaving no room for argument. 'With "outstanding" teaching, he *will* still achieve a Level 4.'

Yeah, sure thing, you fucking imbecile. This was a school with high absenteeism, about 70 per cent of pupils on free school meals allowance, pupils who bit and spat at teachers, chair throwers and frequent 'runners'. Writing some 'Learning Objectives' and 'Success Criteria' on a whiteboard at the start of each lesson is *definitely* going to overcome those issues.

The education system is every bit as fucked as the NHS. For the last twenty years or so, a blind governmental drive to 'raise standards' has blithely ignored the well-being of children and young adults in the UK. We are told we need an excellent system like they have in China, Japan or South Korea, despite the fact that these countries have among the highest suicide rates for young adults in the world (China, it is thought, disguises its suicide data, as their official results are so at odds with other independent figures).

Whichever way you look at it, student well-being is in no way a priority for the government. Whatever they might *say*, consecutive governments failing to make Personal, Social and Health education (PSHE) or Sex and Relationships education (SRE) a compulsory part of the National Curriculum cannot give two shits about the overall wellness of pupils. This is an email you could easily ping off to your MP – new legislation, provisionally including lessons about identity and pornography, is being mooted by the Education Secretary, Justine Greening, as I type.

This is of particular concern for young LGBTQ students, who are vastly more at risk of truancy, self-harm, substance misuse and suicidal behaviour. Since the removal of Section 28, which so blighted my education, very little has been put in place, officially, to support LGBTQ young people. Some schools are great – they reach out to organisations like Diversity Role Models or Stonewall for assistance. I'm a Stonewall Schools Role Model now and I've been into so many wonderful schools who are already phenomenally supportive of their LGBTQ staff and students. It's the schools that *don't* reach out to Stonewall I'm concerned about.

Making PSHE compulsory – and putting guidance in place – is the quickest way I can think of to change the world. Primary age children are wonderfully open-minded and receptive. I remember using the gorgeous *And Tango Makes Three* picture book with my Year 1s. It's about two male penguins who tried to hatch a pebble (I know, heart-breaking) until a kind zookeeper took pity on them and gave them a surrogate egg. Plucky Roy and Silo reared a chick, Tango, as a proud gay couple. Five-year-olds *loved* this story. They could so empathise with how unfair it was that Roy and Silo couldn't have an egg of their own even though they were clearly ready to be parents. How they cheered when Mr Gramzay gave them an egg!

Think of what we could achieve if space and time was given over to emotional well-being on the timetable. If there was one fewer maths or English lesson a week. We could tackle sexism, rape culture, consent, extremism, gender, internet safety, first aid, depression and anxiety, sexual health, contraception, inequality, social justice and so much more. And you know what? Young people would love it.

When I used to have my annual Sex Ed Week for Year 6,

you could have heard a pin drop. I planned the whole week around students' questions from an anonymous box. Of course there were the odd daft ones, but *most* students saw it as an opportunity to ask those burning questions. The one that *always* came up, without fail, was 'why do people have sex if they don't want a baby?' No one ever thinks to tell young people, least of all girls, that sex can feel nice.

I was still teaching when I got my first book deal, and thank god I did get that deal, because I was on the verge of being fired. I'd basically rebelled against the nonsense and refused to complete all and any unnecessary paperwork. Teachers spend half their time ticking boxes, highlighting targets and writing reports that literally no one ever reads. I've seen this – inspectors come into a school and check to see if a file exists, they literally don't even open it. It could honestly be a folder of blank pages or erotic poetry.

That wasn't me glossing over seven years of my life. On the contrary, I think those years were really important. Too often – and again as a result of 'overnight fame' on reality TV – young people think success is easily achieved. I went a different path. I'm not alone in finding success a little later in my twenties.

Best-friend Kerry essentially taught herself how to code while working a shitty office job. She's now employed by a massive tech company and is a leading authority in the computer games industry – not bad considering how much that industry hates women. Photographer Lee Faircloth, another dear friend, developed his talents while working as a re-toucher at a modelling agency.

Like them, I started writing while earning money as a

teacher. How else are normal people meant to break into the creative industries? There were no wealthy parents paying my rent or putting down deposits on flats for me. I wouldn't have *wanted* them to either; I wouldn't have liked feeling 'in debt' to my mum or dad. Like I said before, there's no way I could have done an internship – I would have starved to death.

While teaching, I wrote as a hobby and it gradually became more serious. I wrote for free – a mistake – thinking no one got paid for writing. I wouldn't do that now – agreeing to make art for free is one of the reasons why artists are poor.

I suppose I started writing in a professional capacity for the student newspaper in Bangor. I did music reviews and then – as all the other music writers were snobs – got to interview visiting pop acts who played in the Student Union. These included Atomic Kitten, Steps and Ultra Naté, among others.

That said, I'd always written for pleasure. As a child, I used to cut people out of my mum's home shopping catalogues and write little stories about them. When I was a bit older I wrote the aforementioned *Doctor Who* proto-fanfiction. I used to illustrate these stories and mostly show them to my Grandma Breen, in the absence of the internet.

Even before that, my imagination had been too much to contain. Always, always inventing stories – including the parallel world where I was 'Kate'. Nearly all of these fantasy worlds had me as a female character. When I decided to write a novel, it never even occurred to me to write from a male perspective. It makes perfect sense now

– if I couldn't live as a woman, I'd create fantasy worlds where I was one.

While teaching, I'd developed a taste for Young Adult (YA) fiction. I'd already read Philip Pullman's *His Dark Materials* trilogy, so was well aware that some of the most subversive, imaginative and intelligent books on the market were deemed 'children's books'. I'd also read *Noughts & Crosses* by Malorie Blackman, and was struck by how YA isn't caught up in genre conventions – it can be romantic, thrilling, scary and funny and set in the future or in the past. I thought, *Oh if I ever do write a book, it'll be for this audience.*

Deciding to write a novel was born partly out of boredom. The summer before I started *Hollow Pike*, I went a bit mad. I'd planned to read a big stack of books on the beach, but it rained every single day that August so I went slowly insane watching old episodes of *America's Next Top Model* on YouTube. The internal monologue in my head became that of Tyra Banks: 'There are two beautiful yoghurts before me, but only one can be my dessert.' I vowed that the following summer I would actually do something productive with the six-week holiday.

The second reason – and we'll discuss this more later – was that I was seeing a man at the time who worked for British Airways and was away much of the time. I was determined that I wouldn't cheat on him and the devil does make work for idle hands.

By 2009, having read a fair few YA novels, I was struck by how few LGBTQ characters there were at that time. I figured that if me, Kerry and Phyllis had all been queer at school in 1997, there were probably *lots* of young people going through a similar ordeal. Inspired by the Pendle witch trials, the *X-Men* and the film *The Craft*, I combined the two things: queer youths and witchcraft. I'd spent my whole school career wishing I'd develop superpowers so I could kill my tormentors. That's normal right?

In fact, when I was about nine, I did convince myself I was controlling the weather psychically. It was very snowy and I was pretty sure I was making it snow. It probably wasn't me, on reflection, which is a shame.

They say write what you know, so I took myself, Kerry, Phyllis and Beth, turned us into Jack, Kitty, Delilah and Lis, and transposed us into the fictional world of *Hollow Pike*. Like I said, it never entered my head to write the story from Jack's point of view. Partly because I didn't think a YA book told from a gay boy's perspective would sell, but also because Jack didn't appeal to me in the same way that Lis, a girl, did. Now it's clear why. I never wanted to be a Jack, I wanted to be a Lis.

Until I announced my transition, the question I was asked at events more than any other was 'How do you write such convincing female characters?' I swear it wasn't anything I intentionally did – I was just writing myself into stories, and I am a girl.

I was exceptionally lucky when it came to my book deal. No, really. Yes, I know *all* talented people say 'I've been very lucky' and then fawning sycophants say 'It has nothing to do with luck, oh glorious one, it's your talent!', but they're both correct.

Yes, I read a lot of YA fiction and knew that *Hollow*

Pike was broadly comparable to what else was on the market. I knew I'd written a book I would have adored when I was fifteen (this is still my only assessment criterion when writing novels), however, *timing* is so vital to success and that's a stroke of luck.

My dear friend Sam was working for Bloomsbury at the time and assured me that agents and publishers were always on the lookout for talent. After I sent the manuscript off to a few agents, I found one – the lovely Jo Williamson – who had just returned from maternity leave and was actively expanding her client list. *Hollow Pike* was on submission a) just as the *Twilight* bandwagon was rolling out of town and b) as Orion Children's Books had just started a teen imprint and needed launch titles.

So. Much. Timing.

Had *Hollow Pike* been on submission six months later it wouldn't have sold – all publishers wanted were *Hunger Games* knock-offs. Seriously. Timing and luck are everything. There are extraordinary writers and fantastic novels being rejected every day because the timing isn't right.

Hollow Pike was a foot in the door. I got a 'good five-figure advance', to use publishing-speak, and was able to quit teaching before I was fired. The rest was up to me.

This time, Gender came to my rescue. Publishing is a precarious industry. If a book doesn't sell, and if it doesn't sell immediately, the author is dead in the water – regardless of the fact that it's actually a *publisher's* job to sell and market books. I was one of very few (openly) gay male authors in children's publishing, and I turned it to my advantage. With slightly *Showgirls*-level ambition, I bulldozed my way into the industry. I didn't wait to be asked to events, launches or book fairs, I volunteered. I, and I shudder at the use of this term, networked. I said 'yes' to every opportunity, unencumbered by spouse or child. I travelled the length and breadth of the country, and to Ireland, Spain and the US to promote my books.

The awful truth is that, if I'd been a cisgender woman in the early days, I think I'd have been seen as ruthless, pushy and aggressive, and therefore spurned. I have seen this happen to female debuts – they are labelled as having a bad attitude. Because I was seemingly a man, and had a campy northern sensibility, I totally got away with it. It was positively encouraged. The biggest divas in the publishing world are men, let me tell you.

Some good came out of it too. I was quickly invited to become a Stonewall Schools Role Model. A side effect of my big gob was that I became an accidental LGBTQ spokesperson. I was happy to be one. I figured that gay people in the media before me had made it easier for me to have the career I was having. The Stonewall role entailed me going into a few schools every year and telling my story in a bright red SOME PEOPLE ARE GAY. GET OVER IT! T-shirt.

It was through my position as a 'role model' that I was invited to lots of panel events and schools, consolidating my writing. Had I not carved out a 'brand' for myself online and in person, I doubt I'd have been offered a second book deal in 2013. Again, it's not all about talent, it's about how you 'work it'.

I wonder, had I been a cisgender woman, if I'd have been able to 'work it' quite so effectively.

13.

THE BRIGHTON YEARS: PART 2

AKA Cherry Filth and the Deathlegs

I suppose I should explain about Brighton. If there's *anywhere* in the United Kingdom that LGBTQ people can flourish, it's in Brighton. In 1783, Prince George, who would later become the Prince Regent, first visited the trendy seaside town, already notorious for its wine, food and parties. The prince was told bathing in saltwater – very fashionable at the time, sort of like juicing kale or something now – was the best course of action for his gout.

George was spellbound by Brighton, and commissioned a ludicrous pavilion as his holiday home in 1787, partly as somewhere he could enjoy sexyfuntime with his mistress, Maria Fitzherbert.

In the centuries that followed, Brighton maintained its somewhat seedy reputation as the good-time girl of the south coast. Having fallen into disrepair in the mid-twentieth century, it quite suddenly became fashionable in the 1990s as an affordable escape for burnt-out Londoners who fancied doing a load of MDMA by the seaside. Of course, this gentrification rendered Brighton *unaffordable* within about five years.

Today, Brighton is the closest thing we have to Neverland.

The lack of private sector industry (we do have AMEX, Bupa, some games companies and hotels, but little else other than many, many call centres*) means graduates party relentlessly while working in minimum-wage jobs well into their thirties. Either that or they give up and move to London after college. I expect if we were to look at vegans per square mile, Brighton would be pretty much at the top of the world rankings. A local joke is asking any Brighton resident the name of their garage band. Chances are, they're in one.

I'm allowed to tease Brighton because I've lived here for twelve years. You're not.

Brighton has the third largest LGBTQ community in the UK after London and Manchester, but – as it's much smaller than both of those cities – it feels a lot, well, queerer. It's undiluted. Having lived in London and Brighton, there really is something special about Brighton.

Yes, it often feels provincial in comparison to the capital, but there's also a warmth, an empathy, an acceptance of queerness† that goes far beyond mere tolerance.‡ A few weeks before I first moved to Brighton in 2002, Kerry sent me a copy of Armistead Maupin's *Tales of the City* with

* If you got a cold-call trying to sell you Sky-box insurance in 2003, that might have been me.

† I KNOW some people see 'Queer' as a pejorative. It IS still, sadly, used as one. It is not meant as such in this context and context is everything. I use it in the spirit of the Queer Movement – to represent the fluidity and intersectionality of non-heterosexual and non-cis-gender people.

‡ I fucking HATE the notion that LGBTQ people should be 'tolerated'. Fuck off, you *tolerate* hay fever, not vast swathes of society.

a note saying 'They say Brighton is our answer to San Francisco.'

I think she's right. On arriving in Brighton, I *truly* started my evolution. Mary Ann Singleton, to Mouse Tolliver, to Anna Madrigal.

This was the first time – no offence to Bangor – I was fully able to explore my queer identity. Even in the bedsit days, I started, inspired by Carrie Bradshaw again, to experiment more with my vintage clothes. There were some major lewks involving string vests, neons, leg warmers, sweat wristbands, flares and the aforementioned bleached mullet. At the time, I mistakenly believed *anything* from a vintage clothes store was automatically good.

Jesus fucking Christ I looked a state.

That said, it was a change in me. All through school, and through much of college, I'd tried to get by with my head down (reality TV attempts notwithstanding). Now I didn't care who looked in my direction; in fact I actively encouraged it. In a town where men proudly walk around in crotchless leather chaps, I was still on the conservative side, to be honest.

You'll have noticed by now that all my friends are girls. It has always been thus. When I arrived in Brighton, Kerry thoughtfully 'set me up' with some of her coursemates from Sussex Uni who she thought I'd get on with. Sam, Sarah, Kat and Nic are still among my closest friends, so she curated well.

At the time, both Kerry and Sarah's boyfriends were in terribly serious garage bands. Bored of endless conversations about the Small Faces and The Velvet Underground, we decided to rebel and form our own band. As a joke, we started Cherry Filth and the Deathlegs. Initially, it really was meant to be a piss-take, but my friend Fi had a keyboard, Kerry could borrow a bass and Sarah could sing. I could *sort of* sing so why not? We got together and had a couple of rehearsals.

I wrote our first ever song, inspired by a recent encounter on the now antiquated gay dating website, Gaydar. Having never seen *South Park*, I didn't know what 'Mr Hankey' referred to. I clicked on Mr Hankey's profile and, with utter horror, was confronted by a picture of a man eating poop.

This inspired our first song, 'Poolips'. I got to thinking, what if you discovered your boyfriend was a secret poo-eater? 'Poolips', which would eventually become the song we were known for, features the following lyrics.

> Let me tell you 'bout this boy
> Thought he was my pride and joy
> When it was cold, he gave me his sweater
> I thought it couldn't get much better.
>
> But the feeling couldn't last that long
> Everything started to go wrong
> Cos when I took you to meet my mother
> I found your secret fetish for The Other.
>
> (You're givin' me) Poolips in the morning!
> (You're givin' me) Poolips in the evening!
> I wanted some tulips!
> But all you ever gave me was poolips, wo-oah!

The Gender Games

Every single kiss you gave me
Came with a little gravy
You knew I would start a riot
If I found out about your diet.

CHORUS

I seen your face on Gaydar now you can't deny
It's all over your face, boy, how you gonna lie?
I told the Magic Bird and she thinks it's such a waste
But I can't shake the feeling never mind the taste.

CHORUS

I'm glad we never had no babies
I'm sure they would have all caught scabies
Or maybe even rabies
I don't know much about babies.

CHORUS X 2

OH COME ON! We were like twenty-three. It was supposed to be a spoof . . . we just never expected it to catch on. Over the next couple of years, we gigged and recorded an EP called *A Pudding Made Out of Diamonds*. Our songs were a tiny bit #problematic, but these were in the days before Twitter call-out culture got going. 'Poor Cow' was about that girl we all know whose boyfriend is definitely gay ('*P.O.O.R.C.O.W, don't those nagging rumours trouble you? / P.O.O.R.C.O.W, we've all seen him drinking MALIBU!'*). 'Everybody's Talkin' 'bout the Vikings' imagined how excited a young gay might have been in 800AD at the impending arrival of the Vikings (*'If they're gonna take this village, then they better start with me'*).

We were, and this will blow your mind, very popular with student audiences.

Cherry Filth, in hindsight, was fairly unique in that I was able to experiment with gendered clothes and make-up in a performative capacity long before I even knew transitioning was on the cards. Cherry Filth were a proper pop act and, as such, we always performed in costume – taking our cues from the Spice Girls, Goldfrapp, Scissor Sisters and Gravy Train.

We often themed our gigs – over the years I was a pirate and the Queen of Hearts, we did a Nativity and a Victorian funeral. I styled myself in the same vein as Bowie or Brian Molko – the acceptable alternative for boys: lots and lots of black eyeliner. I was, however, struck by how – well – *pretty* I was. I loved the transformation and how differently I could behave on stage as Cherry Filth.

It's a common theme. Numerous trans people 'perform' as drag kings or queens before taking the plunge; from *RuPaul's Drag Race* alone Sonique (Kylie Love), Carmen Carrera, Stacey Laine Matthews, Jiggly Caliente, Kenya Michaels and Monica Beverly Hillz all announced they were going from drag queen to trans woman. Rory Smith, of Brighton, started out as drag king Rory Raven before initiating his transition. 'At the end of performances, I'd watch fellow drag kings remove their drag and change into their regular clothes. They'd scrub off the fake facial hair and five o'clock shadows and replace them with lipstick and eyeshadow. I wanted to stay in drag and felt at a loss when the evening was over.'*

While obviously not *all* drag performers are going to transition, the fact that *anyone* is able to perform as a drag king or queen is tangible proof that Gender exists. With very few signifiers – a wig, a beard, some make-up – actors are able to convey that they have 'changed gender'.

Of course, by its nature – rooted in theatre, cabaret and comedy – drag is an extreme take on gender norms. It's a (usually†) harmless spoof of femininity and masculinity alike. Through drag, the stereotypes around both genders are dragged into the spotlight and ridiculed. I do not think *most* drag performers seek to mock cisgender or transgender men or women. I think, instead, they highlight how ludicrous gender norms and binary sexuality are: massive breasts or cocks; grotesque, clown-like make-up; hyper-sexualised; very deep, or very high-pitched, voices.

It was the extremes of drag – the wigs, the sequins – that were a turn-off for me. While I understand *now* the cultural role of drag, the caricature held little interest for me beyond enjoying *Drag Race*. I grew up wanting to be a woman, and I never saw drag as a way to achieve that. For some, drag is a 'gateway drug' or a socially acceptable way to engage with Gender, but I didn't get the link.

'Gender Performance' is often a stick used to clobber

---

* Rory was interviewed in 2013 for *This Book Is Gay*.
† Perpetuating stereotypes about black women, especially if you are a white cisgender man, is never OK, hun.

trans people. The criticism is that trans people are 'playing dress-up' rather than 'becoming' or 'being' men or women. On the contrary, feminist writer Judith Butler, who first coined the term in the 1980s, said in a 2017 interview: 'I know that some people believe that I see gender as a "choice" rather than as an essential and firmly fixed sense of self. My view is actually not that. No matter whether one feels one's gendered and sexed reality to be firmly fixed or less so, every person should have the right to determine the legal and linguistic terms of their embodied lives. So whether one wants to be free to live out a "hard-wired" sense of sex or a more fluid sense of gender, is less important than the right to be free to live it out, without discrimination, harassment, injury, pathologization or criminalization – and with full institutional and community support. That is most important in my view.'

In 2015, my dear friend Stuart Warwick and I started a cabaret night in Brighton called *Club Silencio*, named after David Lynch's surreal, unsettling jazz lounge in *Mulholland Drive* (Stuart's a singer – look him up on Spotify). It's through that I now – even as a trans woman – get to 'do drag'. The clothes I wear for the club night are undoubtedly costumes, the absolute extremes of femininity: dominatrix; *Barbarella*; pin-up girl; mermaid; Bond girl. I get to be a fantasy, and it's a woman's prerogative to do so as she pleases. It isn't *real*. At the end of each month's show, I change back into my jeans.

I wonder if *that's* why my Cherry Filth years didn't kick-start my transition earlier; I didn't feel like I was being an actual woman, it was just another gender game.

MUM, DAD: STOP READING NOW,
IT'S ABOUT TO GET SAUCY.
PLEASE TURN TO PAGE 305
IMMEDIATELY AND DO NOT
READ THE FOLLOWING CHAPTERS.

I DO NOT BELIEVE YOU
HAVE STOPPED READING,
MUM AND DAD.
I MEAN IT. GO TO PAGE 305.

SERIOUSLY.
WHY WOULD YOU PUT
YOURSELF THROUGH THIS?

THIS PAGE IS LEFT
INTENTIONALLY BLANK
TO FOOL JUNO'S PARENTS.

14.

SEX AND THE CITY

AKA Doing It

I was a fucking ugly teenager. I was all nose and teeth and elbows. A recent peek at a school nurse report written in 1996 described me as 'very pale and underweight'. Like so many adolescents, I didn't quite grow into my body until I was well into my twenties. As such, sex wasn't really a feature of my teenage years.

That said, I wasn't especially interested in sex anyway. Seriously. If you remember, my revelation about fancying Dean Cain came more from a place of wanting a boyfriend rather than sex. I was quite keen to hear about *other people* having sex, but at sixteen, I knew it wasn't for me. These days, I suspect I'd have proudly identified – for a period – as asexual.

This is probably, in part, due to very poor sex education. I didn't know anything about same-sex intercourse, so was slightly terrified of it. I had also been told – via the powerful messages of the media – that I would almost certainly, if determined to follow the gay route, get AIDS and die. The entirety of my Sex Ed came from *Queer As Folk*, Channel 4's seminal, groundbreaking 1999 drama series. '*But . . . why is he LICKING HIS BUM?*' etc.*

I was a late bloomer. I didn't really do *anything* with guys until I was in Bangor. As I felt nineteen was quite old to be a VIRGIN (is virginity still seen as leprosy for teenagers?), I *told* people I'd lost my virginity younger. I told school friends I'd lost it at uni and uni friends I'd lost it at school. If you're reading this now, friends – soz, I stretched the truth.

Virginity, as we know, is a construct. Use of the term has become so commonplace, I think we've forgotten that both virginity and virgins are abstract concepts. There is no such thing. The term is derived from the latin virginis, which meant maiden. It is, therefore, a gendered term – used initially to describe only sexually inexperienced women. To this day, the onus is still on female virginity. In cultures where virginity is considered precious, there are higher rates of child marriage and female genital mutilation.† The stakes are very different for girls who, in some instances, are victims of familial 'revenge' attacks if their 'modesty' or 'purity' is compromised.

But in Bingley, and naive about such matters, I was desperate to be rid of my V-Card, mainly because everyone else was. In western culture, and for young men, virginity is not seen as a precious gem worth protecting; it's a hot

---

* I later met *Queer As Folk* creator Russell T. Davies and had the biggest, most undignified fangirl meltdown the world has ever seen. It's part of the reason I had to transition – I'm in disguise in case I ever run into him again.

† Bozon, M (2003)

potato to get rid of. Hell, the entire *American Pie* franchise is based on this fact. It's sexism. Girls who lose their virginity are easy, but boys who *don't* are losers.

As such, I'd *tried* to lose the cursed thing before, it just hadn't happened. In my head, having sex was a VERY SPECIAL EPISODE of *Dawson's Creek* or *90210*. It was something that required great planning and forethought. I set aside some time to have sex with a nice bi guy called Matt while my mum and sister were in Majorca the summer before university, but it turned out he wasn't bi, he was just trying to sound more interesting at art college. In Bangor, I'd attempted to engage in grand narratives with boys (Joe by the pier, coming between a couple in the drama society) but when it happened for real it was like falling off a log. Effortless but painful.

His name was Ryan and he was a student at Bangor. He had a boyfriend but we'd spoken on an LGBT forum (very cutting edge at the time) and agreed to meet for a coffee in Wetherspoon's – in Bangor, Wetherspoon's was one of the nicest pubs. He was nice and handsome, although he did like sport, which was quite boring to hear about. That night, my friend Frankie was having a house party and encouraged me to invite Ryan.

I did so and was just *thrilled* when he invited his boyfriend along for the ride. Luckily, his miserable boyfriend chipped off early with a headache or something and Ryan and I talked for hours. It was the night, fact fans, that Will Young won *Pop Idol*.

Looking back, it was so inevitable. I should have been able to read the signs – the fact he didn't leave with his boyfriend, the gentle prying about my sexual preferences – Ryan was blatantly DTF. It got so late that Frankie let us crash on her pull-out sofa bed.

What followed was so traumatic it put me off sex for almost two years. Again, school-based Sex Ed had left me *woefully* unprepared for the moment and, after some admittedly lovely foreplay, Ryan – sans lube or condom – launched into some very ill-advised anal sex. I wasn't to know at the time, but Ryan was also very well-endowed.

It was, obviously, excruciating.

Walking side to side, as Ariana Grande would say, I did the Walk of Shame the next day, conflicted about what had just happened. It was SO not how I'd scripted my first time in my head. Sex was, in my mind, supposed to be the culmination of a long and loving courtship, not an aggressive raw fuck on a sofa bed in North Wales. No violins, no rose petals, no kisses in the pouring rain – and this was Bangor, so pouring rain was plentiful.

Had I been lied to? Should I have said no? Should I have made him wait? I remember thinking, as it was happening, that this was IT. That if this was my one Sex Window, I wasn't going to ignore it, even the lunacy of putting my health at risk by consenting to bareback. I would no longer be a virgin. So I let it happen, even though it wasn't at all how I'd have liked it.

Thus, as my relationship with Gender quietened down a little – I'd begrudgingly accepted I was a boy even if I'd rather not be – my slightly problematic relationship with Sex began.

I went on a few dates with Ryan, but he was very insistent

that he'd like more sex and I was in no hurry to repeat the nightmare. I dropped him soon after, deploying the 'I don't think we've got much in common' clause. It was true, we didn't, but I refocused my romantic attention on the unrequited affair with housemate Joe.

Interestingly, I ran into an older, even more handsome Ryan about eight years later in Brighton and we had sex in a nightclub toilet. By then, that was quite standard behaviour for me. From Madonna to whore in the space of eight years. What went wrong? What went right?

There's probably a whole other book about gay male promiscuity in me, but I probably won't write it because I think my friend Matthew Todd did a jolly good job of doing just that in *The Straight Jacket*. I'll leave it to you to deduce why some of my behaviour might seem a little shocking. Be amateur therapists and I'll just tell you how it all shook out.

I will say this though, if you aren't a gay man – or haven't spent much time in the world of gay men – this will baffle you. There is absolutely a culture of casual sex that exists among gay men, *especially* those in urban areas or 'on the scene'. Much of my promiscuity happened within the norms of a subculture. I couldn't have done the things I did without opportunity. You might think I carried on the way I did because I'm a deeply damaged individual OR you might agree that I was an opportunist and, more vitally as we'll discuss later, passing as a boy.

It started, I suppose, when I moved to Brighton. I'd never been around that many gay men before. From maybe fifty in Bangor to an estimated 50,000 in Brighton. For the first time I had choices, and I was other people's choice.

My lively sex life was a result of messages. Both Gender and Sex had plenty to say on the matter. From the get-go, from a very instinctual, primal place, I knew I wanted to be 'the woman' when it came to sex. Oh, calm the fuck down, let me explain.

Yes, I know that the whole point of gay relationships is that both partners are 'the man' or 'the woman', but – as it turns out – I WAS NEVER GAY. It wasn't about sexual role play; it was a very conscious urge to get fucked, be *penetrated* as a woman would be. I was always the (physically) smaller partner and took a receptive ('bottom' or 'passive') role. I am categorically NOT saying that all bottom guys secretly want to be women, I am just relaying *my* experience of sexuality. I enjoy being . . . not exactly dominated or overpowered as that opens a whole dreary can of *Fifty Shades* worms . . . but certainly *led* by a male partner.

However, although my preference for big, strapping men was bubbling under, I was still receiving transmissions from the female station at Radio Gender. I had been told, via fiction, TV and film that it was *correct* to withhold sex. In fact, I found sexually promiscuous men a real turn-off. I still wanted the dream – the romantic Milk Tray fantasy.

My first relationships fit the mould. Mikey was incredibly tall and handsome. We met in a club over my first ever Brighton Pride weekend. I was out with friends from the call centre where I was working the summer before I started my PGCE, and I'd spent all weekend following some other guy around town. I'd lost sight of him, and me and my friends found ourselves at a foam party.

I realised I was dancing next to a gorgeous guy. I must

have been drunk as hell because I felt brave enough to reach up and wipe some bubbles off his shaved head. 'You had foam on your head,' I said. Smooth.

We talked and kissed in a corner for much of the night. He wanted to come home with me, but I knew that that would be *wrong*. As it was, like a total gent, he walked me all the way home and didn't push his luck. I was so innocent, but felt I'd played it correctly. After that night, we went on a few dates but I found Mikey's attention too much to handle. I wasn't used to it and felt suffocated.

We parted ways until a couple of years later, when I randomly bumped into him while I was on the world's most boring date with an ant scientist. Yes, ant scientist. Mikey was at the bar and he asked if I remembered him, which, of course, I did. He took my number and we ended up dating for a year or so. It was my first *proper* relationship and I suppose I proved to myself that I could do it. I had been starting to wonder if I was missing the 'boyfriend gene'.

Even in a relationship, I was still a little scared of sex. I was learning on the job, as it were. Mikey was patient and lovely. He taught me so much, not least how to end a relationship.

Although I was a little more mature, I still wasn't ready for a big commitment. A few problems were simmering away and I wasn't emotionally literate enough to deal with them – his drinking, which I found problematic and excessive, his slightly right-wing politics. I wanted out and, unable to discuss my feelings adequately (remember I was raised a boy. Boys don't talk about their feelings), I had a meltdown.

This culminated in a monstrous anxiety attack on a train

to Arundel. Mikey had prepared the day as a romantic surprise and wouldn't tell me where I was going. If you've ever suffered from anxiety, you'll understand that being led to a train and being kept in the dark as to the final destination didn't make for a charming mystery. As we got to Worthing, I felt I couldn't breathe. 'I need to get off this train,' I cried, running for the door.

Mikey seemed able to sense that I was already metaphorically 'running for the door' in our relationship, too. I became more and more elusive until he gave me an ultimatum.

I ended things and proceeded to quite brutally cut him out of my life. I was trying to make a clean break but it wound up hurting us both. Poor Mikey was very much the victim of my inexperience. I certainly haven't made a hash of things in quite the same way since.

If Mikey was my Aiden, then Johnny was the Mr Big villain. We'll never know if I was more enamoured with the chase than I was him, but Johnny led me on a merry dance for the best part of five years. The problem was, I could really *see myself* with Johnny in a way that I never had with other men before we met. I was twenty-two. He was an artist and totally my type – rugby build, stubble, big shoulders.

The trouble with Johnny was that he talked a very good game. Over romantic dinners we agreed our relationship goals were Scott and Charlene, he took me on long walks on the beach and bought me ice cream from Marocco's – the best ice cream parlour in Brighton. The sex was hot and I believed I was in love with him.

But this time, *he* couldn't commit. I became a nervous

wreck. I would text him (always me first) and then wait anxiously, for hours, for a reply. I remember once being so paranoid about why he hadn't replied that I turned my phone off for a whole day, so I wouldn't watch it. I was too young to know that that shit is intolerable unless your other half is an astronaut, miner, submariner or in some other profession where it's impossible to fire off a polite 'busy, spk l8r' text.

Johnny's affection yo-yoed for a few years and I always allowed myself to be reeled back in. Here's the thing: had Johnny suddenly said 'OMG, you're The One! I finally recognise that you're the best thing that's ever happened to me!' I'd have probably run a mile. There was a safety, not to mention a predictability, to our relationship.

There were a handful of other meaningful relationships in my twenties. Jerry, who was very clear he didn't want a boyfriend but really took care of me when my grandmother passed away in 2008; Owen 1, who I fancied so much I went legitimately insane (no really, I almost crashed a car speaking to him while driving AND went through his text messages to discover he'd cheated on me); Owen 2, who I moved in with for a while but to whom I was very ill-suited; and Liam.

Liam, I was truly in love with. I was tricked into loving Liam. Liam was a third-year student at Sussex and I was twenty-six. Because we both knew he only had a year left in town, it was meant to be a casual thing. In fact, I found him hugely annoying to begin with. He was crass and immature – prone to finding burping hilarious – but it didn't matter because he was leaving. He was cute, funny and had a big willy, so I went along for the ride. Before I knew it, without the pressure of WHERE IS THIS ALL HEADING, I was completely, utterly in love.

Liam loved guinea pigs and got scared when we watched *Doctor Who*. We both loved 'American Boy' and 'Black and Gold'. My friends loved him. When he left town it hit me hard. I'd never missed anyone like that. That was when I knew it must be love.

A few weeks after he left Brighton, he returned for a visit. I decided I wasn't prepared to let true love get away without a fight. We met at my little attic flat and I begged him to stay. It was too late – he'd already met someone else and I was truly heartbroken.

Continuing to cast myself in soap operas, whenever we crossed paths in the years that followed we'd have nights of sweaty passion – regardless of who else we were seeing – and it'd end in tears and tantrums. A couple of years prior to my transition we mutually decided it'd be best if we didn't see each other again. It was just too difficult.

I do, I confess, sometimes wonder if I'd have still transitioned if I'd wound up with Liam or Johnny. I wonder if trips to Ikea, weekend spa breaks and a family of guinea pigs might have sufficiently distracted me from musings on my gender.

No, is the short answer. OK, I can't skim into the parallel world where Liam returned to Brighton, but I do know I was in a relationship with a wonderful man called Erik and I *still* started to question my gender at that time.

It was in the spaces *between* my relationships, however, that my dealings with Sex continued to develop.

15.

GAYDAR AND GRINDR

AKA Sex Addiction

Before there was Match.com there was Gaydar. Before there was Tinder there was Grindr. As people from the LGB community aren't always able to pick each other out of a crowd and because the majority of people are heterosexual, they have relied on 'the gay scene' as a way to better the odds when it comes to finding partners. In larger towns and cities, this takes the form of gay clubs and bars.

It figured, with the advent of the internet, that 'the scene' would go online. Gaydar launched in 1999 and revolution-ised the way men were able to meet. I was never inclined to go creeping around bushes, so-called 'cruising grounds' or public toilets, but Gaydar was different. I started using Gaydar as a means to meeting men to go on dates – indeed I first met Johnny on Gaydar – but it soon became clear I was being very naive about its usage. Many guys, if not *most*, were using it to hook up for casual sex. Why bother with a condom-strewn bush on Hampstead Heath when you could have a lovely bonk in the comfort of your own home? It was Deliveroo sex, straight to your door.

There's obviously nothing inherently wrong with no-strings safe sex between consenting adults, but to begin with it wasn't for me. If guys steered conversation to 'meets' or 'fun', I'd politely decline. To begin with.

You see, around this time I became versed in a different set of norms to the high school, Judy Blume ones I was used to. Increasingly surrounded by all-male, all-gay company I began to understand that there was, perhaps, a different set of rules for gay men. A far less heteronormative set. For much of my twenties, gay men weren't allowed to get married, or adopt kids, or have all sorts of other basic human rights. Is it any wonder gay men and women might have seen fit to disregard society's 'family values', most of which were dreamed up by a church that historically despised them anyway?

It was not *unusual* for gay guys to randomly go to each other's flats for some casual sex. Lots of people I knew were doing it all the time and they all seemed fine, safe and happy.

The devil makes work for idle hands, as we know. Boredom mixed with the Horn on a Friday night can never end well. I was about twenty-three and living in a grotty terraced house and my housemate, Kat, was out or had gone home for the weekend or something. Little Gaydar messages kept popping up. The guy was hot – killer abs – and he didn't seem like a total monster. After a while, between The Horn, the boredom and his persistence, I invited him over. I figured it was safer if he came to mine – I knew where the knives and escape routes were.

I don't remember how the invitation went, but I recall it being very awkward. I was chatty – offering him drinks and snacks like an excellent hostess – while he was very much about business. He had a shifty, uneasy quality about him. Had we met on a date, he wouldn't have got the invite back, put it that way. Worse still, as I'd invited him over, I felt *obligated* to give him what he'd come for.

In our online messages, I'd made it clear, I think, that I wasn't prepared to do 'full sexual intercourse', but he seemed to forget this as soon as we got to my bedroom. I remember little else of the encounter other than him trying to force himself into me while I tried to wriggle out from underneath him. 'Oh relax,' he said, 'I'm not going to *rape* you, although I could if I wanted to.'

Well, that put me right at ease. He stopped trying, thank God, and I think he gave up, put his pants on and went home. My first experience of a 'hook up' and I came away from it feeling that I had done something wrong. I'd made a mess of it. The experience was enough to put me off for a year or so.

I eventually forgot the fear I'd felt during the first experience. By then, I was living by myself in a cute converted attic in Kemptown – dead in the heart of Brighton's 'Gay Village'. I fucking loved that little flat. It was such a weird conversion – the shower was in the entrance hall as you came in, so if you wanted to shower while guests were over, you had to shut them in the lounge.*

---

* One of the very few trans women I met during my time in Brighton lived downstairs. She was called Mel and I was forever asking her to stop playing loud trance music – the walls were tissue-paper thin. I often wonder where she is now. I wish I'd taken the time to get to know her better.

Living alone, I was now susceptible to that deadly combination of boredom, the Horn and loneliness. I LOVE living alone, because I become much more proactive at organising my social life, but even as busy and popular as I was, there were nights when a quiet flat was a bit empty. Moreover, when you live alone there are no flatmates or family members to judge your promiscuity. You can keep your dalliances as secret as you like.

What I learned, quite quickly, was that, for the most part, sex can be fun and have few negative consequences. Yes, there will always be the guy who's eight years older than his profile picture, but the vast majority were cute guys who were also bored and horny. Most were friendly, nice and vaguely good in bed. Sure, some had boyfriends – some who didn't know they were on Gaydar and others who were in the ubiquitous open relationships.

Like with drinking, drugs and smoking, if you don't *instantly* see the negative effects of a behaviour, you can convince yourself it's harmless. OK, I was *well* aware of the oral gonorrhoea I managed to get (twice)* but I was less mindful of the 'spiritual' damage hook ups were doing to me.

1. By 'spiritual' I don't mean I think I'm going to Hades because I did some sex. I more mean how it impacted on my mood, well-being and psychological state.

---

* Again, while in the straight world contracting an STI is considered deeply shameful, I would be surprised if any gay men on the scene haven't had at least two.

2. I'm sure *some* people are able to have an abundance of sex without it having any emotional impact whatsoever. I am not one of them.

The first way promiscuity affected me was in my attitude to sex. I'd started out expecting violins and white doves, but I soon came to regard sex as a game of squash – something physical but ultimately meaningless. It was also something I came to view as a *hobby*: I could *choose* to have sex any time I wanted it.

If, as a gay man, you really want to have sex, you can find it in minutes. You can either go on Grindr (the modern-day, even more potent, app equivalent of Gaydar) or head to a cruising ground or sauna.

Saunas marked what I view as a bit of a low. I didn't visit a sauna until I moved to London in 2011. I'd viewed saunas as the pinnacle of sleaze – a bathhouse of iniquity. However, on a very ordinary night out at Clapham's Two Brewers, a gay friend of mine thought it was hilarious I'd never set foot in one. He assured me they were perfectly pleasant and we should go at once. As I was more than a little drunk, I agreed.

Pleasuredrome Sauna, near Waterloo Station, was about to become infamous for the chemsex deaths of three young men on its premises, but I was initially taken by how clean and spa-like the venue was. There was a sauna, steam room and Jacuzzi. Men – some very handsome indeed – pottered about in crisp white towels. If you turned a blind eye to the surreptitious crotch rubbing going on, it could have been any high-end leisure centre.

But then my friend gave me a tour of the upstairs section. The first floor – set within Waterloo's railway arches – was divided up into creepy little booths, the floor covered in PE crash mats. Everything was illuminated by red bulbs and porn played on flatscreens. Men hovered at the entrances to the alcoves, waiting for someone to join them. No one spoke; it was deadly silent, the clientele using subtle eye gestures.

For someone who is quite short-sighted, this wasn't ideal.

Without words, we become animals.

It was kind of hot, to be honest.

In the sauna and steam rooms, in the darkroom and glory holes, little orgies broke out: three or four guys pawing each other with anonymous hands and tongues in dark corners, while others spectated. It was like the last days of Rome.

And all for fifteen quid. Bargain.

So exciting was my first visit that I decided to return about a month later by myself on a drizzly Wednesday night. You know that scene in *Bedazzled* where he returns to Hell and everyone is still partying and looks sad and wasted? It was a little like that. The second time, it was much, much quieter. Only a few forlorn-looking men roamed the labyrinthine corridors like wraiths, hoping against hope that some fresh slice had arrived since their last lap.

I pruned in the Jacuzzi for about ninety minutes before I realised that I wouldn't have sex with *any* of the punters in real life and so I shouldn't while here, just to get my fifteen-pounds' worth. I got a quarter pounder with cheese from McDonalds and went home instead.

The other problem with Disposable Sex is that, again

as with drugs (I'd imagine – I've never been one for drugs), you crave a more extreme, more frequent high. We'll talk more about fetishism later (because I'm a living, breathing fetish at the moment), but it became clear to me that for *some* gay men, a lovely kiss and a cuddle – or even a good old-fashioned fuck – isn't scratching the itch.

Sex, I'm sure we all agree,* is a physical and psychological experience. Anyone can *perform* the right moves, but a partner has to *stimulate* you beyond physicality. I think if you have a *lot* of regular sex, it loses some of its shimmering novelty and you veer towards new and interesting takes on it to keep things interesting.

That's probably excellent *Cosmopolitan* advice to keep *any* relationship fresh and fruity, but some of the things I saw went beyond 'keeping it interesting' and well into degrading, dehumanising and downright dangerous. I met men who wanted to wee on me and have me wee on them; men who wanted me to poop in their mouths; a millionaire who wanted to pay rent boys to fuck me while he watched; men who wanted to 'kidnap' me; men who wanted to film us at it; men who spat on me; men who wanted to choke or be choked; men who rammed chair legs up their butts; men who wanted an entire arm, up to the elbow, inside their intestines.

While you can't censor fantasy, and I'm all for safely and legally exploring fantasy, some of those things, clearly, don't do a body good. I think there is a line – a movable line, but a line – where sex becomes self-harm.

* Unless you're asexual.

I was never that extreme. For me, there was a thrill to be derived from 'doing something a bit naughty'. This involved having a cheeky threesome with a hot American couple in a hotel in Prague; being paid for sex by a wealthy businessman;* sex in various nightclub toilets or a quiet corner of a public library. It was about a thrill. I could, so I did.

Those men who engage with the more damaging things . . . I dunno. I don't know if I, or Matthew Todd, or Alan Downs (*The Velvet Rage*), or Larry Kramer (*Faggots*), or any other writer can generalise about why gay men have formed the subcultures they have.

Todd and Downs posit that gay men (and I think trans women who spent any considerable time living as men) grow up with a terrible *shame* that results in what is, essentially, self-harm. They subconsciously punish themselves through self-destructive behaviours. I can only speak for myself, and I think during that period I behaved in ways that, at times, endangered my health.

I came of age post-AIDS and, despite being well aware of the risks, still operated with a somewhat devil-may-care attitude towards sexual health. Only in my late twenties (admittedly after getting gonorrhoea) did I start to take my health seriously. I consider it a minor miracle that I didn't contract HIV in my early twenties. Of course, it's not the death sentence it once was, but as HIV awareness

---

* I didn't actually need the money, I just found the idea dimly exciting. If that's not the very fucking living definition of privilege, I don't know what is.

campaigner Kristian Johns once told me, it's one hell of a life sentence.

It's time to grindr that axe again and say I think it's fucking criminal we don't teach young people sexual assertiveness in schools. What fucking good is putting a condom on a cucumber if we don't deal with the fact that many men will *always* try to find a way to avoid them? It's like the Riddle of the Sphinx: *Ah condoms, I see! Excuses not to wear one, I have three.*

As I was carrying on with wild abandon, not once did I think, 'I am a bad, bad abomination and must be punished', but I do think if I'd been, say, smoking crack as often as I was having risky casual sex, one of my friends might have gently taken me to one side and said 'James, hun, this is an intervention.' It's difficult to say how much of my behaviour was flagrant opportunism and how much was deeply rooted childhood trauma.

I suspect if straight men had the same *opportunity* to have casual sex that gay men do, they'd be a lot more promiscuous too. But more on that later.

Women are *not* encouraged to be promiscuous. Promiscuity and virginity are abstract concepts. They are value judgements. Virginity is not a 'thing' to be had or lost. It's nothing to do with 'breaking the hymen', as many girls break their hymens while riding bikes or horses, and that would mean young men *never* had this virginal state. For centuries, society, culture and religion have placed a premium on female purity. I see no difference in Eve and Snow White. Both give in to apple-shaped temptation, both pay the consequences. *This* is the message girls get. I *heard* that message, but – as a child and teenager – it didn't apply to me.

There is no female equivalent of *American Pie*, where girls try to get rid of their virginities.* Women and girls who enjoy sex openly are deemed sluts. Even *Sex and the City* asked 'are we sluts?' in one episode. 'Slut', like 'promiscuous', is a value judgement and one that does not apply to men.

Hannah Witton is a successful YouTuber who speaks openly about sex and sex education. *Any* woman online is a target for trolls; imagine what it's like for one who discusses sex. 'I get a lot of shit,' she says, 'but I'm quite strong. There's an assumption that because I talk about sex I must be having sex all the time, I'm a massive slag and I treat men like meat. Every once in a while, a friend will pass comment on my sex life and they're probably having more sex than me because they live with a partner! I think people feel entitled to know about my sex life, which is kinda gross.'

She tells me that slut shaming is worse online, but that might be because she has a record of it. 'I get a lot of negative comments on my videos. I did a video about sexism – it was quite tongue-in-cheek but the comments were full on. Most comments are condescending, patronising, belittling. The negative comments are almost always from men.'

I asked her if it happens in real life, too. 'Most slut shaming happens online but it has also happened in bars and clubs. My favourite kind of slut shaming is the beautiful

---

* *Cherry Falls* doesn't count because they only go about losing their virginity because a serial killer is on their tail.

double standard. If you have sex, you're a slut, but when you get propositioned for sex and you say no, you're a slut! You can't win.'

We all have an archetypal slut, slag, whore, ho or hussy in mind, so the schema must come from *somewhere*. We know how she is likely to behave (promiscuously) and how she's likely to dress. Again, these stereotypes, these slurs, tend not to reach men. Calling a man a 'manwhore' is just repurposing a female slur.

'I do not dress for the attention of men,' Witton told me. 'It's the opposite. I don't want men to look at me because it makes me feel terrified and intruded on. It's different when a woman compliments you to a man. She doesn't want anything back from you.' But women *do* slut shame each other. You can hear it on any train or bus. 'It happens. I catch myself doing it. It's awful – I'll see a woman dressed in a certain way and I think, *Oh she looks like a slut* and I have to stop myself. It's been engrained in me from high school. It's a harmful stereotype that women compete for the attention of men, but a lot of stereotypes come from somewhere. There's a grain of truth in it. I think it comes from a place of insecurity.'

The world saw me as a gay man – two types of norm protected me from slut shaming. Oddly, London calmed me down a bit. To be fair, I think I'd reached the point where I'd tried everything I wanted to try and I became rather keener on the idea of finding one awesome man who was great at the sex stuff but was also dead good, clever and funny too.

On a more practical note, London is also really hard

work. Often, living in Battersea, Grindr would pick up men from Fulham, Chelsea or just rolling through Clapham Junction on the train. Who can be arsed to cross the Thames and board two buses for a quick blowie? Certainly not I.

I was no angel, but I scaled it way, way back – I also had a flatmate in London, and it'd be tacky to parade a load of men through our shared space. Perhaps I just grew out of it.

Heading into my transition, and having broken up with Erik, I was satisfied that, if another man never wanted to touch me, I'd had a pretty fucking strong innings. Being the real me was far more important than a trip to a gay sauna or a quick fling in the club. Some anti-trans writers accuse trans women of being 'failed gay men'. Fuck that, if we're looking at sheer numbers, I was – frankly – *slaying* that whole 'being gay' malarkey.

A final trip to Ibiza seemed like the best way to have some going-out-of-business sex. One of Ibiza's most beautiful beaches is Es Cavallet, a clothing-optional cove for naturists and, well, gay men. Sand dunes and wild scrubland stretch into the hillside and it's a veritable sex theme park. Gay men patrol the winding paths waiting to make that all-important eye contact before scurrying silently into a bush for a quick fumble.

This was the nearest life can ever get to pornography. Like some awful Bel Ami production, I had sex in the sea, sex in a bush, sex in a hot tub, sex in sand dunes, sex pretty much up a tree. It was ludicrous.

At one point, I discovered a group of guys standing

around watching something happen in a sand dune. I assumed I'd stumbled onto an orgy, and I had, just not the one I was expecting. A group of (quite clearly) gay men were lining up to take turns on a cisgender woman.

It seems the final frontier of kink for gay men is women. Who knew?

The biggest miracle was that I returned STI-free. Clearly destiny was smiling down on me. It's hard to feel guilty about it to be honest. Like I said, it sort of feels like I've done ALL THE SEX. There are no surprises left. No regrets . . . mostly.

Now I'm ready for something new.

16.

MASC4MASC

AKA Why Men Need Feminism Too

The legend of Narcissus tells of a beautiful man, cursed by the gods to never love anyone as much as he loved himself. So enamoured was Narcissus with his own reflection that, on gazing into a pool of water, he fell in and drowned.

A curious affliction of the gay scene – and one which rarely affects heterosexual couples – is one I called the Narcissus Effect, whereby gay men fervently overhaul their image and bodies until they want to – literally – fuck themselves.

Have you ever seen a set of twins walking around until, with horror, you realise they actually aren't identical brothers, they're a couple? Same styling, same tattoos, same body type. It's eerie.

That's not to say *all* gay (or indeed bi or queer) men (or women) solely go for men (or women) who look like them. It's just a phenomenon you don't really see with straight couples. I suppose if you're attracted to people who are the same sex as you, there's a sort of logic in transforming yourself into your *own* fantasy in the hope that other people share it.

I have always been attracted to big, giant, hairy men. At five foot eight and very slender, I was never going to be my own type, but when I moved to London I decided to invest some time and money in trying to appeal to as many gay men as possible. I was writing full-time by this stage, so decided to properly DO IT and get a personal trainer.

I purposefully went for a trainer I didn't fancy – no one should have to worry about looking sexually alluring while working out. Nate was a Sarf London Jack the Lad with cheeky dimples and a body to die for, but not nearly tall or hairy enough for me.

After the first session, when I collapsed and vomited on myself, I soon started to see results. If you are serious about changing the shape of your body, I would recommend a trainer to help you do it safely. However, I wasn't ready for the brainwashing.

Nate told me it was 60/40: 60 per cent diet, 40 per cent exercise. If I wanted to 'gain', as he called it, I was gonna have to eat 4000 calories a day. The recommended daily intake for a man is 2500. This meant a gruelling, gluttonous regime of eggs and turkey bacon every breakfast, a morning protein shake, chicken and rice for lunch, another protein shake in the afternoon and some sort of fish or meat for dinner. High protein, low carb and MANSIZE portions.

If I wasn't eating I was cooking. It left very little time for anything else.

I went to the gym five times a week and had a weekly session with Nate. I very quickly saw the difference. I gained about two stone – weighing more than ten stone for the first time in my life. My chest and shoulders ballooned and 'male clothes' looked better on me. I developed the much sought-after 'v-lines' over my hips.

Other people both noticed and complimented my more masculine physique. Don't get me wrong, I didn't look like Chris Hemsworth, but I did have the lean, muscular body you might see in a fashion magazine. I felt more confident on the beach and, yes, at that gay sauna. I knew I was looking good.

Because I looked how Gender said a man should look.

Hipster beard reached peak popularity, and I was able to grow one. This changed the shape of my face, broadening my jawline at the same time as my body. I added to my tattoo collection rapidly, trying to emulate the 'alternative' models I followed on Instagram – Chris John Millington, Andre Hamann, Leebo Freeman. I was finally someone I would fuck.

And I was fucked up.

By this point, sex was almost too easy. I stuck a topless pic on Grindr and learned how easy fishing in that pond could be. If I wanted sex, I could find it. Moreover, I was now more confident in approaching men I would have once thought were way out of my league. Now, if I caught the hottest men in London while they were feeling particularly horny, they'd go for it. The peak was a Swiss man mountain – six foot six and all muscle. Sadly, he just wanted someone to fist him, which really wasn't my thing. Too bad.

My body plateaued. I guess I could have eaten *more*, but it was hard. After about a year of seeing Nate, I asked how we could take it up a level. 'Well,' he said. 'To be honest if you wanna make more gains, you might wanna think about getting some shots.' He whispered the last part.

'What? Like *steroids*?'

'Nah, mate. It's just HGH, everyone's doing it. I can get you some if you want, just don't tell anyone I told you, yeah?'

HGH is Human Growth Hormone – basically pumping more testosterone into my body. While HGH or anabolic steroids would certainly have increased my body mass, I was wary of mood swings, 'roid rage', back acne and shrunken testicles.

I was mortified. I'd worked so hard to improve my body – not to mention eating the entire cast of *Chicken Run* every day for the last year – only to be told to cheat. I did see it as cheating. I knew that as soon as I stopped the injections or supplements, I'd just lose any 'gains' I'd made. So what's the point? Even I knew that was a lifetime commitment to drugs – it wasn't like if I got bigger I'd be satisfied with reverting to my normal size. I declined Nate's offer and stuck to my word.

But now I'd seen the Matrix. As Nate explained that *all* the buff guys in the gym were using steroids, I started seeing the signs everywhere. Tiny little testicles like two almonds swishing around in a shopping bag, the telltale keloid 'back acne'. I suppose it's a bit like Photoshopping or filtering pictures – who wants to be the one who does it the honest way when there's a very quick, very easy way to cheat?

Even a few of my friends – who I assumed just had a natural propensity to be muscular – turned out to be using.

It was disappointing because – and it took me a while to figure this out – I'd spent a lot of time feeling inadequate next to them. Turns out, all I ever needed to do was inject a load of growth hormone into my arse cheeks.

It was during these two or three years that I learned that there *are* body pressures to being a man. Gradually, since the Schwarzenegger/Stallone/Van Damme halcyon days in the 1980s, we've seen an increasing amount of male flesh in the mainstream media. Think back to my childhood. He-Man and Lion-O had their bulging man-tits out at 3.30 every afternoon. That, I was subtly being told as an infant, is what normal men's bodies should look like. This arche-type persists. The Marvel films take once human actors (Paul Rudd, Chris Pratt, Benedict Cumberbatch) and super-size them into ripped He-Man figurines, seemingly overnight. There is always that one scene where Captain America or Thor loses his shirt and is attractively sweaty.

Of course, this is nothing new for women. Since Ursula Andress clambered through the waves in *Dr No*,* we've seen plenty of female flesh. Much has been written about the 'male gaze' in Hollywood and how the patriarchal studio system favours lingering shots of women's bodies. Over the last two decades, however, we have inched towards naked parity.

TV and cinema, still overwhelmingly controlled by male overlords, lean heavily towards the 'male gaze'; just look at the boob-to-penis ratio on *Game of Thrones* or *Westworld*

* And before – the first nude outside of pornography was Audrey Munson in the 1915 silent movie *Inspiration*. Only female nudity was featured.

for proof. But social media, as we have already discussed, is not privy to the same gatekeepers. Men suddenly fancied a slice of the naked exploitation pie previously inflicted only on women. Writer Mark Simpson coined the term 'spornosexual'; the modern young man 'branding' his body as a commodity online. Instagram boasts as many male 'fitness models' – half-naked men with insanely toned bodies – as female ones.

Flesh is cash. With thousands of thirsty followers, such men can make a fortune from product placement – protein powders, supplements and the ever-present tooth whitening strips. A girl's gotta eat, and I'm not judging anyone – male or female – who seeks to earn a living this way.

However, the side effect of wall-to-wall naked male flesh is the skewed concept of what a male body should look like. Gym culture is now simply culture, and men have two choices: you can either get into it or admit defeat. But here's the thing: During my time on London's gay scene and gym scene I learned that even the hunkiest, beefiest men weren't especially happy with the way they looked. If they *were* happy with their bodies, they probably wouldn't be in the gym every spare minute of the day.

Sure, there are some guys who simply love the gym. It's a social space, a great way to switch off mentally and endorphins make you feel good. They are also habit forming. But what I *heard* in the gym was guys – even *huge* guys – trying to get bigger. It wasn't really about maintaining a good physique. There is always some goal, something better, waiting just around the corner. Once you're on the treadmill, you can't get off.

Gym culture has bred a general, low-level disappoint-ment with the male body. Triangular cartoon human Johnny Bravo is the new archetype of male physicality. Again, women reading this are rightly rolling their eyes and saying, ''What's new?' I can only speak for myself, but there was a constant hum of anxiety that I *should* be at the gym when I wasn't. I *shouldn't* be eating that bread or cake. There was something very masculine about the sheer *discipline*. If you didn't have the self-discipline to GET RIPPED you were a) a fat loser or b) a skinny loser.

What's perhaps interesting about this dissatisfied thought process is that it was largely self-created and self-fulfilled. Male body anxiety was not entirely pushed onto men by advertisers (although *clearly* sports nutrition brands are massively benefitting) as was predominantly the way for women. No, this anxiety was born of man, for man.

Yes, straight women *of course* compliment men on their physiques, weight loss or weight gain. However, I feel women are turned *off* by overly vain men (it contradicts Gender's teachings on what makes men masculine), so I'm not sure the pressure is coming solely from women. I'm unconvinced that women objectify men in the same way that men objectify women, or indeed other men. Even if they do, the objectification of men doesn't tally into the same rates of rape, sexual assault and street harassment.

Simpson suggests that in the middle of a modern mascu-linity crisis men are suddenly unsure of their value in society. Men are and aren't expected to be breadwinners. Traditional manual labour jobs have evolved in the wake of mechan-isation and globalisation. Men are expected to co-parent fairly. Men are supposed to be, at the same time, sexually dominant and submissive. With an M&S Food on every corner, no woman *needs* a man to hunt or gather for her, although it is expected he will make the effort to go to that M&S and adequately select a Dine-in-for-two option.

Suddenly, in a sea of role confusion, here is a way to be, quite literally, a self-made man. You might not be able to control the societal shitstorm around you but you *can* control your abs and biceps. What's more, taking control of your body is a way to better navigate the rest of society – in terms of perceived sexual currency and opening potential employment doors.

I felt this. During my brief 'hot man' phase, I felt a sense of purpose, a sense of control, a sense that I was doing 'Man' correctly.

And it did not for one second make *me* happy.

Perhaps it took 'being a man' for a bit to realise I was most definitely a woman. I couldn't say I hadn't given it a fair crack of the whip. My male role play, the drag, the dress-up, was exhausting. I felt like an imposter, and not even a convincing one. I cannot say if – for actual men – the gender performance of masculinity is so wearing. I cannot say if all that braying and backslapping, fist- and chest-bumping feels as ludicrous as it did when I tried it. Grayson Perry tackles this subject extensively in his book *The Descent of Man*.

Although there were *many* moments of realisation that I plainly wasn't a man, two spring immediately to mind. The first was at the gay club, XXL, in London. Rarely, during my 'gay years', did I think there was anything 'wrong' with being gay. I couldn't have not fancied men any more than I could stop it raining with the power of my mind. Yet a night at XXL was enough to convince me that many gay men might benefit from a tiny bit of therapy. Don't @ me.

Humans aren't often segregated by gender, and I think that might not be a bad thing. XXL is men-only, and you could smell 'man' in the air – sweat, Issey Miyake, testosterone, poppers, beer. This was during my gym-going chapter and, I kid you not, after about ten minutes on the dancefloor my slouchy hipster vest had been *ripped* from my body. I'd always vowed I'd *never* be one of those shirtless torsos, but I wasn't given a choice.

The sweat-slicked bodies were to 'roid for. Pecs and abs and biceps, oh my. Popping forehead veins and spotty backs. Gurning mouths. And these weren't just the kids – men in their forties and fifties chewing their faces off. Not a judgement, an observation.

At the time, I was knee-deep in writing *This Book Is Gay*, a guide to sexual identity and coming out for young adults. I was with my friend Niall and asked if, purely for research purposes, we could investigate the darkroom. It actually really was just curiosity – we both had monogamous boyfriends at the time.

Have you ever been to Ikea? Much like the Swedish furniture giant, in the darkroom at XXL you follow floor arrows around what can only be described as a sex showroom. For one thing, it's not actually that dark. Health and safety regulations mean the space has to be lit in low-level red lighting. As you shuffle around – not nearly as anonymously as you'd like – little pockets of sexual activity break out.*

The A-list hotties wordlessly attract the most attention, obviously. As fit pairs hook up publically, bottom feeders (in some cases literally) try to get in on the action; cuttle-fish nibbling on humpback whales. Depending on how wasted the hotties are, they either let the B-listers get in on the action or bat them off like a horse using its tail to fan away flies.

Mostly, it's just men standing around waiting for a turn, for someone to give them the eye. Most, I'd guess, compromise. In the dimly lit tunnels, alcoves and archways – which stink of cum and shit – you lower your usual standards. After all, it's dark, and you've come this far.

Let me be very clear. This is not a nice place to be. The only reason the darkroom is in *any way* arousing is *because* it's so fucked up. It's naughty, it's bad, it's taboo. I saw precious little evidence of condom use. HIV is not the killer it once was, but such flagrant disregard for physical health is indicative, I feel, of poor *mental* health. I see little difference between risky sexual behaviours and teenagers unscrewing craft scissors and taking them to their forearms. It's self-harm.

Here we are back on *Velvet Rage* and *Straight Jacket* territory. I'd urge you to read both of those titles. Now

---

* Darkrooms are NOT a uniquely homosexual experience. 'Kink' and fetish nights clearly cater to mixed-sex couples too, they just tend to be a lot more expensive and often involve shit *Eyes Wide Shut*-style fancy dress masks. Ooh, how 'decadent'. Whatever floats your basic boat.

you've all stopped screaming how it's sexual expression, a rebellion against heteronormative attitudes and #notallgaymen, let's actually acknowledge that LGBTQ people are vastly more at risk of addiction, suicidal ideation and depression than our straight, cisgender counterparts*. Something *is* wrong. Whether you *like* that or not is neither here nor there, it's fact.

Why? As mentioned earlier, Downs and Todd say 'shame' is to blame. LGBTQ youngsters are shamed, explicitly and implicitly, into feeling they are fundamentally wrong and require punishment. They dole this punishment out to themselves.

I think there is truth to that. I also think misogyny underpins this 'shame' and misogyny comes from Gender. When young LGBTQ people learn they are 'getting it wrong' as kids this usually comes from not properly 'acting like a boy' or 'acting like a girl'. Long before anyone is shamed for their sexual preference, they are shamed for gender non-conformity:

PUT THAT DOLL DOWN
YOU LOOK LIKE A BOY
YOU THROW LIKE A GIRL
SHE'S GOT A TASH
HE SCREAMED LIKE A GIRL
THAT'S NOT FOR LITTLE GIRLS

* LGBT people are an estimated two to three times more likely to have depression and suicidal thoughts compared to straight or cisgender people. Statistic: LGBT Foundation.

And so forth. Small children (mercifully and hopefully) are not sexual beings, so it's not until adolescence you might start to think your sexual desires are anything other than straight and 'the norm'.

Beyond 'my religion disagrees with it', I feel nearly all homophobia stems from misogyny. When people abuse gay people it is often for gender non-conformity:

YOU TAKE IT UP THE ARSE
(receptively, y'know, like a girl)
THAT DYKE LOOKS LIKE A BLOKE
(because we all know what girls should look like)
FUCKING NANCY
(he's not fulfilling his manly duties)
LOOK AT THAT MINCER
(walking as we'd expect a woman to walk)
HE LOOKS LIKE A WOMAN
(in make-up or clothes I'd assign to women)

I honestly feel that misogyny is one of the pillars holding up homophobia and *that* is why gay men who propagate sexism (disgust at vaginas, 'serving fish', breast grabbing, etc) are complicit in their own ongoing torment.

I don't mean to be 'down' on gay men now that I'm not one. I was one (or at least thought I was) for a really long time. I was clearly fucked up too – and I think I was fucked up by the exact same things they were. I was so busy not abusing drugs and alcohol that I let my attitude to sex go to some very odd places. Gay people can either stick on some Robyn and dance through the tears the way they've always done, or we can all try to remedy decades of institutional homophobia. And we start with attitudes to Gender.

For proof of the misogyny–homophobia link, consider Jeremy Clarkson's former *Top Gear* sidekick, Richard Hammond. In 2016, he commented – in the way that the gobby little Napoleon in any group of ladz might – that he wouldn't eat an ice cream because he identifies as heterosexual.

That's right – for some men masculinity is now so fragile they wouldn't be caught dead enjoying a lovely choc ice or Mr Whippy lest someone, somehow, extrapolate they might not be 100 per cent British Heterosexual Beefcake. Instead, I imagine, such men would select a raw, dripping hog's head on a pike as a tasty summer snack. *Such* fragility. And to think they call *us* snowflakes.

We call masculinity 'toxic' for two reasons: the first is that it's dangerous for women (and we'll discuss rape culture later), the second is that (I'd imagine) it makes the vast majority of men feel inadequate a lot of the time. If you're stressing about a fucking ice lolly, what *else* is throwing your self-worth into crisis?

Poet Anthony Anaxagorou often speaks about the issues surrounding toxic masculinity. 'This pervasive and damaging idea that masculinity exists as a specific set of approved and normalised behavioural patterns results in a wide and profound pathology for many men. There is no fixed way to be, just as there is no fixed way to love or to express oneself – to restrict the organicity of the human being is to limit and control that which secretly looks for freedom. How gender and masculinity forge these myopic and lethal binaries becomes part of the reason why so many men around the world grow up conflicted and emotionally repressed.'

XXL was one of two key moments of realisation. The second was less sordid. My friend Rob hosts occasional 'gay gamer' nights at his flat. Nerdy, 'cutester' types gather and play *Mario Kart* and *Super Smash Bros*. Thinking there'd be some prime geeky, beardy hotness, I agreed to attend one such gathering even though I'm not especially into gaming.

Having always been something of a geek (*Doctor Who*, *Buffy* and *X-Men* are my poisons) these absolutely *should* have been my people, but once more I found myself in an alien, all-male environment. At once, I sensed I was the odd one out. I *looked* like them – beard and plastic-rimmed glasses, American Apparel tube socks – but I strongly, strongly felt I wasn't one of them. Not one little bit. I was an imposter, a bodysnatcher, an interloper.

I am particularly awful at *Mario Kart* (probably because I'm quite awful at driving, period). At one point, one of my 'brothers' turned to me after a disastrous round and said, in all seriousness, 'Why are you even here?'

Well, quite. Couldn't have said it better myself.

I know that by saying 'I didn't feel like a man' it seems like I'm actually saying, 'I didn't like stereotypes of masculinity', and that is true. However, and I can only speak from experience, it went much further, much deeper, than that. My negativity towards traditionally masculine pastimes pales in comparison to how *positively* I felt towards traditionally feminine things.

My transition isn't a *rejection* of masculinity, it's *embracing* a state I feel far more attuned to. How I am now doesn't even feel like *trying*, I am simply *being*. Every day I was a man felt like a day I was failing; a square peg, swimming against a tide; other clichés. To me, being a woman feels as instinctual as breathing.

17.

THE PENNY DROPS

AKA I'm Coming Out 2

I owe my new life to a young woman called Charley. I don't think she'll mind me mentioning her by name. When I met her, she was fourteen years old and in one of my writing groups for gifted young people. She is also trans and had started secondary school as a girl.

This was not, I hasten to add, the school from *Glee*. This was a real, hard core, South London state school. They had stabbings (one, quite inventively, with the pointy end of an afro comb) and gangs and all that jazz. I can only imagine the kind of bravery it took for her to rock up on her first day at a new school in a skirt.

Yes, people talked behind her back, but I guess that's preferable to hurling abuse (or afro combs) at her face. What was interesting was how – three years in – most people had stopped caring. With access to testosterone blockers, Charley would never go through 'boy puberty', meaning she looked and sounded like any other teenage girl and had a wonderful support network of lovely friends.

I was spellbound by the zero fucks Charley seemed to give. Her stresses were about her controlled art exam and poetry, not her gender. She was so, so comfortable. I couldn't help but wonder how my life would have been different if I'd had the knowledge (and access to drugs) that her generation have.

But it was too late. My body *did* go through boy puberty, so I was stuck with it, right?

Wrong. And that was where it began.

The coming out process was slow and laboured, but only because transitioning is a fuzzy-edged, ephemeral beast. Unlike my late-night Dean Cain sexuality revelation, my gender identity took a little longer to solidify. In fact, I can't pinpoint the precise moment I started to think I might be trans.

Gender is *learned* behaviour and *trans*gender is no different. Much as restaurants started to introduce gluten-free options to their menu, a third option was becoming widely available on the gender buffet: male, female, trans.

The media – more powerful than ever – was responsible for this new awareness. Since Nadia Almada won *Big Brother* in 2004, we have seen Laverne Cox, Isis King (*America's Next Top Model*), Chaz Bono, Candis Cayne, Carmen Carrera, Andreja Pejić, Paris Lees and fictional characters Hayley Cropper (*Coronation Street*) and Jason Costello (*Hollyoaks*) on the telly. Conchita Wurst – who fits the brief of performative transgender – won Eurovision. All of these things happened *before* Caitlyn Jenner came out as transgender.

Isis King was living in a homeless shelter in New York when she appeared in the background of a photoshoot on *America's Next Top Model* in 2008. She was spotted by producers and competed in the show's eleventh season. 'I didn't really have any role models,' Isis says. 'I saw *Paris Is Burning** so I'd seen Octavia St Laurent and fell in love with her confidence and poise. Other than seeing that, there were really no girls on TV that I saw myself in. My mom was always my role model.'

Making history as a trans woman on the youth-oriented CW network didn't enter King's head at the time. 'I just wanted to win and have a better life than living in the shelter. I didn't realise the magnitude of the impact it would have. In a way I'm glad, because I would have put more pressure on my twenty-two-year-old self. Not being aware also allowed me to be more authentic, which I believe resonated with many more people.'

King's appearance on *ANTM* was seven years prior to Caitlyn Jenner's *Vanity Fair* cover and five years ahead of Andreja Pejić's coming-out. Awareness was *not* where it is now. 'It was hard across the board,' King tells me. 'The industry wasn't really ready to accept a trans model back then. I had my fair share of amazing experiences but it was an uphill battle. It still is.'

I watched Isis from the other side of the world – a trans woman around my age, who looked absolutely gorgeous. Vitally, she was widely accepted as 'one of the girls' by the majority of other contenders. Whether she knew it or not, Isis was a beacon. 'I heard from kids all around the world. It has not stopped in almost a decade! All age groups, but

* Jennie Livingston's 1990 documentary charting New York's drag ballroom circuit.

now the little kids are like *I was in elementary school and saw you . . .* man I'm getting old, but I love it.'

Isis is philosophical about her participation in this social sea change. She shrugs it off when I ask if she was aware of making a difference. 'I dreamed of the change, and I'm honoured that my story, even if it's a crumb, has helped that progression.' And then the big question: Which comes first: media representation or a shift in public opinion? It's a chicken-or-egg mystery. 'Now we live in a world of social media and quick turnaround, I think it used to be mass media [representation] first, but I believe now it's 50/50, because sometimes the media is very controlled and the only knowledge or footage might start from a Facebook live video that goes viral.'

She's right, of course. Prior to broadband, only the gatekeepers of the mass media controlled who I could and couldn't see in TV and film. Now, the mistress of my own media consumption, I could seek out my own role models.

Before I had only known what being transgender was, but now I had *seen* it. Now I *recognised* it. Importantly, I had also now seen trans women around my age. April Ashley and Caroline Cossey – both trans icons – were so much older than me that it was difficult to align their experience to mine.

It seemed that real-life girls, like Charley, and celebrity ones were living their trans lives quite happily. And, just maybe, so could I. Unlike the last time round, this time I wasn't immediately scared. I was a grown-up, I had relative security and a wonderful network of friends. As such, I was able to vocalise my concerns free from worry.

Transition – contrary to popular tabloid opinion – doesn't start by lopping your genitals off. It starts with a questioning process.

The first person I spoke to was my dear friend Sam. This was late 2013, and we were in a Thai restaurant near Clapham Common. I was eating beef massaman curry (as you do). I had, to an extent, summoned her from Camden, as I wanted to talk through my turmoil. 'I wanted to talk to you about something quite serious,' I told her.

'Is it that you're a woman?' she said, sort of half kidding, I think.

'Well . . .' I began, and it went from there.

Sam has been at my side through various phases (there was a period in 2005 where I dressed like a tweedy country gent á la Guy Ritchie, for example), so – perhaps fairly – she did question my commitment to transitioning. At the time, I was in the relationship with Erik too, so I wasn't sure if it was fair to carry that on while questioning my gender.

Questioning, in my mind, is absolutely part of any transition, so it was where my gender transition began. It starts with opening your mind – just a peep hole – to the possibility that facts about yourself you have previously held true might not be. It's as much about letting go as it is letting something in.

This is not to be sniffed at. For about fifteen years I had truly believed I was a gay man, and been resigned to living as one. If that wasn't true, it was a real ground-shaker. Nothing would be the same ever again.

And so I did nothing.

At various times since I started transitioning, the climb

from the bottom of Kilimanjaro just seemed too daunting. At Basecamp One, looking up, it's fucking terrifying. It's easier to just go home. In my case, although I strongly suspected I should have always been a woman, it was much, MUCH easier to just 'make do' as a gay man.

In fact, I threw myself into 'making do'. My last year as a man was the one where I really went for it. As mentioned, I worked out, I drank gallons of protein shakes, I grew a huge beard, I took full and lively advantage of London's gay scene. I took that trip to Ibiza and had sex with the whole fucking island. It was fun. I was MASCULINE TO THE MAX. I broke up with my boyfriend anyway, but not for wholly trans-adjacent reasons.

Even after speaking to Sam, I very much decided that living out my years as a gay man was infinitely preferable to changing every last element of my being: my name, my body, my career, my family, my friends . . . It seemed to me that transitioning would be a hugely destructive act.

But sometimes you have to burn everything down. Forest fires, as destructive as they seem, have been used and controlled for hundreds of years. They clear away excess grasses and shrubs and they stimulate the germination of more desirable trees. Sometimes you have to destroy everything for something better to take its place.

I benched the idea for much of the next year, but *something* shifted over the winter of 2014. The idea had been a-brewing for the best part of twelve months. Nothing especially eventful happened on New Year's Eve 2014 – I went to my friend's club night in Vauxhall – but on New Year's Day I was more resolute than I had been in a long time. Perhaps there really is something about January and resolution. Whatever the reason, I went to meet my friend Louis at a greasy spoon. He was chomping his way through a fry-up, but I was way too hungover, so sipped on a peppermint tea between emergency trips to the toilet.

I told him I was *definitely* a woman. I told him I *might* transition. The hard part, I felt, was in getting from A to B. What was interesting is how *surprised* those first few people were. With the exception of the protein-shake years, I've always worn my feminine side close to the surface: I was the sixth Spice Girl, I was Cherry Filth. I think when a man embraces femininity, as a culture, we spring to 'gay' rather than any indicator of him being non-binary, gender-queer or trans, which perhaps shows where we are in terms of failing to understand the difference between sexuality and gender.

Louis, as Sam had been, was lovely and understanding, but both admitted this was something of which they had no experience. In fact, Louis was the final nail in the coffin. I told him that I assumed that *all* gay boys had spent their entire childhood wanting to be women. Immediately, without missing a single beat, Louis (a gay man) said he had never once even *thought* about what life would be like if he was a girl.

Oh. Shit.

Having *never* been comfortable with Gender's lurking presence, I guess it figures that I'd never had that sense of Gender security Louis had. It radiated from him in an insouciant shrug of his shoulder. He was a boy, then he was a man. Oh god, how I wish it had been that easy for me.

But it wasn't, so what's the fucking point in booing about it.

Again, feeling very resolutiony, I found a therapist who specialised in sexuality and gender matters. For the first time in my life, I had more on my plate than I felt I could deal with solo, and my friends admitted it was well outside of their sphere of knowledge.

The first few sessions with Therapist Dean didn't go *quite* as expected in that he did a very good job of talking me out of it. His methods wouldn't suit everyone (which is why it's best to talk to a few people before settling on a therapist – I didn't only meet with Dean) but he spoke of the realities of transitioning and it hit me like a ton of bricks.

'You'll never be a woman,' he told me.

WAY HARSH, TAI.

My thinking has always been fairly dichotic – all or nothing – so being told I would never be biologically female was enough to make me file the idea away, possibly permanently.

Instead, the first few months of therapy focused on my lingering feelings of dissatisfaction and inability to feel the full gamut of emotions. It seemed, after much talking, that my hideous time at school had rendered me, for want of a better phrase, dead inside.

It sounds so obvious, but we had to spend a lot of time going through what different emotions look and feel like, given that I was only really experiencing anger fully. If you've seen Pixar's *Inside Out*, you'll know how the inside of my head was functioning. The little red one was firmly in control. Sadness and Joy were often ignored entirely.

The former issue was as important. I've had sexified boyfriends, career success, a nice flat, enough money to survive on, friends and family, but I've *never* felt entirely satisfied. Is this a terrible symptom of modern aspirational living (which instils an understanding that there's *always* something you should be wanting), or is it that I've been living in the wrong gender my whole life?

Dean's point, as strong as it might sound, was this: What if I transitioned and still didn't feel satisfied? How would *that* feel? It was so important that I didn't view transitioning as a way to fix all the wrongs in both my head and life. Transitioning, I believe, will right my gender, but possibly nothing else. Obviously, I hope there are knock-on benefits of living in the right gender (how could there not be?) but there are no guarantees. It's not a magic wand that will fix all my woes.

What Dean was trying to do was get me to understand the realities of transitioning. Instead of hoping I'd simply wake up a woman – and be readily accepted as such – he needed to make me realise I was getting the full deluxe trans package, with all its hardships. I will be a woman – I am a woman – but I will also always be trans. That has its own pride and its own pitfalls.

Whatever we discussed, and although I oscillated between male and female, the desire to live as a woman wasn't going away. At the *Attitude* Pride Awards in 2015, I mingled with the great and good of the LGBT community, but was especially impressed with (award recipient) RAF search and rescue officer Ayla Holdom, whose transition hit the (very mean) headlines because she just so happened to work alongside Prince William.

What was especially cool – although quite unfortunate for her – was that she couldn't actually attend the awards, as she had to work. She sent a video thanking *Attitude* for the award, but her mother and sister were there to pick up the award in person. As with Charley, it was inspiring to see a normal trans woman just living her life. It was especially encouraging to see her family's unwavering support, making me wonder if my family could survive a transition too.

It was time to shit or get off the pot. Absolutely by accident and not being overly dramatic, I went to the doctor's on my birthday in 2015. Yeah, I know. I'd like to take this opportunity to thank my lovely, wonderful and not-uneasy-on-the-eye GP, Dr Clark.

I had been warned by the NHS website that my GP might not know what 'a transgender' was, so I might like to print out a forty-two-page PDF explaining them to him. Given that Dr Clark had 'read my book review in *Attitude*' (if that's not the best euphemism for being gay, I don't know what is), I hoped I'd be OK.

As it was, Dr Clark was brilliant. We sat and talked for about half an hour (sorry patients in the waiting room, your bunions had to wait) and came up with a plan. As waiting lists in London were beyond horrific (two years? I don't think so), he agreed at once to refer me to Northampton Gender Identity Clinic, where the wait list, although still long, wasn't *that* long.

I consider myself very lucky to have a GP who totally got what was going on – he'd even done training at a GIC. Not every trans person is so fortunate. I guess it's a bit like therapists; had the first GP been shit, I'd have found a better one.

The referral, to me, signalled the point of no return. It's never felt like the wrong decision either. Some anti-trans voices, and the media, are fucking obsessed by the tiny minority of trans people who go through a so-called 'detransition'. I don't see that happening for me, although so what if it did? I think gender is fluid. One person's shifting identity is hardly rock-solid evidence that being transgender is harmful or somehow not-a-thing. There are no official figures on this subgroup, but Dr Stuart Lorimer – a gender clinician based in London – has had fifteen out of over 4000 patients cease hormone treatment or socially revert to their original gender . . . that's 0.4 per cent.

It was time to come out to everyone. Bit by bit, I told my friends as and when I saw them. I told my publisher and the publications I write for. It was also time to tell my family – which we already covered.

Now, I don't for one second consider myself famous. Even *within* the world of children's publishing, I don't really think authors get true fame. J. K. Rowling is an obvious exception, but, to be honest, if Stephen King or Jonathan Franzen strolled into the coffee shop where I'm writing this, I doubt I'd notice. Nonetheless, I knew I'd have to come out 'publically', as it were, to my readers and other 'interested parties'.

Initially, there was a half-arsed plan to make an

announcement at the *Attitude* Awards in October 2015 but it a) didn't pan out and b) would have been a bit naff, in hindsight. They were giving April Ashley a lifetime achievement award and me 'coming out' would have definitely hijacked her big moment. However, at that event – by which time I was pretty much 'out' to anyone who cared to ask – I spoke to the very excellent journalist Patrick Strudwick, and he suggested I could tell my story to him for Buzzfeed. Patrick is a fantastic writer who cares deeply about LGBTQ rights and representation, and I knew he'd handle the story with great sensitivity.

He came round to my flat shortly after I'd relocated back to Brighton and we talked for the best part of two hours. I said everything I wanted to say and I'm still really proud of what Patrick and I achieved with that interview.

The article went live while I was the Deptcon YA convention in Dublin. This timing worked out well – I felt sufficiently removed from the situation, a little like I was in hiding. I needn't have worried; the response was nothing but wonderful. My Twitter and Facebook feeds lit up with warm and supportive messages from all over the world.

Initially, I decided to stick with 'James' and 'he' until I was 100 per cent on a name. Also, at the time – and with Gender closer than he'd been in years – I still very much felt I looked and dressed 'like a man' and didn't want people calling me 'she' when I hadn't yet made a single change to any area of my life. That was my personal preference.

By curious coincidence, Germaine Greer had picked that very day to vent her spleen (again) about trans women, so I found myself drawn into that furore, along with austerity chef Jack Monroe, who also came out as trans non-binary on that day. Weird . . . there must have been something in the water that week.

What was especially wonderful was, later that day, I appeared on a panel about writing teen horror with best-selling authors Derek Landy (*Skulduggery Pleasant* series) and Darren Shan (*Demonata* series). Brilliantly, news of my transition wasn't even mentioned and I was just allowed to discuss my expertise – teen fiction – which is the way it should be for all experts: male, female, trans or cis.

That day was wonderfully freeing. To be honest, I was rapidly losing track of who knew 'my secret' and who didn't. Having everything out in the open, and being able to strap the Buzzfeed interview to the top of my Twitter page, meant I didn't have to keep saying the same thing over and over – it was there for everyone to see.

That night I got possibly the drunkest I've ever, ever been in my life. I celebrated by vomiting all over Dublin and having sex in a nightclub toilet. The next morning was spent projectile vomiting in the disabled loos at Dublin airport before I had to visit the sexual health clinic the following Monday for a course of precautionary PEP. It's odd to me that I'd sabotage such a glorious day by getting blackout drunk and fucking in a toilet stall.

Like I said, the only thing that changes is your gender.

18.

TRANSPLAINING

AKA Feminism is for No-One
if it's Not for Everyone

While I was watching the reaction to the Buzzfeed article in a plush Dublin hotel room, journalists started to call. Not just about my transition. No, they wanted to talk about Germaine Greer.

The night before my coming-out article went live, Greer had appeared on the BBC show *Newsnight* and said the following:

'Just because you lop off your dick and then wear a dress doesn't make you a fucking woman. I've asked my doctor to give me long ears and liver spots and I'm going to wear a brown coat but that won't turn me into a fucking cocker spaniel.

I do understand that some people are born intersex and they deserve support in coming to terms with their gender but it's not the same thing. A man who gets his dick chopped off is actually inflicting an extraordinary act of violence on himself.'

So let's talk about that. First things first: Should the BBC be allowing hate speech like that a platform? Greer was already known for her anti-trans views. Would the BBC allow some pointy-hooded monster from the KKK on *Newsnight* to discuss racism and anti-semitism? No, they fucking wouldn't.* Nor should they allow 'debate' about whether trans women are women or trans men are men. I'm not a concept – I'm *here*. I am alive. I am a fact.

I want to get something out of the way. The F-word. No, not fuck, you stupid fuckers, that word is fine. No, I mean a much more controversial word: FEMINISM.

Yep, I'm going there. We need to talk about how women like me – vulnerable women – fit into women's rights.

Feminist, feminism, intersectional feminism, trans-exclusionary rad-fem, fembot, feminazi. How could a book called *The Gender Games* not discuss feminism? If that word is making you bristle, cringe or anxiously look for an unlocked fire escape we must explore *why*.

Gender only survives if men and women are different and get treated differently. Feminism is the best weapon against Gender we have and *all* people, whatever their sex, benefit from feminism.

To *me* (and I'm not claiming to be the definitive expert) feminism is pretty straightforward: it's about making things between men and women fairer. We know, in lots of different ways, that women, societally speaking, are still not equal to men:

---

* I have since attended a training session for *Newsnight* producers and researchers with the pressure group All About Trans. They are committed to improving trans awareness on the show.

- Only one in four MPs is a woman
- As of 2012, women make up only 17.3 per cent of the staff of FTSE 100 companies
- The full-time gender pay gap is 10 per cent, and the average part-time pay gap is 34.5 per cent
- Approximately 70 per cent of people in minimum wage jobs are women
- Up to three million women experience rape, sexual harassment, domestic violence and stalking each year
- Two women a week are killed by a partner or ex-partner

These statistics are but a taster of the inequality women still endure. Those are the BIGGIES. As journalist Laura Bates pointed out in her wonderful book *Everyday Sexism*, it's also about the micro-sexisms that happen on a day to day basis: the creepers who slow their cars to leer; the invasions of personal space on public transport; being ignored by waiters who will only deal with their mankeeper.

So, feminism. To recognise these inequalities, *and then do something about it*, makes you a feminist in my book. I'm not sure, to be honest, if it's enough for someone to say, 'Sure, I'd like things to be better balanced' and then do fuck all about it – especially if that someone is a man.* It doesn't have to be marching on the capital with a placard; even proudly using the word 'feminist' in real life is active, erm, activism.

---

* And no, I don't think retweeting feminist quotes to your feminist followers on Twitter is enough either. If we've learned one thing from 2016 it's that only talking to people who agree with you is ineffective, to say the least.

Supporting women and girls takes many, many forms. I don't think beating yourself up about 'not doing feminism well' is a) helpful or b) something that troubles a lot of men.

For my part, I go into schools and present a talk about negative media representation of women. I've written seven novels in which young women invest as much in their friends, education and futures as they do men or relationships. I try to give them fictional role models and be a real-life one too. It's not much, but my literary audience has often been young adults, both boys and girls, so it makes sense. It's a contribution.

Your contribution could be as minimal as ensuring your partner actually parents (i.e. doesn't 'babysit') or does their share of domestic jobs (i.e. doesn't 'help out'). Like I said, just calling yourself a feminist, openly, helps future generations see it's not a dirty word. Every little helps.

It makes me way sad, like even sadder than when the Tesco delivery man brings me 'replacement' items, when people suggest that men cannot, and can never be, feminists. To such thinkers, any man who talks about feminism is guilty of '**mansplaining**': men using their patriarchal privilege to educate poor, feeble-minded women in the way that missionaries used to teach the savages in Borneo.

Patriarchy: a social system in which males hold the most power, predominate in roles of political leadership, authority, social privilege and control of property; in the domain of the family, fathers or father-figures hold authority over women and children.

The sad part is, often very well-meaning male journalists, writers and commentators are accused of mansplaining in the course of writing about women's issues and women's rights. Many of them are, I suspect, feminists, and are trying to help. They want things to be more balanced and are doing something about it. While it would be *preferable* to have more female voices in the media, it is helpful to have the support of the men who already exist in that space. The hope is they will create more opportunities for women as they rise through the ranks.

What's more, for equality to really, truly happen, we absolutely *need* men on board. Even if every woman was happy to proclaim herself a feminist all that would achieve is a weird gender battle, the likes of which often existed in my Year 1 primary class when I was a teacher: BOYS ARE BETTER THAN GIRLS, and vice versa.

No, to make real change, we need those already in positions of power – both men and women – to create opportunities and demand better legislation for women. We need men who want to close the gaps. That's why it's especially stupid to fire shots at those men who *do* speak out as feminists, even if some of it comes across as 'mansplaining'. Of course, as with anything, there are also just a whole bunch of patronising dicks in the world. Some of them are men. Indeed, ruefully watching women have their own jokes explained to them by men on Twitter is one of my favourite hobbies.*

Some readers may question the need for labels at all. I hear this a lot from teenage girls when I visit schools: Why do we use 'feminist' when we could use 'equalitist' or some

---

* The guy who explained how space worked to a female astronaut deserves a special shout-out here. Well done, bro, you win mansplaining.

such? There's probably some super, super clever PhDs on this very topic, but for me, while there is a pronounced divide between any group in society, it needs a special word so everyone can see the problem hasn't gone away. While we have inequality for people of colour, we need the word 'racism' and #BlackLivesMatter, while people discriminate against gay or trans people we need 'homophobia' and 'transphobia', and while there is still a pay gap, and FGM, and girls who aren't entitled to an education, I believe we need the word 'feminism'. Overwhelmingly, men and boys do *not* suffer **on a societal level**, although masculinity has its own downfalls, as we've seen.

Sadly, there will be some people who think all of the above is mansplaining because I am transgender. This is where we get to the most vicious divide in modern feminism. And it's a *nasty* one. For some, because I was unlucky enough to be born with male sex chromosomes, I should not be telling *anyone* how to define feminism or patriarchy.

It boils down to one yes/no question: do you think I'm a man?

This is shittola for two reasons IMHO (as dicks say on the internet before they say something dickish). Fundamentally I *don't* think I'm a man. Nor was I ever. Hopefully I've convinced you of that now. If the world was fair, I would have popped out with a vagina, but I had no say in that, and that's not what happened. I never *consented* to being a boy, my body was forced on me. I was born a *baby* and then Gender started to teach me what men and women were.

Now, if, after everything, you still think I'm a 'man in a frock' and if you are a person who thinks gender is a rigid biological cage into which we are all inescapably locked from birth, we might have to, as my gran would have said, 'agree to disagree'. But I believe in hope and I *hope* I'll convince you otherwise. Please do continue reading.

If anything, I'm 'transwomansplaining'. I'm not sure it matters though, if we're all on the same side, and we all want the same thing. I am *certainly* not using this book to *tell* women how to be women. Holy fuck, we get enough of that every time we turn on a television or radio, open a newspaper or magazine or log on to the internet.

Instead, this is a *plea* that we need modern feminists to come together – now more than ever. I truly believe women need to support other women, regardless of our bodies.

PRIVOLYMPICS

'Privilege' is the term often used to describe the way rights, advantages or rewards differ between different social groups. Many writers (OK, people with blogs) over the last few years have tried to, for want of a better word, 'rank' who has the most or least privilege in society. A foolhardy mission if ever there was one, for a number of reasons.

As *any* of us has multiple overlapping (or '**intersectional**') identities and as these also fluctuate as our lives and circumstances change, it would be nigh on impossible to evaluate our *own* privilege, let alone homogenise entire subsections of society. As a transitioning woman – sometimes skint, sometimes less skint – who spent seventeen years as a white gay man, I literally have no idea what privileges I have and haven't had (oh I've 'checked my privilege' many a time), so neither do you.

The other problem with privilege is that it's not ONE THING. It's not like unboxing a phone where you have a handset, charger, headphones and privilege bundle. For different people privilege means different things. It can be money; it can be access to healthcare; it can be access to education; rape culture. All biggies. However, it can also be period pain, body shaming, flexible working hours, feeling safe, freedom to eat in fucking public and many, many more.

I think, when we discuss privilege, it's important – as in *The Hunger Games* – to remember who the real enemy is. It's phenomenally disheartening to read or hear sniping among disenfranchised groups. BAME people who won't tolerate homosexuality; gay men who mock gay women and, yes, cis women who won't accept trans women.

The distribution of privilege, I think, looks a bit like this:

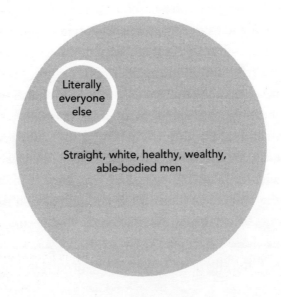

Look at the people on the news – the politicians, the 'experts', the business leaders, the police chiefs – how many of them are plucked from that big circle? All but two of our Prime Ministers in almost THREE HUNDRED YEARS have been from that dominant group; one of the other two is an immigration-obsessed fascist. And the other was Margaret Thatcher.

I can dimly hear a few white men saying 'Juno, I worked really hard to get out of poverty and start my own business.' That's not really what we're talking about. Money is but one type of 'privilege'. What we're saying is, as a white male, the climb out of poverty was likely easier than the climb a woman or man of colour would have had to make. Can you say *with certainty* the bank clerk who approved your business loan wasn't a massive racist or misogynist who made assumptions about you based on the colour of your skin or your gender?

When those of us in the little bubble speak out, we're accused of being 'militant', disruptive, bother-makers, 'snowflakes', rabble-rousers or aggressors. How? How can people with so little power possibly be anything other than a scream into the wind?

The awful men in the big bubble, the ones who *wouldn't* seek to expand the little bubble,* must fucking LOVE it when the people crammed in the little cattle truck pick, argue and fight among ourselves. How they must cackle with delight as they see us split hairs about people 'getting

---

* 'Rape culture is a myth'; 'What wage gap?'; 'If you listened to God, you wouldn't need Planned Parenthood'. All tweets I've been personally sent.

feminism wrong' or who has the most or least privilege.

Shall I tell you who never has to sit down and assess how much privilege they have? The rich, white, straight, cisgender, healthy, able-bodied men. They don't need to talk about privilege because they are too busy having it. It's rested around their shoulders like an invisibility cloak since the day they were born. I know – I was handed one too, remember. They've never wondered if they might not get that job in case an employer *might* worry they *might* fall pregnant. They've never had to butch up their voice in case a lisp gave their gay away. They've never had to 'pass' as anything other than themselves. I wonder, honestly, if they're even aware of this power they possess. If a white, straight, cisgender man has ever worried about his perceived masculinity, and I've acknowledged they do, it's but a child-size portion of the multiple anxieties he'd face if he was also BAME, gay, trans, poor or disabled. Simply put, women and minority groups are spinning more plates. All of the time, every day.

There is already awareness and conversation surrounding the importance of intersectional feminism. Populist, trendy 'white feminism' with its Girl Squads, cultural appropriation and misogynoir has come under fire for not acknowledging the differing needs of minority groups, while prioritising those of white, straight, able-bodied and, yes, cisgender women.

'Kimberlé Crenshaw coined the phrase "intersectionality", which explains that gender, race, class and economic background are inseparable within the experience of black feminism,' writer Bola Ayonrinde tells me. 'This is exactly what I have experienced. For example, after receiving a First Class classification for my teaching degree, I was asked to accept an award for outstanding academic achievement for black pupils. I remember thinking that I had achieved this as a black woman, despite my background. I couldn't separate those aspects. This interlocking wasn't something that society readily recognised.'

I ask what I – we – can do to help. 'White feminism tends to be colour blind. In order for it to be more inclusive, it would have to acknowledge that black women experience oppression in a completely different way. The intersectional oppression that black women face needs to be acknowledged in its entirety and then a move towards eradicating this will lead to a source of empowerment. It's also important to be mindful that one black woman's experience doesn't equal all.'

'White feminism is way too broad for my liking,' adds *Black Girls' Picnic* founder Chardine Taylor-Stone. 'White working-class women working in factories are not having the same relationship to power as someone who went to Oxbridge. For me, a class analysis in feminism is vital. Class is such a barrier in the UK, so yes, a woman of colour will be experiencing racism, but she may have a PhD and be sitting in government. What's her relationship to patriarchy compared to a white working-class single mother on the dole? What is both of theirs compared to a poor trans woman of colour? What are all these relationships to power compared to someone like Caitlyn Jenner or Janet Mock?'

Ayonrinde adds: 'The other thing that white feminists

need to do is listen. They need to realise that by not actively acknowledging *all women*, they have themselves become oppressors. Therefore black women automatically become the "other". Even when some white feminists have listened to the experiences of black women, some have dismissed them as merely "being angry" or that one experience represents the majority. It's one thing to face oppression that is sexist, but coupled with racism it's even harder. We have to realise that feminism is for everybody. It isn't *just* about women. If those barriers aren't broken down with men, women and children, then there will always be oppression.'

As a trans woman, I feel the same. Either feminism is for all of us, or it's for none of us. It's either building walls or bridges. I find it interesting that Ayonrinde uses 'oppressor' to describe some feminists – I was about to feel the full force of that. But I'm getting ahead of myself.

Trans people are uniquely positioned to discuss privilege – we've experienced both sides. Remember Ayla Holdom? She was an RAF helicopter pilot, about as masculine as it gets, and *then* transitioned while still in that role. I asked her if she noticed a change in how she was treated as she transitioned, surrounded by men. 'The short answer is yes, I absolutely noticed a shift in attitude – both in me and towards me,' she tells me. 'I don't think I became less ambitious though – if anything, more so – but the *way* in which I competed totally changed. Suddenly on my terms and in a way that finally made sense to me. Part of that was not putting up with the masculine nonsense any longer. A negative, of course, was the absolute shift to being near invisible in conversation. Being assertive became a tricky thing to achieve. I actually find being trans and having experienced both sides of misogyny feels like a distinct advantage – both professionally and personally.'

I ask her to expand on this advantage. 'For me, the sense of advantage stems from an improved confidence in my ability to empathise with those around me, also playing the gender game. I feel I can relate in my own way, how both sides of misogyny experience that and wish to challenge or perpetuate it (consciously or otherwise). It helps me recognise the individual nuance and context, often limited in modern life. That feels really empowering to me as an individual, not on a grand political scale, but in tiny day-to-day interactions and ultimately everything we do in the world comes down in some way to a game of communication.'

Conversely, diversity consultant Leng Montgomery came *into* male privilege once he started to 'pass': 'Privilege is something I think about a lot. I have an uncomfortable relationship with it,' he told me. 'I definitely acknowledge that if it's late at night, I feel safer walking down the street – unless I "look gay". Men in groups still make me tense. It's a hangover from before my transition, but also because I'm not a big, shouty, tough guy. In my core, I don't have that . . . grrr. I'm also wary that I don't want to intimidate women if we're alone on a street or a tube.'

But Montgomery believes entering manhood wasn't a wholly positive experience. 'It was expected I'd know everything about football. I can't abide situations where it's expected I'll be "served". Typically the bill, or tasting the wine, comes to me. A few years ago my depression got really bad and there was no support for me. I said I wasn't coping and I was told to "man up" or that I should be able to cope because I'm a man now – "Chin up, boys don't cry."

'I was seeing a girl who complained men treated her like shit, but would then tell me to toughen up and that I was "too soft". I said "What is it you want? This is such a mixed message.". I don't believe there's a typical man. So much of my behaviour now is attributed to my being a man. I think this brainwashes us.'

Montgomery thinks it's impossible to ever fully move on from the socialisation we receive in childhood. 'I wasn't brought up as a man. I grew up a woman. I feel I've had a different experience. Therefore, I don't feel that just because I have facial hair I have privilege.

'I hated men. It stopped me from transitioning for a long time. My role models perpetuated the worst attributes of male behaviours. I was scared of men. Now I'm bi, but I struggle to emotionally connect to men. I hate men-only situations.'

I wonder if all the big and tiny 'privileges', melted down and re-formed into one meaty lump are this – being able to live free from fear. OF COURSE there are straight, white, able-bodied, cisgender men living in fear right now: war zones, soldiers, sickness, divorce and all sorts. But those are life events that have *happened to them*. In general, as children in particular, if nothing goes *awry*, what do straight, white, able-bodied, cisgender men have to be afraid of? Racism? No, white racism doesn't exist. Rape? Not impossible, but rare. Domestic violence? Sure, but less so than women. Being thrown out by their parents? Sometimes, but certainly not as much as LGBTQ youth. The bottom line is, if you're in the little bubble there is more *fear* and I think that's what I think of when I discuss privilege.

I acknowledge just how fucking exhausting masculinity can be, and men are *very much* at risk of mental health issues and suicide,* but I don't think that's the same thing as living in abject, constant *fear*.

As a trans woman – even one who 'lived as a man' – I have spent a good many years being scared in a way that I don't think I would have if I'd been cisgender (or, previously, heterosexual). As a child, teenager and adult, my innate difference singled me out for bullying and ridicule. As a gender-confused child I never got to fully enjoy male privilege. I was simply too girly to pass as male. I was shamed by peers and teachers alike.

It is *still* very scary to be trans. It's scary every day. Sometimes you momentarily forget you're a freak of nature, and that's usually when some charming little twat on a bike cycles past you and screams 'TRANNY'.

If the warring factions in the little bubble pulled together, I wonder if we'd see real societal change. Those white, gay men in the media – what if they made more room for women? Publishing and teaching have always attracted women – what if they actively recruited from the BAME and disabled communities? What if we addressed potential societal barriers in *all* these examples? Perhaps each group

---

* The suicide rate in the UK is highest for men aged 45–49, although it's worth noting the male suicide rate is declining in comparison to the female rate, which increased by 8.3 per cent in 2016. Data from Samaritans.

has had to *individually* fight so hard for anything resembling progress, we're not yet at a stage where we have a free hand to help a brother or sister out.

It would also be insane to turn away allies, to bat away helping hands, from those already *inside* the big bubble. Let those men, the good men, the *feminist men*, be our moles and instigate change from within. However, the most important thing for me, as a trans woman, is that we *have* to be able to rely on support from each other *inside* the little bubble. Otherwise, what hope do we possibly have?

19.

STEPPING OUT

AKA The Prom

Now that everyone knew I intended to start my transition, there was a certain expectation that I would 'perform' as a trans woman. Unlike coming out as a gay, this time there was supposed to be a physical change even though, so early in the transition, there hadn't really been one.

Free from the shackles of male gender expectation, I'd already started doing bits and bobs: I'd started growing my hair, dyed it red, I'd got my eyebrows threaded, given up on the gym and protein shakes, but there would be no Caitlyn Jenner 'reveal' on the cover of *Vanity Fair*. Jenner's considerable wealth has lent her huge advantages in access to private healthcare I – and most trans people – could only dream of.

Instead, I was invited to the final Stonewall Awards in November 2015 and I decided this was to be my inaugural voyage. I could have just gone in a tux, but having done the 'big announcement', I felt bound to give at least a nod to traditional female attire.

Right from the offset, I didn't feel like a drag queen. I am not a drag queen. I do, however, watch *RuPaul's Drag Race* and I know the tricks: the bum pads, the cinctures, the breastplates, and I know they're not for me. I think that to strap on a fake female body or sellotape my penis up my butt is somehow pretending the transition part of transitioning doesn't exist. My body is my body, and it will change over the coming years. If we say that *all* female bodies have to have big boobs and curves to qualify as female, I don't think that really helps anyone, cis or trans.

This did mean, though, that a lot of clothes didn't fit me properly. Women's clothes are cut with boobs and curves in mind. Evening gowns, in particular, would have looked awful unless I was prepared to pad (which I wasn't). I wanted to go as *myself*. This is also why I only wear wigs at *Club Silencio*; there I'm in character.

I had a test run the week before. I went to the Brighton genderqueer club night, Traumfrau (translation – 'dream woman') in a load of make-up and some heeled boots. The friends I went with were surprised I wasn't *more* female. What were they were expecting? A tutu? A gingham pina-fore á la Dorothy Gale? Leopard print and PVC? Nope, just skinny jeans and a slouch vest, clothes I already owned and wore 'as a boy'.

In my head, I knew *exactly* how I wanted to look at the Stonewall Awards. Think Kate Moss meets Faith the Vampire Slayer meets Tilda Swinton. I knew I wanted to wear a top designed by my friend and some pleather pants.

And so I did. This involved a trip to the women's changing room in H&M (utterly terrifying, needlessly so given how few fucks the staff gave). Side note – how the fuck trans women coped before ASOS I have no idea. They deliver the clothes to your door, nine times out of ten they would only fit a child of seven, and then you send them back; it's all delightfully worry-free.

I got ready at my sister (not my biological sister) Matt Cain's house. His lovely cousin, Rosie, did my make-up (so my contour was 'on fleek') and I wore the pleather trousers, the Dom&Ink vest, a vintage tuxedo jacket (sleeves rolled to the elbow, *Miami Vice* style) and some *ambitious* pewter heels.

Matt and I Ubered to the venue, the V&A in Kensington, to meet former *Attitude* editor, Matthew Todd (Toddy) in a hotel bar. Toddy was up for an award and feeling très nervous. Walking into the hotel, I got my first taste of what the next few years would be like. Our arrival was perfectly timed with a busload of American tourists trying to check in. As we walked across the brightly lit lobby, every last tourist fell silent and stared at the trans woman with orange hair and pleather pants.

Welcome to London!

I could have quite happily crawled into a taxi, gone home and never come out again. Luckily, with Matt and Toddy supporting me (quite literally in the heels), we got to the V&A and my life, in a very small way, changed.

For one thing, I didn't have to introduce myself. I was pulled over to have my photograph taken. People fell over themselves to tell me how beautiful I was – which was both weird and quite nice. I don't think it was a case of 'let's instantly objectify her now she's a woman', more 'wow, that's quite a difference'. My appearance, however, was more under scrutiny than ever, ever before. More on that later.

My feet soon felt like they were on fire – the balls of my

feet were in agony – but it felt *right*. I didn't once feel like I'd made a terrible mistake. Obviously, I wasn't the only trans person in the museum (Stonewall started defending the rights of trans people in 2014) and at the heart of the LGBT community, I felt both safe and welcome. It felt, and this sounds uncharacteristically mushy, predestined.

Matt Cain and I finished up in McDonald's in Archway eating McChicken Sandwiches and nobody batted a single eyelid. It was Juno's first night out.

Only, at that stage, I was still called James. I knew that I wanted to go into 2016 with my name all sorted out. More pressingly, Hot Key Books needed to know what name to put on the front cover of *Mind Your Head*, a book I'd written about teen mental health the previous year.

An unforeseen difficulty of being a trans person is the crushing weight of responsibility that comes with choosing your own name. Far from being a moment of liberation, it's a curse, let me tell you. Whatever name your parents lumbered you with, you can resign yourself to the fact it was out of your control. Not so for trans people; we have the job of finding a name that's truly 'you'.

To be genuinely 'me' would be to name myself Grumpy, Sleepy or some other dwarf name. If I were to go with what my parents would have called me had I been born a natal female it would have been Katy. I neither look, nor feel, like a Katy, and some infinitely more famous member of the Kardashian dynasty has claimed Cait.

I love my parents, and their support has been the most significant part of my transition, and so I wanted to honour them by keeping the initial they gave me. I was born 'James', and despite Ryan Reynolds and Blake Lively trying to make fetch happen, James remains very much a boy's name. Honestly, had I been a Sam or Alex I'd have kept it the same for pure ease.

Jamie, Jaime, Jaimie, Jaiymeeeeee all felt a bit cutesy, not to mention reminiscent of *Summer Heights High*'s Ja'mie, so I initially opted for 'Jain'. Sounded like James, wasn't as straightforward as Jane. One of my dearest friends, however, is called Louis, pronounced 'Lewis'. He spends a good degree of his life spelling his name out and I got a glimpse of introducing myself as 'Jain like rain' until my death. Jain like pain, more like.*

Adopting a new name was a once-in-a-lifetime opportunity to find a name that reflects how I view myself and how I feel on the inside. Choosing Jain, simply as it sounded like my old name, didn't sufficiently do this.

Juno, in mythology, was the sister (and wife – controversial) of the god Jupiter. The queen of the heavens and goddess of women. In statues and artworks, she is depicted as victorious, wearing armour, furs and peacock feathers. In short, she is the strength in all women. I've taken some internet flack from the anti-trans brigade for taking a goddess's name. 'I see she thinks she's better than cis women . . .' and the like. Not at *all*. I just wanted something pretty and unusual that started with J. I was all set to go with 'Juna' until my friend Joe leaned in quizzically and said, 'Did you say *tuna*?' and that was the end of that.

Trans people hear 'brave' a lot. We are 'brave'. I always

* Also, yes, it's a religion and comes with religious connotations.

think it's a shame we have to be, but I do feel strong. Going forward, I have cast off the worries and doubts I had about making such a big change. The dissenting voice in my head is silenced and I am boldly marching into the unknown. I will need a thick skin, an armour, to fend off people who would attack and mock me and people like me. Like Juno, I will be victorious. And so, I'm taking her name.

I also quite like the 2007 Ellen Page film.

In the early stages, people seemed to worry about what to call me. At events, in traditionally female clothes and make-up, I got stick for calling myself James and using male pronouns. Before events, worried librarians and book-sellers called to make sure I was still 'he'. It's possible you, dear reader, have wondered how to refer to or address a real life trans person or even good old Caitlyn Jenner.

It's like the run-up to a bad joke: What do you call a trans woman?

Answer: Ask her.

Here's the thing. I'm very quickly learning there are as many ways to be trans as there are trans people. Every trans person is different. I will not let anyone tell me I'm 'getting it wrong'. Angry internet people (AIPs) on Twitter get their panties in a right old twist, and yes, for some trans people getting names and pronouns right is a very sore spot.

No trans person I know would be offended by you asking, 'Would you like to be called "he" or "she" or "they" right now?' Many trans people express their preference on their websites or social media channels. DO respect their choice, to not do so is plain belligerent.

It's a shame language is so gendered; it does make life hard. What follows now is a special message to all public-facing workers. This is a plea to the baristas, bartenders, waiters and receptionists. Can we please not use 'man' or 'sir' or 'mate' after every transaction? Since starting my transition, I've become hypersensitive to how often this happens. Of course, no one who's called me 'man' is trying to cause offence, but it's so needless, and every time is like a little poke in the eye reminding me how much bloody work I've got to do to convince a random stranger I'm not a bloke. Wouldn't it be easier if we just said 'thanks' and 'see ya'? While we're at it, how do we feel about 'love' and 'darling'?

Words can be so powerful – they can be an incredible force for love, or for hate. Some words, and here I refer in particular to the word 'tranny', are terrible weapons. It is used against my community like a grenade. For far too many women, it was the last word they heard before they were murdered. While I concede I used it jokingly earlier in this book, there is a conversation – as you well know – about the reclamation of slurs *within* oppressed communities. I would urge you to treat it as you would racist or homophobic language. A curse as unforgivable as Avada Kedavra.

In folklore, knowing someone's 'true name' gives you a power over them. Be careful how you wield it. By sharing my new name with you, I'm letting you in and hope it will be reciprocated.

My name's Juno Dawson, what's yours?

20.

DARK DAYS

AKA December 2015

As I write this, I'm on about day five of a bout of insomnia. I'm too tired to transition. I just can't do it any more. I have the face of living meth addiction. I don't think all the make-up in MAC could make me look like a woman. I'm too tired to care that not all women wear make-up and it shouldn't matter what I look like. I'm too tired to shave the beard that stubbornly continues to grow despite several hugely painful laser hair removal sessions. I have eyes like The Hamburglar. What the fuck was I thinking? I should have just stayed as I was. I wasn't even that sad. I could have just been a nice, handsome, beardy gay man for another fifty years and then died. I was quite hot. Men really went for that beard. It would have been a hundred times easier if I'd just stayed a man. I might still be miserable after I've had many major surgeries. I've upset half of my family and I could have just stayed quiet. Every time someone talks to me I want to bite their head off. I've been waiting six months for an appointment at the gender clinic. I'm pretty sure my hair is falling out. My new haircut looks like Rose West meets Linda Thorson in *The Avengers*. It looks like a wig. Anyone who says transitioning is 'trendy' can fuck right off. No one would do this for a laugh, for shits and giggles. If I'm making this look fun or glamorous or aspirational, it's a lie. It's gruelling.

21.
FEBRUARY 2016

AKA Early Days

I'm a bit shit at keeping an actual diary, but I wrote this in February 2016 as a snapshot of early transition life . . .

If you've ever had a gym membership, you'll be keenly aware of the inner sludge of dragging yourself there on dark winter mornings. You lie in bed until the last possible second before forcing yourself to get up and go, driven by the guilt of the monthly direct debit that seeps out of your account.

The gym is a faff. You need to pack a change of clothes, water bottle, protein shake thing if that's your bag, shower gel, hair stuff – and all these things on top of anything you'd already need as a part of your normal day. By the time you're ready, you're basically wheeling a suitcase in the direction of Fitness First.

This is what the early days of the transition are like. Still waiting – nine months on from my referral and yet to be seen by a gender clinic – to start my hormone replacement therapy but fully living as 'Juno'. Every morning starts with a groan in anticipation of the EFFORT required to get through the day.

As I predicted, I now understand the easier option would have been to carry on as a boy. This is because it's easier to be a boy.

- If you don't want to shave, you don't have to
- Male gym wear is socially acceptable in dining establishments
- If your hair is pissing you off, you can legitimately shave it all off without making some sort of edgy fashion statement
- Men don't have to set aside between ten and thirty minutes for applying make-up
- More importantly, men don't even have to wonder if they can be arsed to set aside ten to thirty minutes to apply make-up

I worry about a number of things cis women could worry about but with a doubled-up second hit of trans-specific worries. It's trying. It's exhausting. Many days, I wish I hadn't bothered.

These moments are, without fail, when my alarm goes off in the morning.

I'm expending a glut of energy trying to convince a world that may never entirely accept that I'm a woman that I'm a woman. The day starts with having a tiny breakfast of Special K, oatmeal or fruit and yoghurt with a cup of tea. It's not that I'm starving myself, it's that I believe if I am small and compact I will be more feminine. I have to shave every day, sometimes twice a day. My face is sore and red.

Depending on what I'm doing I choose whether or not to apply make-up. I have three levels of make-up.

1. *'Emo Boy': This involves no foundation but just some eyeliner. I opt for this if I'm not trying to 'pass'. It's Brighton, a lot of skinny boys look like this.*
2. *'Natural Day': To cover the blue-ish tinge of my moustache area, I have to first apply a fine layer of orange base to cancel out the blue tones. This goes under my normal foundation. It often requires two or three applications before the beard area is sufficiently covered. Once you have the foundation there's a risk that you look a bit 'deathmask', so a bit of bronzer is also necessary.*
3. *'Evening': As above but with either a statement eye or lip.*

Dressing is also a conundrum. The more 'female' I dress, the more people stare, so I have to balance what I want to wear with how much scrutiny I want to squirm under.

At the moment I do not 'pass' as a woman and it's deeply painful. Every day is Juno Horror Story: Freakshow.

Back in the autumn of 2015, I met my friend, author Dawn O' Porter, at her pop-up shop on Carnaby Street. It was the first time I'd seen her since starting my transition and she was delighted for me. 'Are you going to write about it?' she asked.

I told her that I might pitch a transition diary to *Attitude*, for which I already wrote. 'No,' Dawn said. 'That's preaching to the converted. I want to read about this. I think a lot of women will. I'm going to tell Jo Elvin you'll email her.'

Jo Elvin – I already knew from pre-*Next Top Model* reality show *Model Behaviour* – is the editor of *Glamour Magazine* UK, which Dawn also writes for. I thought that sounded like a wonderful idea.

I emailed Jo and we met at the Riding House Café the next week to discuss a potential column. Jo reiterated what Dawn had said – that she was forever worried about 'getting it wrong' or saying the wrong thing in relation to trans issues and was keen to get a transgender voice in her magazine.

I realise now that they're both right. Trans people will only ever make so much progress if we exist in an echo chamber – only talking to other trans people. *Attitude* already features a wonderful monthly column by trans writer Paris Lees, so it made sense to take the column to a women's magazine if I could.

With both the column and this book, I'm trying to take the marginal to the mainstream. Yeah, there aren't all that many trans people compared to cis people, but referrals are going up year on year (rapidly), so it's likely everyone is going to experience trans people – and their issues – more widely.

The column became my way of keeping a diary. Written in March 2016, this entry sums up how I was feeling at the time:

9.00 a.m.

I head to Brighton station. I'm at the stage in my transition whereby if you don't look too closely you'd probably think I was a 'regular' woman. But who are we kidding,

I'm tall and leggy and wearing a ton of make-up so OF COURSE people are going to stare at me. Women get stared at, why would I be any different?

Most people, once I've registered the recognition that I'm trans in their eye, just go about their business – the coffee barista, the train conductor. I appreciate their polite professionalism. Some call me 'Miss' or 'Ma'am' and bless them for trying.

Some look at me with pity, or the 'Who is she trying to kid?' scowl (answer: no one). Some are less kind: the girl who turns to her boyfriend and giggles something in his ear. I've had parents point me out to their children ('That's a man'). I've had people oh so subtly take pictures of me on their phones. Oh, and the ever-present child asking 'Mum, is that a boy or a girl?' Parents, do me a favour and pass on the following wisdom: 'Son, some people are trans.'

Sometimes it's downright scary. Heaven help any woman alone in a train carriage with a beery stag do between Clapham Junction and Waterloo. It happened to me once, it wasn't very nice. 'Show us your cock, love . . .'

10.30 a.m.: Meet some writers at the Royal Festival Hall. People still stare at me, but I'm with friends now, so I don't really care. I feel safe.*

2 p.m.: I head up to a school near Finsbury Park to run my weekly writing workshop. My writing group is cool, as are the teachers, but I often have to answer questions

---

* See what I mean about privilege? How many people do the daily commute IN FEAR they'll be mocked or hurt?

from other students. Cisgender people are not responsible for educating anyone about gender, transgender people, apparently, are.* I guess if it makes life easier down the line for young trans people, it's worth it.

5 p.m.: Central London for a book launch. I find a disabled toilet because I wouldn't feel at all comfortable shaving in the ladies OR the gents. Yep, it's time to shave again because my face is getting stubbly – it looks like you have oatmeal on your face when mixed with foundation.

I've developed a technique to take make-up off just the lower part of my face, shave, then reapply without having to do my eyes again. This is quite a skill, let me tell you.

9 p.m.: It's time for the train back to Brighton. I try not to get the last train – the Burger King Express – as it's always packed with drunk business people and I feel awkward. The earlier trains are quieter and I can keep my head down.

10.30 p.m.: Take the mask off, peel off three layers of control underwear, put on pyjamas and make a cup of hot chocolate.

It's exhausting, because being a woman is exhausting. I have all the regular issues – stupid shoes, retouching make-up, white van men trying to lure me into sex – plus an additional bunch of trans-specific problems.

Transitioning is not a glamorous experience; it's not a Top Model makeover. But here's the thing, all these things, these annoyances, are practicalities. Yes, I'm shattered,

* Another privilege.

but on a much deeper level, I feel more serene than I ever did when I was faking it as a man. I have to trust things will get better as I progress, or I'd go mad, but despite everything, I know absolutely this is the right thing to do.

And I'll do it all again tomorrow.

At the time of writing some of the practical things have eased. For instance, monthly laser hair removal has meant I don't have to shave all the time now and that will continue to get easier, but it is still tiring. That provides a snapshot of what the early days of transition were like. Hard. I once again recall Rebecca Root's warning about going into transition because you *have* to. Anyone who thinks that transitioning is a choice or trend should be very aware of how *gruelling* it is and I don't think anyone would stick it out for more than a week unless they absolutely *had* to.

22.

BODY TALK

AKA Objectification

Remember how I went to the *Attitude* Awards in 2015, just before I publically came out as trans? Yes? Good. By that point, I was quite happy to tell people I was about to start my medical transition. I was still 'James' but was looking pretty androgynous.

On my table at the awards dinner were Patrick Strudwick, journalist Owen Jones, some wazzock off *Celebrity Big Brother* and a member of a now-disbanded girl group. I shan't name her. We got talking over dinner, and while she was very sweet, she did say, in her best outdoors voice, 'SO THEN. YOU 'AVIN' IT ALL CHOPPED OFF OR WHAT?'

I mean, really.

As dearly departed Carrie Fisher recently demonstrated before her appearance in *The Force Awakens*, women's bodies are under a kind of scrutiny, always, that men's just aren't. Who cares if Harrison Ford looks more leathery than Louis Vuitton on Regent Street, because Princess Leia failed to defy the natural law of ageing.

But trans women? I think our bodies are under phenomenal scrutiny, a scrutiny particularly focused on what's between our legs.

At the start of the televised trans-revolution of 2014, both *Orange is the New Black* star Laverne Cox and *RuPaul's Drag Race* alum Carmen Carrera were asked about their genitalia on breakfast television. Can you imagine? 'Welcome back to *This Morning*. Today we're joined by the cast of *Call the Midwife*. Tell us, ladies, who has the most flappy vagina?' And yet, UK news programmes *do* feel it's quite acceptable to ask those sorts of questions of trans men and women. Last year, Channel 4 ran a hugely patronising season of documentaries called *Born in the Wrong Body* (which I'm pretty sure was an episode of *The X Files*), which focused almost entirely on trans people as walking, talking genitals. The gist was very much 'men who loved women with dicks' or 'girls who want dicks'.

This is wildly, wildly insensitive. With grace and poise, both Cox and Carrera told the newscasters why they weren't willing to discuss their bodies on TV. One: it's inappropriate. Two: cisgender people and especially cisgender men don't have to talk about their bodies on TV, so neither should I, and three: it's creating a culture whereby trans people are both misunderstood and objectified.

Misunderstood because people can often make assumptions about trans people. Some people still call us 'sex change people', for instance. This assumes that all trans people are having the same experiences and that all of us are having surgeries. Depending on where you are in the process, a trans person may have had no medical intervention. Some transgender people may never have medical interventions if they don't want them. You guessed it, it's about identity, and identity – how you feel on the inside and how you want to present yourself to the world – has absolutely nothing to do with your genitals or what medical procedures you may or may not have had.

Is this a good place to briefly discuss public toilets? What the argument about trans usage of toilets boils down to is some anti-trans voices saying, 'I don't want a penis in the ladies' loo.' It's boring – why must minority groups constantly have to defend super-basic human rights? While there are **no recorded incidents of trans women attacking *anyone* in public toilets,** toilet cubicles are *private* anyway. It's not like anyone is asking to share some quality piss time. Increasingly, many pubs and restaurants have unisex, single-occupancy bathrooms in any case. Early in my transition, I had disgusted tuts and side-eye from women in the toilets at Victoria or Waterloo station. It's still actively scary for me to use women's toilets, but not nearly as terrifying as it would be for me to be alone in a men's one. I just need a wee. 'I don't see why I should have to explain to my daughter . . .' What? Explain you're a fucking bigot? That's not my problem, it's very much yours.

I can think of no other group in society right now – other than possibly Muslims or EU migrants – who have to continually justify the oxygen they use up more than trans women. And it is particularly trans women as the 'are trans people safe' question doesn't always extend to trans men, who do not, we are told, pose a threat to women in public toilets.

We'll discuss my post-transition sex life shortly, but I feel more objectified than I ever, ever was as a man. Women are objectified all the time: clothes horses; sex toys; baby ovens; naked flesh used to sell everything from shower gel to sandwiches. Trans women are no different. Whole women are reduced down to body parts, only with trans people, onlookers seem to think what's happening in our pants is some modern-day Riddle of the Sphinx that must be solved at once.

And then you get people like Barry Humphries – who made a fortune as a parody of womanhood – saying we 'mutilate' ourselves. This conjures the image of desperate trans people bleeding on the floor like Penny in *Dirty Dancing* having tried to hack at our genitals with rusty screwdrivers and cheese graters. Consenting adults seeking medical interventions (for what many would describe as birth defects) is their business, right? Because they're our bodies. I also think referring to gender reassignment procedures as 'mutilation' suggests trans people are, in some way, unhinged and unable to make rational choices. We are, I assure you. Non-trans people weighing in with opinions about trans bodies is very much like men weighing in with opinions on childbirth.

For all women, objectification is deadly. Literally. Being an object, a thing, dehumanises us. It strips away our souls, our names, our individuality, our humour and personalities. If I'm not Juno Dawson – friend, daughter, Chihuahua owner and author – and just some nameless 'tranny', I'm that much easier to discuss; easier to troll; easier to criticise; easier to mock; easier to batter; easier to rape; easier to kill.

I'm not being a drama queen, and it's also true of nameless 'women'. Various studies have shown there are correlations between the degree to which men objectify women and, for instance, how likely they are to coerce a partner into sex or blame a victim for rape.

Statistics about violence against trans women are sobering. Last year forty-two trans women (that we know of) died violent deaths. So what? Just another tranny, right? No, that's forty-two women. Women like you and me.

So, I know you've come here to read a 'warts and all' account of my transition, but if my bits did have warts (which I stress they don't) I wouldn't be discussing them here. My transition started four years ago when I identified I was a woman, and it's my life that's shifting, not just my body. And it is my body and I can choose to keep it secret. This isn't a coquettish fan dance where I'm trying to tease and conceal, it's just that by not talking about my genitals, you might have to listen to what's on my mind.

23.

THE NEW MESSAGES

AKA How to Be a Woman

I feel like a traitor for admitting this, but the first major turning point, once my transition was underway, was having a job lot of hair glued to my scalp. Like I said, transition is *not* exclusively about getting a makeover. By now we have established that there as many ways to transition as there are trans people and *some* trans or non-binary people's external appearances won't change *at all*, even if their gender identity does.

I, on the other hand, had a very particular idea of how I wanted to look. I always have. Remember 'Katy', my parallel self? She *always* had ideas and preferences about hair and clothes. At various times, as a child, I wanted to be Peri from *Doctor Who*, Sheila from *Dungeons & Dragons*, Dana Scully, Farrah Fawcett-Majors. Even as an adult, I mostly enjoy *Pretty Little Liars* as hair pornography.

I learned quite quickly that being Juno is much more freeing than trying to be James, even if it has practical hardships. Now I can do exactly what I want. Being LGBTQ often comes with the expectation that you'll hide, conceal or play down certain behaviours. My whole goddamn life

I've had to dress in shit clothes that I mostly hated. Well, now I don't have to and I won't apologise for it.

There's a locally famous trans woman who lives near Clapham High Street. She's, I'd guess, in her fifties and favours the sort of clothes Julia Roberts made famous in *Pretty Woman*. People make fun of her a lot. I'd say it's probably hard for her, but then I think, there's a woman who's dressing the way she's probably *always* wanted to dress. And that, let me tell you, is both fun and liberating. I doubt she has a single fuck to give.

My clothes shopping started in secret – again, thank God for ASOS and the like. It took me twenty-five years to figure out fashion isn't just about what you like but what suits you. And now I had to start over with a lot more people paying attention.

I quite quickly figured out that clothes fall into several categories for me:

- NOT FOR TRANS WOMEN: Again, I don't want to go into my body too much, but for 'pre-op' trans women, some clothes are just out.
- NICE BUT NOT ON YOU: Just because something's nice doesn't mean it suits me or is even my style.
- JUST BECAUSE IT'S IN FASHION DOESN'T MEAN IT'S GOOD: applies to all women.
- ADAPTED BOY CLOTHES: I am not Caitlyn Jenner and I can't afford to bin an entire wardrobe and start from scratch.

It's taken me a little time to figure out my 'style', but Kate Moss, Faith the Vampire Slayer, Taylor Momsen, Gwen

Stefani, Kristen Stewart, Eva Green and Shirley Manson all feature heavily in my Look Book. I am, and always was, a rock chick at heart. 'Pretty' clothes don't especially suit me and neither do pastel pinks. This does mean I now look like the world's oldest teenage goth girl and I'm not sure what's wrong with that.

Establishing a style takes time and transitioning is like being thrown in the fashion deep end. Clearly, I've made some errors. I think my 2016 *Glamour* Awards dress was a misstep. Wrong colour dress, wrong colour hair. For that event, and knowing I'd be in a room full of journalists, I thought it safest to buy a vintage 1950s dress with a pleated skirt and a pussy bow. While very *Mad Men*, it was much too frilly and the jade green clashed with my hair at the time. Six months on at the 2016 *Attitude* Awards, I think I cracked it. Brand new Vivienne Westwood gown (listed incorrectly on eBay so only £80, should have been £450) with goth make-up and wild curly hair. I'd go vintage again, for sure, but would stick to my Courtney Love/ Lydia Deetz/Nancy Downs fashion guides. Leather and lace suit me.

Before I got my hair extensions, I don't think I 'passed' especially well. Let's discuss passing, for the uninitiated. 'Passing' is trans shorthand for 'getting away with it' or convincingly presenting as your preferred gender. In the early days, I did not pass. However pretty my clothes or make-up were (and that's not a humblebrag), I think anyone with working eyes could – and probably still can – clock I was 'born male'. I still aspire to the hallowed halls of Passdom, and kind of hate myself for that.

No one especially loves a trans person who harps on about how well they pass. 'Good for you, hon,' the rest of us say, while strapping down breasts or liberally applying matte emulsion to cover five o'clock shadows. It's probably the trans equivalent of those incredibly toned women who gleefully profess 'I can eat *anything* I like and I've *never* set foot in a gym! Can you imagine!' while you dip a bit of celery in some air for lunch.

Although I'd been growing my hair for about six months, I still looked very much like a boy in a lot of make-up. It was heartbreaking and frustrating. I definitely didn't pass.

We attach numerous social cues to hair. Beards are for men; long hair is for ladies – unless it's unwashed boy-hipster hair; smooth legs are for women and swimmers; skinheads are for blokes and that one plucky model trying to get her face in *Vogue*. Pornography would have men believe women do not grow pubic hair.

Who says? Well quite. All of these 'truths' are as ephemeral as skinny cut versus boyfriend cut. If we go back a couple of hundred years both men and women were wearing flowing ringlet wigs. In Revolutionary France, women's hair was worn up, men's down. Christ, even Christ sports bouffant *Because I'm Wo-ath It* Cheryl curls in almost every religious artwork in the Louvre. It's also a cultural thing; some Hindu women, for example, shave their heads as an offering to the gods.

But even while acknowledging 'rules' about appearance are 100 per cent societal bollocks, I wanted hair. Lots of it. In fact, worry over losing my hair very much put a fire under my ass when it came to making the first steps into transitioning. With a heartier hairline, I may well have put it off for another couple of years.

And so, with shameless abuse of my power as a *Glamour* columnist, I approached stylist to the stars Adam Bennett and a hair extension manufacturer called American Dreams to conduct a SERIOUS SOCIOLOGICAL EXPERIMENT. In short, did I look 'more like a woman' with a job lot of hair glued to my head?

The short answer was a resounding yes. Adam attached the hair over the course of three hours in the salon at the W Hotel, Leicester Square. As I made my way out to the lift, I was greeted by a chirpy concierge: 'Ground floor, madam?'

Yes.

All I ever wanted was to be a girl. And now, finally, random strangers thought I was one. It kept happening. In coffee shops, restaurants and ticket offices. At long last, creepy men called at me from their vehicles. This truly is the dream, right?

The transition isn't making me blind, dear reader. I'm well aware that I'm a total Monet – look closely and you'll see the five o'clock shadow and Adam's apple – but twelve inches of hair tipped the gender see-saw in my favour. People, whether they clocked the trans part or not, now recognised I was *presenting* as a woman. It was clear what I was aiming for. No ambiguity, no more androgyny.

An unexpected side effect of the little experiment was the demise of 'boy days'. Those were days when I didn't shave, didn't wear a shred of make-up and stuck on a tracksuit. Of course, women can do all those things, but now when *I* did it, l looked like a very dressed-down

Conchita Wurst. The hair was a very feminine cut. The rest of me had to match. It was quite sad some days, a real sign that a thirty-year chapter of my life was now definitely closed.

It's exhausting. I get it now. One day I was ready to go grab a Sunday paper and a coffee. I stopped at the mirror. I had stubble. I went to shave. It wasn't enough. I needed foundation. Then I looked pasty so I needed bronzer. Before I knew it, I was in full make-up and my pyjamas.

In a way, it's depressingly predictable and slightly concerning that a bit of hair convinced so many people I'm a woman. What does this say about women's choices in society? We all have to have long hair if we want to be considered female? That girls with crops are less womanly? Or does it just mean that we all (myself included) need to expand our limited concepts of masculine and feminine? I think we know the answer.

I won't lie. Getting my hair done has blown my mind. Number one, it's radically changed my whole appearance. I don't think I'd truly understood the power of a haircut until then. Think Mia Farrow, think Farrah Fawcett, think Jennifer Aniston. A haircut can truly make a career, build an icon. But for me, the extensions were a disguise to hide behind while I was doing some changing, and I think that's OK too. If it helps, it helps, right? Sometimes we all need – OK *feel* we need – a little *something* to feel a smidgeon better about ourselves: new shoes, a manicure, a few extra inches of hair.

Also, I don't half look like my sister and I like that.

But passing – and the ongoing *pressure* I feel to pass –

hints at something darker. *Why* do I want to pass? The first reason is vanity, plain and vain. Trans women (and trans men) are susceptible to the exact same beauty demands that cisgender people face. What I'm *really* feeling is the pressure to be thin, pretty, dainty, under thirty, feminine and hairless. What woman isn't?

This isn't our fault. Society and the media – as we know – propagate beauty standards. It's up to you, as an individual, to decide how much of our vanity comes from within – a drive to impress others – and how much is outward pressure.

I can't lie. My Instagram pictures are mostly for other women. I want to be part of a complimentary conversation about hair and make-up. I want women to ask where I bought an outfit or what brand of make-up I'm wearing. They're not for men to lust over – or at least, that's not the intention. I can't help it if I'm just so powerfully sexy sometimes men spontaneously die in proximity to me.

But there are messages. Gender – convinced I was male – fed me one set of instructions for thirty years:

BE MUSCULAR
BE TALL
BE HUNKY
BE GRUFF
BE MANLY

. . . and so forth.

Then, almost as soon as I started living as Juno full-time in January 2016, I downloaded a new, fully formed second set of instructions. The instructions to be a GOOD WOMAN:

BE THIN
BE THIN BUT ALSO HAVE BIG BOOBS AND A BUM
BE BEAUTIFUL
BE SEXY – BUT NOT SLUTTY
BE DAINTY
SHAVE
SHAVE EVERYTHING
SHAVE THAT TOO
AND THAT
EVEN *THAT*

I don't think Gender's rule book for women is any longer than the one for men, from my experience. What I do think is that Gender's rule book for women is more *expensive*. The things in the male book (being tall and broad and gruff) are largely free. The messages for women (beauty regimen) are often things you have to *pay for*. Obeying women's rules costs. Both men and women might well feel pressured into a gym direct debit, but then women are *also* paying, if so inclined, for waxing, threading, manicures, eyelash tints, facials and the like.

As Mark Simpson observed, with the rise of metro and spornosexuality, men *are* now spending more on grooming, but there's also a cost of time. I now spend *at least* thirty minutes *extra* a day on getting ready. The hardship of men applying a bit of moisturiser or shaving balm is nothing, I assure you, compared to the *daily* trembling fingers one gets when trying to apply the perfect liquid liner flick.* I miss that thirty minutes. I used to do all sorts of shit with that thirty minutes but, yes, I also like (and want to wear) make-up, so . . .

THE WOMEN RULES

It doesn't take a fucking oracle to work out why I feel a pressure (and it is absolutely a pressure) to be skinny, toned (not the same as skinny), hairless and just, well, gorgeous. I believe at any given point in history, messages about how you should look have been transmitted. Botticelli's Venus was easy, breezy and beautiful in 1480; Michelangelo's David was ripped (if disappointingly hung†) in 1504; Da Vinci's Mona Lisa looked like a magazine cover in 1517.

If there is a difference between modern times and the renaissance, it's the acceleration of the way images of beauty travel. In 1480, no one was able to google 'Venus Botticelli' in under five seconds. No one was flicking through Mona Lisa's Instagram account and double tapping five selfies a day (in each of which she looked pretty much the same). Since the advent of the internet we are now *bombarded* with images from advertisers in a way we simply haven't been until now. Hell, at least in the 1990s

---

* And the ten minutes taking it all off and putting it back on when you accidentally make yourself look like fucking Cleopatra.
† Interestingly, David has a little winky because at the time big willies were considered stupid or intellectually inferior. Sure, Jan.

buying *Vogue* or *Glamour* was *consenting* to see adverts. Now, wherever you are on the internet – and even with ad blockers – you're still bombarded with advertising, whether you've consented to it or not.

Do advertisers exploit women's bodies to sell perfume, cosmetics, clothes, food and just about anything else you can think of? Almost certainly. Are men's bodies also exploited? Increasingly so. However, I am mindful of the chicken-and-egg catch-22 of advertising. Either the sort of flesh we see trussed up in adverts was already 'aspirational' and this was capitalised on to sell us things OR advertisers *made* a certain body type aspirational.

I agree that, to cut through clutter, artists, advertisers and magazines resort to increasingly lurid, shocking, sexualised and pornographic images. I *don't* know if I agree that models are THINNER THAN THEY'VE EVER BEEN because Twiggy and Jean Shrimpton were pretty fucking skinny in the 1960s. I think there have only ever been slight variations in what we consider physically aspirational. I'd hazard mere inches separate 'curvy' Marilyn Monroe from Jennifer Lopez or Kim Kardashian. I've been in the same room as Kim Kardashian and she is TINY. I don't see much difference between 1970s icon Farrah Fawcett and 1990s template Kate Moss.

Stripped down to the basics, women are meant to aspire to being tiny, hairless and doe eyed.

I do want a killer bod. But I don't feel like a BAD FEMINIST saying that, because I wanted a killer bod when I thought I was a man too. I'm perhaps more clued up this time around to realise a killer bod isn't going to make me any happier, however. Even knowing that, for the first time in my life I'm 'dieting' in a way we recognise as dieting. I try to not eat shit, I eat plenty of fruit and veg, I eat smaller portions (although remember I was gorging on ridiculous portions in my gym days). That said, I don't ever, *ever* let myself go hungry. I think that's when problems start, when you start to see hunger as a competition with your body that you could potentially win.

Am I spending any *more* time being body conscious than during my gym and protein-shake years? Probably not, to be honest. I'm doing all sorts of extra shit with that hour a day I don't spend at the gym frantically pumping iron.

Now. There will be readers thinking 'Yes, but have women's magazines very much like the one you work on not contributed to setting impossible standards of beauty?'

'People like to say that women's magazines are dictator-ships,' *Glamour UK* editor Jo Elvin tells me over scrambled eggs and tea at Café Liberty, 'but as someone who grew up on women's magazines and has worked for them all her life, I just don't see it that way. What I strive to create is – although I hate the word – *companionship*. I'm not looking to tell women how to live, guide them or instruct them. I want the magazine to sound like a friend. For the most part, it's a community. Shared experiences from different voices. Ultimately I set out to entertain and do that in a reassuring way.'

Elvin acknowledges the magazine can only exist with the backing of advertisers and most of them tend to be clothing labels or hair and beauty products. 'Some readers do have an issue with that, and I think it's fine to have an issue with that, don't buy the magazine. We're not forcing anyone to read us.' As a WOMEN'S MAGAZINE, *Glamour* is instantly gendered, and Elvin is aware of that. 'I don't know how to unpick that,' she tells me. 'It's about women's clothes; it's about women's make-up; it's about sex from a woman's perspective. But it's targeted at a particular sort of woman – women who like fashion and beauty. A magazine can't be everything to everyone. Like, if I wanted to read about the economy, I'd read the *Financial Times* like everyone else does. Women don't *only* read women's magazines.'

I think women's magazines are probably more diverse than people who haven't read them since 1995 think they are. *Glamour* hired me, a trans woman, to write for them, and my personal standard of beauty, believe me, is eminently achievable. *Elle UK* also employs trans writer Rhyannon Styles. Meanwhile, *Teen Vogue US* is leading the way in political discourse around feminism and the Trump debacle. 'I think we've always been quite feminist but social media has made it a more overt dialogue. It's made me look at the wider experience of women. We try so hard to be diverse. You're a good example,' Elvin tells me. 'I don't know if your column would have been on the agenda ten years ago.'

There's still a long way to go, however. The message of mainstream media is overwhelmingly racist, with white women very much presented as the norm. 'Why are there no adverts showing black women's hair products on TV?' asks Bola Ayonrinde. 'I think that this is a case of omission. If we are omitted, we are unimportant, we do not exist.'

A quick look at the shelves in Boots or Superdrug sees rows and rows of beauty products specifically for white women with products designed to meet the needs of BAME women squished onto the corner of the bottom shelf.

In February 2017, Radio 1 DJ Clara Amfo called out a 'braid bar' on Instagram who celebrate black hairstyles – corn rows and braids – on almost exclusively white models. Nicki Minaj highlighted a similar discrepancy in the reaction to her bum in the 'Anaconda' video and Miley Cyrus's self-proclaimed 'invention' of twerking. The beauty industry almost uniformly ignores BAME women, suggesting Caucasian beauty is preferable, or at the very least, usual.

If I asked you to sketch a woman, what would she look like? Hopefully all of your drawings would be infinitely varied and reflect the fundamental truth that ALL WOMEN LOOK DIFFERENT. We shouldn't only celebrate the tiny, hairless, doll-like ones. I *slowly* see this changing. The media has allowed some women (Melissa McCarthy, Rebel Wilson) to slip through the net because they are also *funny*. Funny women are allowed to be plus-size as long as they self-deprecatingly ridicule their size or some shit. IDEK.

'Men, women, children . . . we're all bombarded with images all the time, every day,' Elvin says. 'Great lives, great holidays, great wealth. It does a huge disservice to people with mental health issues or eating disorders to say their illness came from a picture in a magazine. I find that offensive. They're not ill because they want to fit into a size six. It's an easy tabloid headline. Beating magazines over the head doesn't make the issue go away. But I think that argument has died down somewhat because consumers are much more vocal about what they will and won't accept in terms of Photoshop or very thin models.'

Being tiny, hairless and doe-eyed is, tragically, out of my reach. Because of the generation I was born into, I was unable to take delicious hormone blockers as a child, so I'm a bit fucked.

I won't lie, I have decided to embark on a bit of facial feminisation. Thus far, I've had laser hair removal (this is agonising and ongoing – it's slow progress. I've had about twelve sessions and anticipate the same again); lip fillers and Botox. Lip fillers I would recommend. I saw a great doctor – Dr Firhaas Tukmachi of Dermadoc – who is morally sound and committed to giving women natural features over profit. When I asked for my lips to be a bit plumper, I was firmly told no. That's what you want in a cosmetic surgeon – someone who knows better than you. Botox I'm *less* convinced by, but my forehead does look less frowny and stern – my brow less pronounced.

I will probably have more facial feminisation. I would like surgery on my chin to make it less prominent. And that's about it. Honestly. I do NOT want *that* surgery face. You know, 'Surgeryface'. I always think if you have too many fillers and lifts you run the risk of looking like that one girl Gremlin from *Gremlins 2*. I was offered cheek fillers but turned them down. I am very wary of 'pillow face'.*

Facial feminisation is a curious thing, as we're essentially exploring what makes a female face look female. We know

* Why do I have a horrible feeling this paragraph will come back to haunt me in about twenty years when I look like Amanda Lepore?

from various studies that symmetry is what's thought to be key to *beauty*, but what about gender? A 1993 study showed that, when parts of male and female faces were isolated, people were able to rank which facial features most 'give away' a person's sex.* In descending order, the most telltale were: the brow and eyes; brow alone; eyes alone; the jaw; the chin; the nose and mouth; and the mouth alone. The nose alone was not found to offer clues as to an individual's sex.

It's these areas, therefore, that are targeted for facial feminisation: softening of the brow and altering the shape of the eyebrows; lowered hairline; lip fillers; chin implants; cheek fillers; and rhinoplasty galore.† Obviously, this opens up a gaping chasm between trans women who can and can't afford these treatments. The NHS only supports facial feminisation in the most extreme circumstances, meaning many women get themselves into huge debt for the privilege of passing.

In the name of research, I visited surgeon Mr Christopher Inglefield of London Transgender Clinic to ask what facial feminisation entails. I was shown into a plush treatment room and asked the consultant what the key differences between male and female faces were. 'The classic female face,' he told me, 'has arched brows, open eyes, the widest

---

* Brown & Perrett, 1993.

† I already had a nose job in my teens. My sister threw a plastic jug at my face – don't feel bad for me, I was being an asshole and deserved it – and it needed fixing. Oddly, the surgeon at the time told me the 'perfect nose' was Audrey Hepburn. Maybe he knew something I didn't.

part of the face is the cheeks, which taper down into a refined chin, creating that oval or heart-shaped face. The hairline should be proportioned to the rest of the face – not too high or low. A nose that's in balance to the upper and lower third of the face. In regards to the mouth, it's about a sensual mouth – the lips will be fuller than a man's with less distance between the nose and the mouth.'

The clinic is a leading specialist in facial feminisation. 'It's always about what the individual wants to achieve,' Mr Inglefield explained. 'My role is to guide people through what they want to achieve. What do you *think* makes you look male? It's usually a strong nose, strong chin or brow bossing. We make a list of the features that suggest maleness – usually the prominence of the brow and Adam's apple – because we just don't see them in females.'

I'd always assumed I don't 'pass' because of my chin. Not so. Mr Inglefield, in a matter of seconds, said it was my hairline, brow and thyroid cartilage (Adam's apple). The brow operation doesn't sound like it's for the squeamish. It involves creating an incision along my hairline to shave down my skull before pulling the hairline *down* to reduce the brow.

And then we got to the money. I'm told how much the procedures will cost and my eyes widen. It costs a *lot*. A *full* facial feminisation (with multiple procedures) could be between 40 and 50K. '[My patients] are not wealthy women – they're women who've saved up for twenty years and planned this journey for a long time,' Mr Inglefield told me. 'The best part is the confidence we see in our patients – how much better they feel in themselves. They no longer have to feel self-conscious of features they consider male.

'When a trans woman walks into a party, she doesn't want to stand out. She doesn't want to feel like everyone is staring at her. I find my "natural" women patients *do* want to stand out. Trans women just want to blend in. That's what I keep in mind.'

As it turns out, I was later contacted by the clinic again. An ITV documentary crew is already at the clinic following the Journeys™ of various trans women and were keen to feature me. It's something I'm presently considering. It's an opportunity to have some facial feminisation by one of the very best surgeons in the world and also represent the trans community on Prime Time. We'll see. I have a consultation later this month.

Of course, *all* women aspire to an archetypally female face. *All* women are forced to make the same choice: do I work with what nature gave me or do I fuck about with my face? This, again, comes back to financial privilege – not all women can afford cosmetic treatments, although *all* women are being clobbered around the head with the pressure to look a certain way.

I don't know how one does it: how we stop caring about what we look like. I really, *really* do care. The dysphoria that I have around my appearance fuels a deluge of worry, anxiety and stress, not to mention time and money. Hair dye, make-up, beauty treatments and clothing take up brain space that I could, I don't know, be curing Ebola with or something.

I wish I knew the magic words, the yoga teacher, the Buddhist parable, the secret to offloading the fucks I give about my appearance, but I'm a long way off. I do want to be beautiful and that's annoying as fuck. It could be because I wasted time trying to be a man and now I'm catching up. I'm still new to this woman business, so maybe it figures I'd be somewhat adolescent in my mindset. Perhaps there will come a day, after years of pressure to be young and pretty, that I really will lose the will to care.

For now, however, passing is more important than pretty. I'm still in the early days of getting from man to woman.

There isn't a final exam to pass on passing. It really is, in my mind, a tipping point at which people don't stare at you and point you out to their mates. The abuse and mockery that trans women get for not passing is the same misogynist abuse ANY woman gets for non-conformity. Case in point: a while back, a group of teenagers were giggling at me on the Bakerloo Line until an overweight woman sat next to me. Then they giggled at her instead.

And this brings us to the second reason I want to pass. It's depressing, but my life will be *easier* and I will be *safer* if I can go about my daily life without people scrutinising my gender. Last year, Crystal Cash, a trans woman from the USA, was shot in the face by Christian extremists. She survived but is now unable to talk. When people ask why any trans woman would 'go stealth' or pass completely under the radar, this is why. There are still people out there with hearts full of hate for minority groups.

That is an extreme case. What makes me squirm on a day to day basis is being stared at, snide comments and giggles. In my mind, if I pass, those things might stop. In an ideal world, I wouldn't *have* to pass, or conform to a very limited construct of what a woman must look like. In an ideal world, *all* woman could proudly and safely dress and look however they wanted, free from judgement, shaming or ridicule. The depressing truth is, we're a long way off, but maybe we can all – you and I – do our bit.

The other day, a super-drunk woman staggered down the train aisle towards the bathroom. Holy cow, she was a mess. I turned to my friend and said something unkind. I made fun of her. And now I feel terrible because I've been the woman on the train people are being unkind about, and it feels like shit, let me tell you.

Next time, I solemnly swear I'll bite my tongue. Perhaps making the world a nicer, safer place for women starts with us.

24.

SEX AND THE TRANS WOMAN

AKA I am Not a Porn Star

Last year, I embarked on a strange and slightly sordid affair with a Premier League footballer. And no, I won't name him or the team he plays for. We met on Grindr – on which you can filter your searches to just trans women and their admirers – and hooked up a few times.

He explained that he'd first discovered his attraction to trans women through a fellow player who regularly bought the services of a trans mistress to dominate him. They'd once had a threesome, which he'd found particularly arousing. Unfortunately, his teammate was quite territorial over his trans sex workers and told his friend to chip off and find his own.

Apparently, that's where I came in, thus answering the timeless question, 'What do you get the millionaire twenty-two-year-old who has everything?' Unfortunately for him, I'm not a sex worker and have no plans to start.* Furthermore, the man in question had quite specific fetishes. Not only was he turned on by trans women, he also had a *thing* for hair. Not *my* hair, his own.

---

* That's not a judgment. I just don't think I have the time, to be honest.

In order to euphemistically 'finish', he needed me to tie him to the bed and threaten to shave his hair off with a set of electric clippers. I obliged in this complex set-up a couple of times (he was really hot) before realising I was seeing a terrifying glimpse of my new sexual reality.

He offered to pay me to continue the arrangement, but I was done. I imagine some other trans woman is waving shears around his head as we speak, and good on her, but it wasn't for me.

When I made the decision to plough ahead with my transition, I did so fully aware that it might be the death blow to my love life. But, like I told my mother, that had hardly been a glowing success, had it? I thought – especially given my disastrous track record – it would be better to be single forever as Juno than be a gay man for a moment longer.

By this stage I knew other trans people and I knew they had boyfriends or girlfriends, but I also knew that shouldn't be an issue. No one transitions to aid their love life. I figured I'd get going with my transition and worry about men in a few years' time.

In the words of bad clickbait everywhere, what happened next will astound you.

Things started simply enough. In 2015, having decided 100 per cent to start my medical transition, I also decided to move back to Brighton after four years in London. This was because a) I was living on a slightly scary council estate in Battersea and didn't fancy wandering around there of a night and b) my oldest, dearest friends were still here and I wanted their support.

I'd only been back in town a matter of weeks when I started talking to Chris, again on Grindr. He was very lovely. He worked for a bank, liked rock music and tattoos and was bisexual.

Bisexual people get a really shitty time both on 'the scene' and in the media. Gay people regard bisexuals as part-time interlopers. Female bisexuals are, in the eyes of the gay community, straight clit-teasers, while bi men are invariably 'bi now, gay later'. To straight people, bisexuals might as well be gay if they're not going to conform. The media portrays bi people as 'slutty', 'not choosy', 'hedging their bets' or simply confused. Bisexual people seem to reap neither the privilege of straight or the community of gay.

I admit, I was dubious of bi men until I dated one (while I was still James). I realised that out bi people aren't in any way *benefitting* from claiming the bi label. There is no reason someone would purport to be bi unless they actually were. So there.

Chris told me on our first date – in Brighton's wonderful Marlborough pub and theatre (one of few genuinely queer spaces in town) – that he'd seen Tim Curry's Dr Frank N. Furter at a very impressionable age and had been into androgyny ever since.

Chris was lovely. *How easy is this?* I thought to myself. There I was thinking my love life was doomed and here comes a new boyfriend! It was a bit of a headfuck, though. I was confused about what he would find attractive in me. When we first met I was still firmly in the androgyny camp, but changing quickly. I was also very impressed with Chris's devil-may-care attitude. When we went on dates to bars and restaurants, people stared at me (as is a trans woman's lot) and I felt bad that I was bringing scrutiny onto him as well.

One evening in a Thai restaurant, I thanked Chris for 'being seen with me in public'. He took my hand over the table, much to the intrigue of the family sat opposite, and told me how proud he was to be with me and that he couldn't believe his luck that he'd met me. My swollen heart almost burst all over the prawn tempura.

And that's where our story ends! I had the big white wedding of my dreams and we lived happily ever after!

Sadly, not so. I can't say why for certain, but I just wasn't feeling the *thing*. You can't marry someone just because they are into trans women, and that's a little how it felt. Chris is a great man and I liked him a lot, but I could sense he wanted more. I think perhaps it was timing. When you're so unsure of who *you* are, it's probably not a great time to be getting into a serious relationship. A friend of mine who's in alcoholism recovery said they tell you the same thing in rehab.

While I was having a nice time pootling along and having dates here and there, Chris wanted something more serious and I felt unable to give any more and so we parted ways quite amicably. He went off around the world to do some travelling and, for me, the real fun began.

After the aforementioned fling with Mr Footballer, I decided to join dating app Tinder. I was very, very clear in my profile about my trans status. The joy of Tinder is that it only pairs you with a suitor if you are mutually interested. This saves a lot of time. I figured that if a man was repulsed and horrified by my existence he could simply swipe me left and into oblivion. Easy.

What I was *not* ready for was how many men would swipe *right* and 'match' with me. There have been many. A lot. Hundreds. More than I would have dared hope for. It turns out a *lot* of men are, at the very least, curious about trans women.

However, these men – almost exclusively – have been less than gentlemanly in their communications. Again, having never been on Tinder as a cisgender woman I can't tell you if this is the universal experience of Tinder or not (please do tweet me your experiences), but almost immediately these guys have propositioned me for no-strings 'kinky' sex. It is *very* clear to me that *they* see trans women as something straight out of a sexual fantasy.

Is this because of porn? There is a lot of trans porn out there. Is it because they have experience of trans sex workers? There are a disproportionate number of trans sex workers. There's a lot of material on the second point – if interested do search out Paris Lees's essays on being a trans sex worker – and some trans women feel scrutiny and transphobia makes 'regular' work difficult or impossible. Cash-in-hand sex work is also a way to make money fast; especially important if you're privately paying for hormones and/or surgery. I am very fortunate in that I am both self-employed and work in the liberal arts sector.

I have been on a couple of dates with men whose *only* experiences of trans women prior to me was either porn or sex workers. One guy, seemingly having his epiphany, pointed out our date was nicer because I actually wanted to be there, showing a stunning insight into how sex work, well, works.

A girl's gotta eat, and I did start a casual thing with a *very* handsome young PE teacher, but it quickly became depressingly predictable. He'd drive over, we'd have a bottle of wine or dinner, we'd get it on and it was nice. *Then* he'd freak out, grab his pants and sprint for the door, leaving a PE teacher-shaped hole in the door. You didn't see him for dust. I then wouldn't hear from him for about two weeks, during which time he was clearly freaking out, and then he'd get back in touch to arrange another session.

While Mr PE teacher is apparently on some voyage of self-discovery regarding his sexual identity, I'm in the same place I was with Mr Footballer – a service provider. What's in it for me?

I have a theory about fetishes. I think if society has no issue with your tastes (tall men, big boobs, leggy, beards, tattoos) it is a 'type'. If you're into something society frowns upon (plus-size people, trans people, leather, rubber, watersports) it's a 'fetish'.

Minority groups are oh so easy to fetishise. While *most* people* are now wising up to how it's *not* OK to wax lyrical about how you only like getting fucked by 'thug black cock' or whatever – because it's racial objectification – the same courtesy doesn't yet seem to extend to trans

---

* Speak to any POC about their experience on a dating app for awkwardness of fist-gnawing proportions. 'But where do you *really* come from?'

women. We are *things* to use and enjoy. We are a sexual deviation on a sordid flesh checklist.

'I've always fantasised about being with a trans girl,' start a good number of my Tinder chats, and herein lies the fatal flaw with fetishisation. Unless a trans woman has a burning desire to shag someone who objectifies her entirely, it isn't going to work, is it? Never once have I thought, *Oh my gosh, I'm a kinky conquest for a bored, suburban married man, that gets me so horny*. There is a total disinterest in what pleasure *I* might get out of the arrangement.

I know. Welcome to Porn Culture. A generation of young men who've *always* had access to high-quality streaming pornography and *never* had access to decent sex education at school. You'll be unsurprised to learn that most of the guys matching with me on Tinder are aged 18–25. Older guys are, shall we say, less experimental.

This follows. A 2011 study in *Psychology Today* found men who regularly watched porn habituated to the dopamine spikes released in their brains and therefore required novelty, or more extreme sexual encounters, to achieve the same dopamine 'high'. While recent research suggests there is no correlation between excessive porn consumption and sexual aggression,[*] I'd argue that as sex education, porn is shit.

A 2012 literature review[†] showed that in adolescents, porn may lead to early sexual experimentation and sexual

* Ferguson & Hartley, 2009
† Owens et al, 2012

permissiveness. Women do not come off well in porn. They too often cater to the man's desires, with little attention given to her pleasure. If there is, her pleasure comes very quickly and with very little effort on the part of her partner. In the absence of adequate sex education in schools, you can see how teenage boys are learning that sex, primarily, is an activity in which they will gain pleasure and dominance and their female partners will be delighted to receive it.

This attitude – that I should be delighted to serve a man – was wholly absent from my gay years. On Grindr, it went unsaid that both partners would get something out of the arrangement. Since joining Tinder, I'm a sex toy. An animated blow-up doll.

If men are still dividing the female population into 'Madonnas' and 'Whores', you win nothing for guessing which camp trans women have been sorted into.

This is where we truly see where Gender is pouring toxic waste over men's sex lives. The most telling, and discouraging part, is that what my new Tinder friends really seem to want – and there's no polite way of saying this – is a winky up their bott-bott.

We already talked about the objectification of trans bodies, but it seems that these chaps don't even want *most* of a trans body. There is a fundamental mismatch in what I want as a woman – a good rogering – and what they want – also, so it seems, a good rogering.

I'd argue that if they want a willy (over and above their girlfriend's index finger or makeshift household dildo), they'd be better off sleeping WITH A MAN. I haven't gone to all this trouble to be a woman in order to fuck men with a penis. That's (strap-ons aside) not how women do sex. Or want to do sex, I'd hazard.

It is, however, sad that so many men – and there have been dozens – want something sexually, but don't feel it's societally acceptable to ask for it. That's Gender again, telling them it's not what men do or what men want. This taps into some very murky themes of fragile masculinity, homophobia and repressed desire.

All cisgender men have a prostate up their bum. Prostate massage feels nice and that has nothing to do with a man being gay or straight. Ladies and gents, perhaps it's time for us *all* to talk more openly about the butt, so these men don't have to bother unsuspecting trans women on Tinder. Or is it again a case of porn rendering good old-fashioned vaginal sex boring? Is the new frontier for straight men getting fucked in the arse? You might well be shocked, but, like I said, I have dozens of 'receipts' in my Tinder inbox if you don't believe me.

Girls, it might be time to *ask* your boyfriends if they want something up their butt. Or, as Caitlin Moran told me: 'Ask if they want to go up Big Tesco.'

I'm sorry, but to me – and other trans people – being trans isn't a twenty-four-hour kinky fetish party. It's a bit like when men think women are aroused by simply having breasts. As a lived experience, it's just not exciting, I'm afraid. In short, I cannot be a sexual fantasy. What woman has the time? I'm not a fetish, I'm not a prostitute, I'm definitely not your mummy.

I want the same things as everyone else: scintillating

conversation; dinner dates; sex; someone to moan at about Southern Rail; Netflix and chill(ed wine); someone to stop me eating an entire bag of Haribo Starmix and getting type II diabetes.

It seems my future will contain three types of men: straight men who want anal sex but are scared of being called gay; men who fetishise trans women – and thus will never see me as anything other than a sexual object; and finally men who are simply comfortable to love whoever they fall in love with. I already met one of the last category, and I have to pray there are more out there. Men who see past the trans part and just see the woman.

Casual sex for women, I'd argue, is generally less casual than it is for men. In 2010, Stephen Fry courted controversy when he suggested that all men want casual sex and all women do not, essentially suggesting all women are a) identical and b) frigid. Clearly this is nonsense. Women like sex every bit as much as men.

However, casual sex for women – in my experience – isn't very casual at all. I mean that. When two guys randomly hook up on Grindr (or similar) you can (if need be) get away with the most perfunctory, basic pre-sex prep. I'm talking about, on occasion, putting on a pair of pants to answer the door and checking your bits are passably clean.

No one is going to think any less of men for having hairy legs, bum, armpits or back. While perhaps frowned-upon, no one is going to be *repulsed* by having to wade through a jungle of coarse pubic hair to find a penis. Now: many cis girlfriends assure me no man is going to walk away from sex because of slightly prickly legs or mismatched bra and pants, but just *exerting thought* over these things is often enough to dissuade me from entering into a random hook up.

If someone wanted to 'pop round' for some 'fun', I'd feel the need to shower, shave my legs, put on a face full of make-up (just to have it all smudged off), select nice underwear. I don't even think I'm trying to 'impress' a man, it's more about feeling desirable in myself. If I feel desirable, it's an intrinsic turn-on.

There's biology at work here too. Now, I'm on a mixture of oestrogen (the same meds you might be taking for HRT) and testosterone blockers (actually a medication for prostate cancer). Both of these things interact to impact on my sex drive. Libido (in both men and women) is partially driven by testosterone and mine has recently taken a nosedive. Unlike Stephen Fry, I have no intention to speak on behalf of all women, but *this* woman is certainly feeling a lot less sexified since actively blocking the hormone that inspires the horn.

It's not that I don't want sex – I do – it's just a less pressing want than it used to be. To use the *Inside Out* model again, a little brain character called Libido used to be at the driver's seat a fair amount of my week. I did spend a lot of time thinking about where my next shag was coming from and, with the possibility of a shag in sight, all reason would often fly out of the window. I often felt, in hindsight, drunk on libido, and it was addictive. The more sex I had, the more I wanted.

These days, I still enjoy and want sex, but it's like Libido has been banned from driving. He can tell me what to do, but it feels like he's less in control. He's in the passenger seat. When men pop up on Tinder and start a conversation with 'Fancy a fuck?', the answer is almost always 'No, hun, *Strictly*'s about to start.' Like WHY would I throw a load of my precious, precious time after someone who started a dialogue with 'Fancy a fuck'? If I'm going to invest shaving and grooming time on a man, I want to know he's worth the effort. That's on top of the new perils of being 'slut shamed' and an awareness that many men think I'm a hooker.

A cisgender friend of mine once explained why she chooses not to sleep with men on a first date. 'Once they think you're just there for sex, it's impossible to change their mind,' she told me. 'So, if you think they're worth dating, you have to just date them.' Another gendered double standard, but given that a lot of men think all trans women are prostitutes, I have to swim against that tide – on behalf of myself and all trans women.

It is thought cisgender women's libidos are synched to their menstrual cycles; they reach peak horn when they are ovulating. Clearly, that not only rules me out, but also any woman on the contraceptive pill. I'm new to oestrogen, but this feels like the beginning of a whole different rela-tionship with my sexuality. My attitude and desire towards men feels *clearer* somehow, like I know what I want un-befuddled by the very real hunger for sex. I feel more patient, more discerning.

At the time of writing, I've just had a wonderful first date with a hunky tall Australian. Obviously much, much too early to say if it'll go anywhere, but he was another man who falls into the category of men who simply fancy who they fancy. He's had a trans girlfriend before, he liked it and it works for him. He thinks I'm smoking hot (he told me so), so that's a promising start.

It's funny. As James, I had little interest in getting married. A partner did once propose but I turned him down as, at the time, I felt civil partnership was state-sponsored discrimination. Even once 'gay marriage' became legal, I was still ambivalent. Now as Juno, now that I can be a *bride*, I'm quite into the idea. I want to wear a big dress (again, think Jennifer Connelly in *Labyrinth*), walk down the aisle and take those vows in front of my friends and family. If nothing else, I've had to suffer their weddings and I'd like to reap my revenge.

But I'm in no rush. I once said that I'd rather be single forever than be in a bad relationship, and that stands true. Now that I'm the right woman, I'm happy to wait for the right man.

25.

DADDY ISSUES

AKA The Problem with Patriarchy

It took my mum some time to adjust. After I initially came out, she briefly reverted to THE SKY IS FALLING mode but, as transitioning is such a glacially slow process, she had time to calm down. I think she realised there wasn't going to be a striking overnight change. When young people write to me for advice on how to come out, I always tell them they'll need a whole fuck-ton of patience. You can't expect people to swallow such life-changing news quickly. Think of it more as a boa constrictor slowly masticating a goat-sized bolus. It'll take some time to digest.

She still sometimes calls me James and 'he'. It is starting to get grating, but I figure there's a direct correlation between how long you've known me and how much getting it wrong I'll tolerate. My mum has known me for longer than anyone, so she gets the biggest pass.

On the advice of Dean, my therapist, I chose to tell my father in a letter, an old-fashioned envelope-and-stamp job. This format offered several benefits:

1. I couldn't bottle it once the letter was in the post.

2. I could take time to draft and say exactly what I wanted to say.
3. Sending a letter also gave Dad a chance to think about his response.

This way, Dean told me, no one would say anything in the heat of the moment that they might regret later.

As I'd gone through adulthood, I'd almost entirely drifted from my father. We'd had some pretty gnarly disagreements about things and while there wasn't bad blood as such, we seemed content to see each other once or twice a year and managed, on those occasions, to not kill each other.

I always thought it was curious that he'd also had a highly terse relationship with his own father – my biological grandfather. I say 'biological' as I never knew him for that very reason. My grandmother's second husband was always considered 'Grandad'.

This all ties in nicely to my issues with Toys R Us segregating their dolls into a section clearly demarcated for little girls. We, as a society, actively encourage girls to nurture dolls, equipping them (if so inclined) with basic parenting skills. Little boys aren't encouraged to nurture toys, nor do we teach parenting skills or emotional literacy in schools.

Then we scratch our heads in confusion and ask why fathers leave; why they cheat; why women still do more domestic labour than men. Societally, we have never prepared men for fatherhood and then we exhibit shock when men fail to parent effectively. Anti-feminist, 'men's rights' groups or 'meninists' whine about why (overwhelmingly male) judges still predominantly grant custody to mothers.

WHY MIGHT MALE JUDGES THINK WOMEN MAKE BETTER PARENTS? I CANNOT *THINK* WHY THAT MIGHT BE.

Patriarchy fails everyone.

The outmoded stereotype that fathers go out to work, and parent only as a noun while mothers parent as a verb, needs to be burnt at the stake immediately. Gender is responsible for life-long awkwardness between my father and me.

Gender, remember, had done a number on both of us. My father was told he had a son and that came with numerous assumptions about what he was getting. My childhood memories are awash with patchy images of my dad leading me to masculine water and me refusing, steadfastly, to drink. He tried to teach me how to ride a bike (not interested) in Myrtle Park. I accompanied him to Bradford City football matches (couldn't have given two shits). He bought me tool kits and skateboards (gathered dust in the garage).

It's pretty clear now that my general attitude of trying to get away from him and these stereotypically boyish activities must have hurt him too. Whenever I could, I sought the company of my mother over him, and that must have stung.

Add to that the fact our house *did* follow the old-school rule of Mum looking after my sister and me while my dad worked hellishly long hours. He would often get home long after we'd gone to bed. I don't think I can be blamed for wanting to spend more time with my mother given that I had an actual relationship with her.

Patriarchy benefits no one.

I imagined my transition could spell the definite end of our already-troubled relationship, but there was also a tiny glimmer of hope. Maybe this third-act twist actually made sense of a lot of our difficulties.

You see, my dad always had a much more harmonious relationship with my sister. My sister was successful at being a girl. He had her figured out. She did the things that were expected of her. I, as a 'boy', did not. I hoped that rather than being the end, this could just maybe be a new start.

In the end, although Kerry offered to post the letter in case I freaked out, I did actually manage to drop the blasted thing into a postbox.

And then, all you can do is wait.

I didn't have to wait very long. The next day I got a text message – yes, a text message, how modern – saying: 'Got your letter. All I ever wanted was for you and your sister to be happy. Sometimes I know I can be hard to talk to but I'm always here for you. Love Dad.'

I do not cry very often, but I did have a little cry at that.

He then went over and above by offering to have THE TALK with my grandmother too. My dad's mum isn't a regular gran, she's a cool gran, so I figured she'd be fine anyway (and she was) but he certainly saved me a job. I think his understanding made my mum re-evaluate her panic as well. If Dad could remain calm, then so could she.

It wasn't so much as mentioned during the Christmas of 2015. I decided to have one last Christmas as James before changing my name, passport and driver's licence as soon as we went into 2016. It was important, I felt, to ease my family into it. No one likes change, however inevitable it is.

Six months passed and it was six months full of change. By June 2016, I had a new name, a new passport, a lot of new hair and a new wardrobe. It was time to go home again, almost a year after my fateful voyage to come out to my mother.

It wasn't that bad. It really wasn't. The dust had settled and I think my family had peeked out of the bomb shelter to see the world was still standing. I arranged to see my dad and stepmother for lunch in unlikely hipster enclave Saltaire.

We had lunch and things felt more . . . serene . . . than they had ever been with my dad. We chatted for hours, about me, my sister, his health – he is presently struggling to get diabetes under control. It was nice. I think my dad understands he *always* had two daughters and now we can have the relationship we were always meant to have.

'I must say, Juno,' he said over artisan full English breakfasts. 'You don't half look like your sister.'

'Yeah,' I said. 'I get that a lot.'

26.

THE KIDS AREN'T ALT-RIGHT

AKA The New Sexism

Breitbart News is an online news outlet started by right-wing conservative commentator Andrew Breitbart. He wanted somewhere he could be 'unapologetically pro-Israel' in his writing. Since 2007, the website has aligned itself with the self-proclaimed 'Alt-Right'.

A bit like Slenderman, Bloody Mary or Nigel Farage, the phrase 'Alt-Right' was uttered enough times to gain traction on Reddit, 4Chan and 8Chan. It's not organised, or tangible, enough to be described as a movement or organisation, so it's more of a hugely loose ideology fuelled by anonymity online. Alt-Right thinking covers, but is not exclusive to: white supremacy; anti-Semitism; meninism; anti-feminism; homophobia; transphobia; conspiracy theorists; and Islamophobia.

While some commentators – who I'm not going to name here because I suspect they desperately *want* me to name them – have said the whole point of the Alt-Right is to cheekily thumb one's nose at political correctness,* I think

---

* Well, I mean, it has gone mad hasn't it? I mean look at me, a trans woman writing a book! Whatever next?

for many, if not most, it goes a lot deeper than that. When people look to far-right politicians and commentators and say, 'He/she just says what we're all thinking' they OF COURSE mean, 'He/she says what I'M thinking' and that's very different.

I'm honestly, *honestly* not sure why we don't call Alt-Right thinkers what they really are: fascists.

As someone who isn't a massive wanker, I have no direct dealings with the Alt-Right (although I can think of at least one ex-boyfriend who probably haunts their Reddit), but I do think this is Gender's newest game and we *have* to talk about it here if we're to hope to understand Gender in 2017.

You see, this is *absolutely* Gender Games territory. It's once again about the messages boys and girls are getting about how to be boys and girls.

A core facet of Alt-Right thinking is that of 'neoreaction', the notion we should return to the good old days of society with a more 'traditional' (see limited) role for women. This way of thinking is also called 'Dark Enlightenment'.

I mean for fuck's sake.

One look at the phrase 'Dark Enlightenment' should tell you precisely everything you need to know. The theory (in as much as you can trace anything that starts online) stems from writer and computer scientist Curtis Yarvin, otherwise known by his pen-name Mencius Moldbug, although it was christened 'Dark Enlightenment' by philosopher Nick Land.

Google them. They look exactly as you'd expect someone who calls themselves Mencius Moldbug to look. They look like nerds.

In a world where I wasn't trans or hadn't been gay, I could have been Curtis Yarvin. I, like he, would have grown up listening to Gender's messages about what men should be – He-Man, Rocky, Rambo, Arnie, James Bond, Vinnie Jones – and, like so many of us, felt unable to live up to the macho stereotype.

Luckily, a *new* archetype rose to prominence in the 1970s, 1980s and 1990s. That of the heroic nerd. Ever since Princess Leia kissed Luke Skywalker over Han Solo (before she knew he was her brother), this stereotype has grown and persisted: that 'goodness' will be rewarded by female attention. It's in *The Goonies*, Marty McFly (Jr and Sr), *Mannequin*, *Karate Kid*, any man in a Judd Apatow film, *Weird Science*, *There's Something About Mary*, whoever Michael Cera or Jesse Eisenberg play. The nerd is always morally and intellectually superior to the popular or trad-itionally masculine characters (jocks or meatheads) and *always* gets the girl in the end.*

When I met Hannah Witton in a Shepherd's Bush coffee shop to discuss slut shaming, I mentioned I was writing about male entitlement. Like so many of the women I spoke to when writing this book, she laughed ruefully. 'Oh God,' she said. 'I can tell you a story about male entitlement.'

'Go on, then.'

With a sigh, she started her tale. 'I was at a mate's big work party thing – I won't say where he works – and

---

* *Pretty in Pink* (1986) is a notable exception, where writer John Hughes felt precisely no one would buy Molly Ringwald picking nerd Jon Cryer over smooth Andrew McCarthy.

everyone was staying at a hotel. It got late, and I was pretty drunk, so I went up to bed. I was sharing a room with another girl and when I walked in the room she was having sex so I was like "Whoops! I'll leave you to it!"

'My mate said, "You can stay in my room." I told him there'd be no funny business and he seemed quite shocked I'd even say that. I felt bad!

'We went to his room and got ready for bed. I was falling asleep, and just as I nodded off, he started to feel me up. I told him to get off but he wouldn't. I can't remember exactly what he said but it was something like "Oh we might as well . . . we're here now . . ." I got out of the bed and, in shock, sat on the floor crying.

'Another friend came in and asked if I was OK. I said I wasn't so he took me to another room. He said I could sleep on his floor with a blanket. I finally felt safe, until HE then started feeling me up too. I was like ARE YOU FUCKING KIDDING ME?

'I went back to my original room and just stopped them having sex. Male entitlement. It's real. The second guy thought he'd *rescued* me and was *owed* something. Neither guy thinks they did anything wrong. I still see them sometimes. I feel like I can't confront them.'

I wonder if either of the guys in Hannah's story *knows* they did anything wrong? The media, stories, films, have all told them that women will always try to withhold sex, so they should always press for it. They earned it, right? Why does every woman I speak to have a similar story to tell?

The message is this: if you are 'good' you are entitled to good things. What happens when life doesn't work out that way? What happens when the Biff Tannens of the world, the jocks, the monied, the privileged few who *always* came on top *still* come out on top? The girls still don't want to fuck you even though you created an app and sold it to a tech firm for half a mil?

Entitlement breeds resentment.

A sure-fire way to spend a day muting people on Twitter is mentioning Rape Culture. This sense of having 'earned a woman' is a key element to the multi-headed Hydra of Rape Culture. Meninists will tell you this culture is a 'myth', that women have invented it to attack all men. Not so.

Rape Culture – or fostering a society in which rape and sexual violence can thrive – encompasses but is not limited to: overexposure to pornography; attitudes to drugs and alcohol; poor sex education at home and in schools; the 'policing' of female clothing; low reporting and prosecutions in rape cases; slut shaming; victim blaming; 'locker room talk' or making apologies for misogyny; rape jokes; normalising nude photography; and the ever-popular catcalling.

Just a week before writing this, I had to get off a Victoria Line tube and wait for the next one. Why? A group of laddish builders boarded and felt the need to talk very loudly about my sexy boots. Yes, I made the terrible error of wearing some over-the-knee boots so I was probably asking for it, right? Mortally (I mean that) terrified that they'd clock I'm trans, I pressed my head into the fold of my paperback and pretended I couldn't understand English until we pulled into Victoria and I made a dash for it to a chorus of 'Don't get off love, we were just admiring your legs in them boots.'

Writer Shon Faye recently made a joke on Twitter that there should be a mandatory 9p.m. curfew for all men. You can imagine the reaction that got (#NotAllMen), but Faye followed up with the following point: women already live under curfew. We feel we can't go out alone late at night, and if we do, we worry about it. We police our own clothes or get rape prevention cabs and just hope the cabbie doesn't rape us.

Of course these nouveau fascists – and the men on the tube train – aren't just joystick jockeys. Much has been made of a 'forgotten', 'silenced' white working-class male.* His entitlement was that if you work hard you're entitled to work, to security. Globalisation has increasingly seen industry cheaply farmed out to the East. While this is clearly not the fault of front-line workers in India, China or Pakistan, globalisation is an abstract concept and is, as such, very hard to blame. Much easier to scapegoat 'foreigners'.

Gender has been telling men they *deserve* things for years. Race has been telling white people the same. This message is very much transmitted through Breitbart and the like. Being left-leaning, liberal or democratic is sneered at as deluded, whiny, politically correct, regressive. On the Left, we haven't 'swallowed the red pill' and seen the 'truth'

---

* Read Joan C. Williams' excellent November 2016 essay in *Harvard Business Review*, in which she argues 'working class' is actually 'lower middle class', as the hard-work ethos actually scowls at benefit claimants, migrant workers, etc.

about race, gender and sexuality. Both Gender and Race are telling them they are CORRECT and they DESERVE GOOD THINGS.

Women, people of colour, LGBTQ people, immigrants . . . we're all teaming up and coming for the things these people think they are *owed*. Note this generation of men is the same generation as the girls (in the West) who have always lived in a world where they have the vote and an expectation (although some would say it's an illusion) of choice regarding work and their bodies. Hard-earned, recent steps forward for women, POC and LGBTQ people have deeply unsettled Gender's applecart. What's ludicrous is that you'd think, from reading tweets and blogs, that disabled, lesbian, transgender refugee women of colour were leading an elite societal empire from which white men are excluded. Are you insane? Women, POC and LBGTQ people may have hoovered up *some* societal crumbs, the most basic rights, but we are in no way 'the elite'.

Of course, if you can't see that the *expectation* that white men *should* have a better deal in society than POC, or women, or LGBTQ people is deeply fucked up, you are stupid. If you *do* acknowledge that and that's your stance too, you are a fascist. Good, glad we cleared that up.

In a community that refers to feminism as 'cancer', and describes rape culture as a myth, the games have taken a turn for the worse. All we can hope is that the vast majority of young men *have* swallowed the red pill and can see this shit for what it is: woman-loathing misogyny, white-supremacist racism, homophobia, xenophobia and transphobia.

27.

TERF WARS

AKA Some People Aren't Gonna Like This

Having dealt with one extreme, let's deal with another. TERF, or 'Trans-Exclusionary Radical Feminist', is a label sometimes bestowed on rad-fem commentators who suggest that trans women are not, and will never be, women. It's not a label you'd choose – in fact they claim it is a misogynist slur – although some academics seem rather proud of the *stance*.

Like 'Alt-Right', the phrase TERF manifested online. I'm personally a bit fucking sick of talking about it, to be honest, but the voices we hear in the media probably aren't the only ones who feel that way, so I think it's right and proper to explore *why* some people think I'll never be a woman.

Whether you prefer TERF or 'transphobe' or 'bigot', I really don't care. Following my November 2016 *Glamour* column, I found myself thigh deep in a Twitter shitstorm because we'd used the term TERF. I – admittedly naively – thought it fairly accurately does what it says on the tin: people who exclude trans women from conversations about feminism. For some, this extends to trans inclusion in womanhood because, in their eyes, trans women are men.

The day the column went live started well enough. People tweeted me and shared the link, saying 'Wow – I hadn't thought about that' or 'I think you're so right'. But about twenty-four hours later, my Twitter feed went *off*. 'Another man in a dress thinks he can tell us about feminism'; 'ha mansplaining feminism'; 'TERF IS A SLUR'; 'Glamour Magazine supports violence against women'; and even 'another man wants to get his penis in safe spaces'. I was basically accused of being a rapist.

Instead of 'TERF', these people (of whom there are men and women; this isn't a female-only witch-hunt) sometimes use 'gender-questioning', 'gender-critical' and terms like 'male-bodied' and 'female-bodied'.

Hopefully I've convinced anyone reading this book that I too am both questioning and critical of gender. We all should be. The problem is that, for them, 'gender-critical' actually means challenging the notion of gender as an identity. Gender isn't an identity, they would argue, it's your body. I find 'male-bodied' and 'female-bodied' troubling. The argument goes – and I got this from a website that claims TERF is a slur with the same impact as the n-word – that *some* women seek to exclude trans women from female-only spaces (toilets, changing rooms, women's shelters) because they are male-bodied and male-bodied people (statistically speaking) are more likely to carry out violence against women.

But what this insidiously does is slide a wedge between how I view myself – a woman – and how they see me – 'male-bodied'. However eloquently the argument above is made, it implicitly suggests that women are at risk of harassment, rape and violence from trans women. This, quite clearly, is prejudice. Making sweeping, awful assumptions or accusations towards *any* minority group is prejudice.

Moreover, I have experienced rape and violence. As well as the aforementioned debut Gaydar experience ('Relax, I'm not going to *rape* you'), I was later sexually assaulted on a date.

This was during my time as a gay man. I had met my rapist for a drink on the sunny terrace at Brighton's Amsterdam bar a week earlier. He was handsome, but kind of smarmy. He told me how much money he earned and how he was renowned for being well-endowed. I was about twenty-four at the time and wasn't especially impressed. He was flashy. Maybe I should have sensed danger.

Nevertheless, he invited me on a second date. He spoke of his culinary skills and offered to cook for me in his swanky seafront apartment. I thought, *Why not, saves me having to cook.* I went along and we ate Parma ham and melon, stuffed chicken breasts with asparagus, and chocolate fondue for dessert.

Things nose-dived after dinner when he steered me to the sofa to watch *The Scorpion King*.* We were only about five minutes in when he pounced. It came out of nowhere. Without warning he was all over me. He was six foot three, I am five foot eight; there wasn't a lot I could do about it.

I told him, worried I was being impolite somehow, that I was too full from dinner to make out. That was true. He

---

* Clearly, *this* should have been my cue to leave.

continued, trying to squeeze his semi-solid erection into my arse. He pinned me to the sofa, reeking of much too much Jean Paul Gaultier Le Male.

In the end, I pretended I needed a poo. Turns out, this is quite a handy rape deterrent. No (well almost no) man wants shit all over their cock. I locked myself in the loo for about fifteen minutes and returned, saying I had an upset stomach and needed to call a taxi at once. Fortunately – and I know I got off relatively lightly – he didn't try to stop me.

The smell of Jean Paul Gaultier aftershave still makes me nauseous to this day.

I'm not sharing that story in a bid to one-up any other woman who may or may not have experienced sexual harassment or sexual violence. What a fucking winner-less contest that would be. For the longest time, I didn't even think of that evening as rape or sexual assault. I never even told my friends. I just figured it was a bad date. I wonder if I subscribed, subconsciously, to the notion that 'male-bodied' people can't be raped. That's why I'm sharing. It just *isn't* as simple as 'men are rapists, women are victims'.

I know we all eye-roll over #NotAllMen, but I don't want to live in a world where I view all men as potential rapists. I think we've established by now I've had more than a few sexual partners and only two (thank God) assaulted me. I know, it's fucked up. It's fucked up I think that's normal, acceptable *or* that I didn't register the incidents as crimes either in my head or with the police. But that's why *I* need feminism too. I need it to change that mindset – the mindset that makes me think what happened to me was part of a perfectly normal mating dance. It *wasn't* OK.

Surely we aren't saying the world is divided into two types of people: women and potential rapists? I suppose what I'm trying to illustrate is that it isn't *nearly* as simple as the world being divided into two types of people, least of all based on biological determinism.

Biological determinism: The belief that our lives, bodies and behaviour are strictly controlled by genetic or physical factors.

So, an adherent to the church of biological determinism would argue that because I have an XY chromosome and was born with characteristically male genitalia, I am a man. I will always be a man. I am trapped in the cage of my biology.

There are some high-profile subscribers to this theory. As mentioned, Germaine Greer said trans women were not women because they 'do not look like, sound like, or behave like women.'

Greer is not alone. Journalist Julie Bindel wrote in 2004: 'I don't have a problem with men disposing of their genitals, but it does not make them women, in the same way that shoving a bit of vacuum hose down your 501s [jeans] does not make you a man.' Author and columnist Julie Burchill told fellow writer Paris Lees she was a 'big white bloke with her dick cut off'. Sisterly.

Before Greer, Burchill or Bindel, feminist writer Janice Raymond accused trans women of 'appropriating' the female body. Countless other writers, 'experts' and journalists use trans people's bodies as punchlines.

In all of the above cases, we see the unmistakeable finger-prints of biological determinism – men and women are wholly defined by their bodies, and, in particular, their genitals.

You may well be reading this and thinking, '*Yes, I also think that women have vaginas and men have penises and that's all there is to it*. I hope I can change your mind. Now, I used to teach my class of eleven-year-olds that when writing debates, it's important to predict what the oppos-ition will say. I've also been accused of 'silencing' my critics. So here goes, let's air the common issues thrown at me and other trans people, and I'll tell you why I think each is a pile of steaming shite.

1. 'YOUR BODY IS MALE, YOU ARE A MAN, MAN. MAN, I TELL YOU . . . MAAAAAAN.'

Well. The first obvious problem for TERFs/bigots/whatever is that of intersex people. Being born intersex – people whose bodies do not fit conventional notions of male or female – is a lot more common than you might think. Such cases are proof positive that the body cannot always be trusted as a definitive measure of gender. Nor do intersex people need 'fixing'.

In January 2017, supermodel Hanne Gaby Odiele publicly revealed she was intersex, bringing the issue to media prominence. Teaming up with charity InterAct, Odiele said, 'It is time for intersex people to come out of the shadows, claim our status, let go of shame, and speak out against the unnecessary and harmful surgeries many of us were subjected to as children. Intersex children born today are still at risk from these human rights violations.'

Like many intersex children, Odiele received 'corrective surgery' without consent as an infant.

Increasingly, thinkers and writers – if not yet all doctors – are moving away from old-fashioned X or Y definitions of gender, partly because of the increased awareness of intersex people but also because, regardless of body type, dysphoria is more readily discussed. For some people, neither male or female accurately describes their identity. Even Miley fucking Cyrus is able to get her head around this one for crying out loud – in 2015 she 'came out' as gender non-binary, and is unwilling to describe herself as female.

Whether this is because traditional, basic-bitch concepts of male and female are becoming so tedious the younger generation don't want any part of them, or because gender is truly a state of mind, remains to be seen. Either way, does someone shunning binary gender affect anyone but the individual? Well, maybe the bank and their GP, but I don't see how it affects *us*.

Of course, 'gender critical' feminists would say gender non-binary people are kidding themselves.

If we can move past gender as bodily (and remember the WHO agrees) it shouldn't be too hard to understand that a person might *feel* like a girl even if their body was outwardly male and vice versa. Again, what fucking business is it of anyone else anyway? You have your gender identity and I'll have mine. *No, I want you to think exactly the way I think!* Well I don't, so fuck off.

So yeah, I personified Gender and made him some scary presence that lurks under every child's bed, but actually, if you think about it, gender is no more corporeal than a bogeyman. It's an abstract concept. If gender isn't a real, solid thing we can reach out and touch, then why shouldn't we be able to change it? All of us.

For me, my transition *is* about changing my body. While I may have had a MAN BODY at birth, I certainly didn't ask for it. If a person was born with a cleft palate or some other physical deformity that made their life physically and/or mentally difficult, would anyone argue that they shouldn't be allowed to fix it if they wanted to because it would impact on the identity they'd been handed at birth? I really think the mismatch between my identity and my body counts. I did not *ask* for this discrepancy any more than a child born with a cleft palate does.

I think – as women – we can all agree on one thing: sometimes biology fucks us over. Those of us who can't get pregnant – does that make a woman less of a woman? Women who choose IVF or surrogacy? Those of us who need mastectomies – less of a woman? Those of us (including me) on HRT – less womanly? I think I'm just one more woman who was royally fucked over by biology and now I'm in the process of putting that right.

If the issue is 'women with dicks', what about those who've had gender reassignment surgery? There is precious little agreement about what to do with such individuals other than mock them as 'men' who've 'mutilated themselves' and are still not women.

If you would exclude trans women on the grounds of biological determinism, be prepared to get ready for filth on every other aspect of biological determinism. Cisgender women are usually biologically equipped to bear and rear children . . . agreed? Therefore, the contraceptive pill is in some way tampering with NATURE'S LAW, amirite? Homosexuality becomes against NATURE'S LAW, as surely only men and women are meant to have sex, and in order to reproduce. It's this kind of biology-based thinking that inaccurately assumes women are unable to parallel park or read Google Maps.

The irony is that those early feminist writers, like Greer, were among the first to denounce biological determinism with the advent of the contraceptive pill; women being able to control their biological destiny changed what it meant to be a woman forever.

Societies change and evolve. Only the fruitiest of fruit-loops would now dare suggest, like Galton or Zola at the turn of the last century, that intelligence or morality was linked to race and inheritance. A hundred years ago, people really believed that.

In a new millennium, perhaps we need to move away from the notion that sex (and *definitely* gender) is as simple as XX or XY. Clearly, the way we feel isn't always connected to our bodies. We are so much more than a clump of genes, proteins and hormones.

That said, there *are* studies showing that the brain

chemistry of trans people is often in line with their gender preference,* while other studies found a genetic component in MTF transsexuals that reduced efficiency in binding testosterone.† I'm not a big fan of looking for excuses for my existence (again, no straight, white, cis person *ever* had to do that), but if you're going to rigidly throw biological determinism at me, be prepared to have it thrown right back.

2. 'DANGER! TRANS WOMEN POSE A THREAT!'

There is ONE terrible example of a sexual predator, in Canada in 2012. Christopher Hambrook claimed to be called Jessica and gained access to two shelters in order to assault women. The judge who jailed him rightly called him a 'dangerous offender'. I don't know what sort of monster would so coldly lie their way into a safe haven, but I would argue he wasn't actually trans.

That case is undeniably an atrocity, but a one-off. Saying trans women pose a threat to women based on this example is as logical as suggesting women shouldn't be allowed to be nurses because of Beverley Allitt.

There are no reported cases of trans women assaulting women or children in public bathrooms. That sort of accusation harks back to similar tabloid witch-hunts of gay men.

* Zhou et al, 1995
† Hare et al, 2009

In the 1980s and 1990s, gay men were often likened to paedophiles in the press. If trans rights are truly about twenty years behind those of gay men and women, this seems to be where we're at now. Trans people are gaining ground in the media, and so we're being backlashed through none-too-subtle scaremongering.

I can't say this enough: if I'm in a public toilet, it's to take a piss (and presumably because I'm really desperate – public toilets are usually fucking gross). If I'm in a changing room it's because I exist somewhere between a size ten and twelve and can never be arsed returning things if they don't fit. God forbid I ever need to seek out a women's shelter, but if I do, it will be because I fear for my life at the hands of an abuser.

There is a very serious and valuable conversation about safe spaces for women that I feel is being derailed by anti-trans voices. I strongly feel – based on the scarcity of any solid evidence that trans women pose a threat to other women – that we have been unfairly scapegoated. Let's instead talk about rape culture, pornography, the leniency of judges on sex offenders, police response to domestic abuse, the poor quality of sex education, date rape.

Women DO need safe spaces, but I don't think it's because trans women pose a threat. Among the abuse hurled at me following my *Glamour* column, some more rational Twitter users suggested I lacked empathy for the way 'most women feel'. God, I really hope that's not true. I mean, *I* can't imagine for a second any trans man or woman is going to want to parade around nude in a big open-plan changing room at a swimming pool or something. That would be placing *ourselves* in terrible danger. If this is something you've witnessed first hand, I'd be genuinely, honestly surprised – like why would we do that? A group in Brighton runs a night called *Trans Can Swim* in a private swimming pool for this very reason. We are *petrified* of public changing rooms. I'll give you the same advice your mum used to give you about spiders: it's more scared of you than you are of it.

Also, I don't see anyone suggesting cisgender lesbians should be banned from women's changing rooms and bathrooms. I'm not suggesting for a single second that all gay women are predators, because *I'm* not a massive bigot, but, like, if anyone was going to have a good old perv – wouldn't it be them?

Given that all my friends, all my life, have been predominantly female, the idea that I would now lose the support of women is profoundly upsetting. When posing as a gay man, I was surrounded by girls. The idea that they are now scared of me breaks my heart. Do women really think I pose a threat?

I spent a lot of time thinking about this.

After sweating it for a while, I thought to myself, *Oh fuck off.*

If those Twitter users had said 'I just don't feel safe around black women. They're so angry and aggressive' or 'I don't like getting on planes with women in hijabs, I am concerned they are terrorists' we would quite rightly have accused those people of being racist or bigoted. I don't think telling them to fuck off would be 'silencing them'.* Perhaps bigotry, whether it's coming from women or men, does need to be silenced.

3. 'YOU ARE APPROPRIATING OUR BODIES, BODYSNATCHER!'

Next is the accusation that trans women are somehow appropriating or distorting what it means to be women. Greer, in 2009, referred to trans women as 'ghastly parodies' of femininity with 'too much eyeshadow', which *is*, I'll grant her, the point of DRAG QUEENS.

If we go back to Greer's original worry that trans women don't sound, look or behave like women, we're into a whole quagmire of sexist shite. Tell me, reader, what does a woman sound like? Marilyn Monroe? Billie Holiday? Britney Spears? The Queen? What does a woman look like? Is she tall? Does she have big boobs?

I'm sure you see my point. God, let's not even begin on 'what does a woman behave like?' because that takes us down the highly questionable path of 'appropriate female morality' (hint, there's no such thing).

Clumping all trans women together is no more rational than saying 'all Muslims are terrorists' or 'all women can't read maps'. Her comments do a huge disservice to both

---

* And I firmly believe nine times out of ten people only ever start whining about FREE SPEEEEEECH when they want carte blanche to say absolutely awful things.

a) trans women who don't wear make-up – of whom there are thousands – and b) *any* woman who wishes to wear eyeshadow.

Janice Raymond, in the 1970s, posited that trans women perpetuated myths about female bodies by transforming into some sort of Jessica Rabbit female caricature, one which, in 2013, *Guardian* columnist Suzanne Moore suggested was becoming the impossible ideal for cisgender women. '[Women] are angry with ourselves for not being happier, not being loved properly and not having the ideal body shape – that of a Brazilian transsexual.' That's a bit shady.

In the aftermath of my *Glamour* column, some kind Twitter person suggested me being a woman was like an able-bodied person pretending to be disabled. I'm doubtful of that claim to say the absolute very least, and they are suggesting my gender is some wacky, whimsical choice. I don't think my medical transition is TAKING ANYTHING FROM or HURTING any other woman.

If I thought for a second my choices were seriously harming any other woman, any other person, I wouldn't make them. That's why I sought my mother's approval before steaming ahead.

In terms of setting impossible standards of beauty, while Andreja Pejic, Hari Nef and a handful of others have been singled out by fashion designers, I'd still say a good 99.99999 per cent of the 'models of beauty' we're confronted by are cisgender. I don't think many women look at themselves in the mirror and think, *God, I'd be flawless if only I were transgender.*

4. 'TERF IS A SLUR! TERF IS A SLUR!'

Yeah, but is it a slur though? Or is it a valid term for people who are derailing a perfectly legitimate conversation about safe spaces, women's rights and intersectionality? It's TERF or bigot, you choose.

The inclusion of trans women in discussions about feminism is about *expanding* the concept, not *changing* it. Moreover, trans women have been at the coal face of the feminist movement since the 60s and 70s.

'I strongly believe in trans-inclusive women's spaces,' activist Chardine Taylor-Stone tells me. 'Black Girls' Picnic, which I run, is for women-identified people, leaving it open to all women. I understand why some may see this as binary and prefer to have "all genders", but my experience in all gender spaces is that sometimes cisgender men (straight and gay) and those who are non-binary/genderqueer but are still read as male often forget that their experience of patriarchy is not the same as mine or that of a trans woman. I also feel and have heard that for some trans women their inclusion has felt like an undermining of their identities as women. It's kinda like saying, "Well if we are gonna include trans women we might as well include everyone."

'The underlying meaning of that is that it is no longer a "women's space". I find this to be, ironically, transphobic, even though the same could be said about Black Girls' Picnic for not being "all gender".

'A safe space for one is not going to be a safe space for

another. So, as an organiser, I try my best. I have to make tough decisions on who I am making that safe space for and sometimes it will be controversial.'

The other day, I unwisely clicked on a Facebook post in which someone politely requested protesters didn't bring 'PUSSY POWER' placards to a pro-immigration march for fear of upsetting trans women. I sighed, because I saw immediately where this was heading: shit-storm time.

One girl stood out. She looked about eighteen. She commented 'LOL – when bae is trying to show how woke AF she is and misses the whole point.' I had to agree. This urgent march was about President Trump stopping desperate immigrants and refugees – many of them women, some of them almost certainly trans women – from entering or re-entering America, and here we were arguing the finer points of placard etiquette. I mean, come on, priorities.

The thing with endlessly arguing about feminism is that those arguments, from where I'm sat, are killing feminism. We're getting further and further and further away from helping. It's the reason that, when I go into schools and ask who's a feminist, about three girls out of a hundred put their hands up. Feminism has become a horrid, women's version of the Bullingdon Club – exclusive to the point of empty. Everyone is doing feminism WRONG.

It's become just one more thing for women to clobber themselves with that men don't have to. 'You're doing feminism wrong' arguments are dull as fuck (not to mention counterproductive), but I think, fundamentally, feminism has to be for *all* women. I also think it has to be for men, because – as discussed – I don't think living in a patriarchy benefits the vast majority of men either.

My mother, a single parent who has always voted and worked, would *not* describe herself as a feminist because she thinks that feminists are mean, angry people who seem to hate everyone. In my mind, feminism is a protest, but it's a protest against patriarchal *systems*. Systems that still overwhelmingly benefit 'man', but not always men themselves.

I do not believe patriarchal systems benefit trans women. We saw how Leng Montgomery started to experience privilege as he started to 'pass', but the reverse was true for Ayla Holdom. I would argue that no trans woman is trying to *take* anything away from *anyone*. **All we want is what we should have had in the first place – *ourselves*.**

It goes back to everything we've said about intersectionality. Cis and trans women share very similar concerns. Conversations about 'pussy grabbing' have become worryingly normal due to the events of 2016, and the January 2017 Woman's Marches around the world rightly focused on that vocabulary. But, even with our slightly different biology, *all* women are more at risk of sexual violence; *all* women are struggling with access to healthcare (whether it's abortion for some or access to affordable medication for others); *all* women are disadvantaged in the workplace (employment statistics for transgender people are sobering). We must also remember that many trans women are also BAME or disabled, and are encountering issues surrounding race and disability on top of their gender. Like a lot of women, trans women cannot access housing and a disproportionate number are sex workers.*

No, these are not the very cute and sexy 'girl squad' feminist problems, but they are the ones where women are being failed. So no, I don't think we should 'exclude' trans women from any conversations about women, even if you are polite about it and don't scream 'you're a rapist man' in my face.

Either we acknowledge that different types of women have different needs or we propagate a one-size-fits-all feminism which, as we know from clothes, actually fits no one.

I am trying to stay civil, because in 2017, what else have we got to stop us spilling into a primordial vortex? Julie Burchill's uncivil attack on Paris Lees suggested that no trans woman has *earned* the right to be a woman because we haven't been through the rites of passage (both positively and wholly negative) that young women go through. There's a whole chapter dedicated to this but the message I seem to hear is: I AM A VICTIM, THIS IS MY PAIN AND YOU CAN'T HAVE IT.

You're welcome to it. Would you like some of mine? I could bleat on and on about thirty years of feeling like a freak, praying to transform into a girl, the bullying at school (largely down the fact that I crashed between Gender's stools), the failed relationships, fighting against

* Notably, sex workers are often excluded from feminism in the same way that trans women are.

my stupid wrong body, the surgeries and procedures I'll have to go through so I don't get openly mocked, attacked and murdered, the fact I *can't* give birth to a baby (like thousands of other women who've been fucked over by biology). But I'm not going to complain, because I will **not** be a victim and I will **not** be defined by my pain. Who wants to be defined by struggle? I want to be defined by success.

When I was about eleven, I started to pretend to have girlfriends so that I could hang out with girls at school without anyone picking on me. I remember watching *Dirty Dancing* at my girlfriend's house and going shopping around Tammy Girl in Keighley, longing to buy a brown suede Posh Spice dress. I belonged at sleepovers, not on a football pitch. I want the same thing now as I did then – I simply want to be a woman, nothing more and nothing less. I'm not asking for anything additional and I'm not detracting.

If you aren't trans, it seems likely you're never really going to know how I feel or what it is I've been through to get here. You can't have this lived experience just as I can't really have yours. In fact, I don't think I've ever seen a trans person claim to know what it's like to be cisgender, so it's annoying as burning herpes when cisgender people offer up hot takes and opinions on my existence. Just fucking let us be.

If anything good came out of my Twitter pile-on it was the support of women. When the *Independent* published a (very poorly written) piece (it's still online if you can be arsed) called 'Why Does Juno Dawson Think She Can Tell

Us About Feminism?', the wave of *support* I received washed the attacks clean down the drain. At my lowest ebb, when I really thought I was no better than a rapist, a cavalry of women rode to my defence – calling the writer a transphobe, a bigot. These were not trans women, I add. They weren't friends, they were just women. I was – and am – so, so grateful.

Perhaps I'll personally retire the phrase TERF, and meninist, and Brexiteer, and Alt-Right, and any other made-up internet tribe. Perhaps I'll use 'Shitty' and 'Non-Shitty' to describe people. People online calling me a man, a rapist, a misogynist, a woman-beater, a liar, a pervert? People sending me death threats? That's pretty Shitty behaviour. Over the course of 2016, between Brexit and Trump, my eyes have been opened to how many Shitty people there are in the world. It seems the current political and social climate is emboldening Shitty people to be that bit more vocally shit. Donald Trump is now the President of the United States of America. I fucking despair for ALL women, all the world over.

And another thing. If you are using 'TERF', or any other word, to threaten rape and violence on anti-trans voices, then you are part of the problem, fuelling the shittiness. This isn't 'victim blaming' at all, but if trans people engage in that level of discourse, we're proving our critics right.

We *do* have to use the word 'feminist' at every available opportunity so that girls know it's here for them; that it's going to protect them; that we have each other's backs regardless of our body types. If it's a viper's nest of bickering and one-up-womanship, they'll never want to join the club. I delved into the Reddit forum about my column and someone commented 'oh another case of pretty Beyoncé feminism . . .' Yeah, because that sounds *awful*.

Can't we all get along? As women, we have so much fucking work to do.

I have to bear in mind that for every very vocal person attacking me on Twitter there are a hundred more women who've done nothing but support me every step of the way. To the women who've sent me kind messages, who've included me in conversations, who've invited me to parties, lunches and drinks, who've complimented me on Instagram, who've come to my book events, a massive, heartfelt THANK YOU. I hope to repay the favour.

Some days, I know it looks like the Shitty people are going to win. But no, I have faith there are vast swathes of Non-Shitty people out there and we'll find each other somehow. I think it's hard for trans women to feel like 'one of the girls', but with your continued support, I'm getting there.

28.

PUBERTY II

AKA The Rites of Passage

In the summer of 2015, powered up by my meeting with Ayla Holdom, I swooshed through Battersea to see my GP. As mentioned, Dr Clark was utterly wonderful. We hatched a plan. He saw, at once, that waiting lists to be seen at a specialist gender clinic were going to be hellish. The Charing Cross clinic – the UK's longest-running gender clinic – had a waiting list of eighteen months.

Dr Clark spotted a new clinic that was running out of Northampton and had a waiting list of six months. Clearly, that's what I opted for. I went away satisfied I'd probably be seen by a specialist gender doctor before the end of 2015.

But as winter crept closer, and with no appointment in sight, I called the clinic to be told waiting lists were *somewhat* longer than they had anticipated. In the end, I received an appointment for April 2016, some ten months after my referral. Hearing horror stories about three-year waiting lists in some parts of the UK, I gladly accepted this. Once I had a date in the diary I could work towards it.

I trundled to Northampton for my initial 'diagnosis' appointment. Luckily, I'd been briefed by *Catastrophe* actor Nicole Gibson. 'When I went for my first appointment,' she told me, 'there was all these blokes with beards in trucker caps. I thought they were trans men, but they weren't, they wanted to be trans women. You know, I'd been Nicole for *years* at that point and didn't think anything of it – but you do have to convince them you're a woman. Play the game, babes.'

On one hand, that's a really depressing state of affairs, but on the other, I decided now was not the time for a gender protest. Like Nicole, I went to my appointment in a dress, wore chicken-fillet boobs for the first time and a face full of (subtle) make-up. At the end of the day, I figured I was asking the NHS for a life-long commitment to treatment. They need to be sure.

I was quizzed for about an hour. What toys did you play with as a child? What do your parents do? Were you a happy child? Did you always want to be a girl? Have you ever felt suicidal? I answered honestly – I didn't feel the need to tell him anything other than the story I've written in this book. My childhood was *fine*, my gender was *wrong*. I have had my anxiety issues, but I'm not sure how much of that is tied to my gender or not.

Either way, I 'passed' and was diagnosed as having gender dysphoria. 'You look great!' the doctor told me. 'But you *sound* terrible! We have to do something about that voice.' I'm not sure what you're meant to say to that, so I just smiled and nodded. I was referred for speech therapy.

So that was it, right?

Wrong.

That was just the *first* diagnosis. To receive care on the NHS, I'd need *two* doctors to agree I was transgender.

'When will I have my next appointment?' I asked with trepidation.

'Very soon,' said Doctor One. 'Usually a couple of months.'

I could deal with that. I returned home and waited. And waited. And waited some more. No word, no nothing. With no date in the diary, I became increasingly needy and anxious. Eventually – after chasing – I was given an appointment for June.

Only then another letter came telling me the appointment had to be cancelled due to unforeseen circumstances and would be rescheduled to 10 September.

OK, fine, whatever.

Only then another letter came in August explaining that due to unforeseen circumstances, my appointment would need to be rescheduled to 21 December.

And then I lost my fucking shit.

Look. I *hate* that I'm slagging off NHS services. I love the NHS. The NHS has saved my life and the lives of the people I love the most. The NHS puts the great in Great Britain. But, on trans issues, the NHS isn't doing a very good job.

It's true that for people with mental health problems, the NHS isn't great either. People with depression, anxiety and eating disorders are waiting weeks to see a specialist. But I do question if, after referral, they're waiting EIGHTEEN BLOODY MONTHS.* I'm impatient and anxious, not depressed or suicidal, but a great many transgender people

* If they are, they fucking shouldn't be.

are. I don't think it's OK that *desperate* people are being made to wait so long for therapy and medication that will impact on their mental health.

Unfortunately, lovely GP Dr Clark was not able to initiate my hormone therapy without the second diagnosis. I felt like both my life and my body were on hold. Listening to really bad lift music.

Some trans people feel they do not want or need hormone therapy to feel like they're getting it right. I was NOT one of those people. Taking oestrogen (or testosterone for trans men) is an inexact science. Indeed, there has been very little scientific research performed on the reliability of the outcomes of taking these hormones. What we do know is that, for trans women, taking oestrogen (in the same forms that menopausal women use) usually brings about physical changes: redistribution and storage of subcutaneous fat makes hips and bum swell and natural breasts develop. The face appears softer, more feminine. Hair changes, becoming glossier. Body hair decreases and facial hair, although it doesn't cease to grow, becomes easier to remove by laser therapy.

It can't undo what puberty did to my body (which is precisely why trans youths are given hormone blockers to delay the onset of irreversible changes), but it can make it easier for me to 'pass'. As it was, given that it was now almost a year since I'd told the world I was trans and I was *still* not on any form of medication, I felt utterly dejected and frustrated. Following Nicole's advice, I felt I'd done my bit: I'd walked the streets as a woman; been stared and laughed at; changed my name; changed my passport; told my family. I'd done everything I could do without a doctor, and now I wanted something in return.

I needed *something* to feel like all this was heading *somewhere*. In my head, hormone therapy was that something.

When the Northampton clinic moved my appointment back *again*, I broke. I went private. This came about via participation in a training day at *Newsnight* with the media watchdog, All About Trans. A group of trans people in the public eye gathered at the BBC to discuss trans representation with the editorial team. Over drinks afterwards, artist and film-maker Fox Fisher expressed shock and horror when I told him I still hadn't started my hormone therapy. 'Just go private,' he told me. 'Everyone else does.' Leng Montgomery agreed, and suggested a couple of names who'd helped him out with testosterone in the early days.

Three days, yes THREE DAYS, later, I was sat in an unassuming clinic on Wimpole Street, London. The doctor gave me the same set of questions as the NHS doctor had done and told me to come back after a three-week cooling-off period (after all, hormone therapy is a big step). As scheduled, three weeks later – and three hundred quid poorer – I had a six-month supply of oestrogen gel.

Typically, I then received a cancellation NHS appointment just a couple of weeks later. I returned to Northampton and got my second diagnosis and a prescription (albeit with *another* six-week delay, as that's how long it takes, apparently, to type a letter to a GP).

The care I received on the NHS was no better or worse than the private care, the private care was just two years *faster*. As a friend of mine who worked for the NHS said, somewhat slyly, 'Oh, I'm sorry the systematic cuts to the NHS have affected you on a personal level.' He's absolutely right. The NHS is being subtly killed off by a government that doesn't want to subsidise it any more. This is bad news for all of us, especially in an aging population.

I am terrified we're rapidly seeing two levels of healthcare – those who can and cannot afford their treatment.

What's interesting is – and ask any trans person – *they* saw the upswing coming. Fox Fisher was one of the trans people who took part in the 2011 documentary *My Transsexual Summer* – at the time considered groundbreaking. I asked him how much of a role he thinks the media played in the upswing in referrals. 'When I agreed to take part in *My Transsexual Summer* it was because I was coming out as trans into a world which *really* didn't "get it",' he tells me. 'Having done a lot of activism for LGBT rights previously, I knew that in order to make change, I had to step up and talk about my gender identity not matching what I was assigned at birth because the biggest barrier was ignorance.

'When the series was released, *My Transsexual Summer* had a massive impact, as a mainstream show which started a dialogue with the nation and did the rounds online and was shown twice in Australia.

'Despite being personally upset with the final edit of *My Transsexual Summer*, it sparked the imagination of the general public and for many trans people who watched, it was the catalyst to come out. I've have had many people get in touch to tell me so.

'Similar to *My Transsexual Summer*'s ethos of real trans people sharing real trans issues, I believe that organisations such as All About Trans are also responsible for the shift in public understanding. All About Trans contacted me just after *MTS* aired in 2011, and I have worked with them for five years, going into national organisations like the BBC, the *Sun*, the *Mail on Sunday*, Mail Online and the NHS to give gatekeepers a human reference point of what it's like to be trans.'

It seems churlish to pretend Caitlyn Jenner hasn't impacted on global understanding of trans issues, but I do question her influence *within* the transgender community. I asked Fox if he thinks Jenner has had any influence. 'I was aware of Caitlyn coming out before she did publicly, because I was contacted by a production company to ask if they could use my films. Caitlyn Jenner's coming out interview on the Diane Sawyer show actually had clips from *My Genderation* films, a project I set up immediately after my experience on *My Transsexual Summer*, in an attempt to cut out the middle men and tell stories about members of my emerging community.

'Despite the conversation on trans issues having a celebrity stance, I am not sure how relatable Caitlyn is to trans people, with her connections, money and fame. I believe the real heroes and inspiration are the stars of YouTube, documentaries and books on the topic of trans.

'Perhaps the real battle is actually fought in the grassroots, by people who are in activism, working for organisations and having personal conversations with people. These days, it's almost impossible for people not to know someone who is trans. Once people have that personal connection, it changes something in the way that they think about trans issues.

'So, despite the impact people like Caitlyn might have upon some people, she isn't the one paving the way for change more than any one person is. It's all a joint effort of the community as a whole.'

For whatever reason, trans people are coming forward in swelling numbers, and the NHS – although closely monitoring the increase in referrals – wasn't prepared for the tide. Well of course it wasn't; it isn't properly funded.

I am aware this ship has now sailed into tabloidy, turbulent waters. Some people think the NHS has no business funding medical gender transition. That it's wholly elective and unnecessary. Clearly, I'm going to disagree with that, and many, many trans people will tell you their NHS treatment has been life-saving.

For one thing, not all trans or genderfluid people access NHS care, because we don't all medically transition. And yeah, if you want to be cold about it, funding hormone therapy and surgery might well be cheaper in the long run than anti-depressants, patching up suicide attempts, issues surrounding alcohol and addiction or therapy.

But, if we're not cold about it, I think the NHS has to be for all. As you start discussing moral issues around free healthcare it gets super murky. Smokers, obese people, immigrants, drug addicts, alcoholics, promiscuous people, people who eat fatty foods, sex workers, people who didn't wear sunscreen; should they get NHS treatment? I'm sure you see where I'm coming from. Christ, if we go down that path I imagine a good 80 per cent of us probably wouldn't qualify for free healthcare.

No one *asked* or *chose* to be transgender. I promise. Sure, you choose to seek medical interventions, but that's not without reason. I think we should all stop what we're doing right now and form a protective circle around the NHS. It might come to that. I really hate that I 'cheated' and went private; I felt like I was betraying my boyfriend.

With my hormones secured, I felt more at ease than I had done in months. Every morning I showered and applied a thick gooey gel to my tummy and waited for it to soak into my skin. When I got my NHS prescription, it changed to one pill a day and an injection of testosterone blockers every three months.

The transformation had begun.

THINGS I HAVE CRIED AT SINCE STARTING OESTROGEN

- My dog looked sad
- A (different) dog with two legs
- Any guide dog
- A dog on Facebook that found its owners after it got lost
- (Maybe I should just avoid dogs for a while)
- *Planet Earth II* (every episode)
- *Frozen*, because Elsa is very trans, I think
- A small child, because they had to wear glasses
- A man with Tourette's on *First Dates*
- The mere *idea* of old people

- A documentary about miners
- My own novel
- Hillary Clinton's concession speech

About three months after starting the medication, I started to notice physical changes on top of the emotional ones listed above. My face looked a little softer – less angular. My nipples became tender to the point of painful and I could feel the flesh hardening underneath them. Within a few weeks, I could see definite breasts taking shape. My girlfriends nodded along: 'Welcome to puberty,' they told me. I suppose it is puberty, only without the period part.

When I was young, I was hugely curious about periods. This could partially be because I missed the day Year 6 was sat down to watch the education video about what a period was. Anthony Barraclough fainted from the horror of it all. I was off sick and returned the next day. I remember the first girl in our year group to start her period (a gaggle of girls gathering around Catherine Barrett like she was recently bereaved, a female teacher telling her, with little sympathy, that she wasn't going to die), although it later transpired that a) she was faking and b) Becky Tyler had started long before her anyway.

I also remember my sister starting her period. Or rather, I remember she and my mum having secret, hushed conversations and surreptitiously ferrying sanitary products to the bathroom. I don't know why we didn't just keep them in the bathroom tbh.

It's clear now that periods are the first time you get told VERY DEFINITELY that 'this is only for girls'. A chasm opens between the sexes. At the time, I wasn't especially disappointed that I wouldn't be bleeding every month, but I think it was the final nail in the coffin as far as my magical thinking about 'transforming' overnight went. Biology was telling me YOU ARE A BOY.

And I was gutted.

Going back to my internet spat with transphobes, they made one thing very clear: YOU ARE A MAN, YOU HAVE A PENIS, YOU WERE BORN MALE.

Fuck, you think I don't know that? Gender dysphoria takes many forms, one of which is disgust at your body. I wouldn't say my body *disgusted* me, but I certainly never enjoyed it or took any pleasure from it. When I would look at my body in the mirror, I would see a formless, asexual, alien thing. Possibly a hairless stoat, or some such.

When I later had sex, as discussed, I didn't really use my peen penetratively. That just did nothing for me on a psychological level whatsoever. If anything, it was a turn-*off*.

I acutely feel the *absence* of those rites of passage that women go through. Well I *think* I do. How do you miss something you never had? I guess I fantasise about the parallel world where I'd had a 'normal' girlhood. Where I'd had a first kiss; a hideous satin prom dress and cheap corsage; lost my virginity at an under-eighteens' night at Maestro's in Bradford. Through my teens and early twenties, being a gay man was a bridesmaid position alongside my girlfriends' engagements, weddings and babies.

And then there's the recognition that passing as a man for so many years undoubtedly brought me some privileges. Many of the unpleasant rites of passage that girls inevitably go through – heckling, harassment, slut shaming – diverted around me.*

Laura Bates of *Everyday Sexism* writes so powerfully about the drip, drip, drip of sexism and misogyny that are so commonplace a lot of girls think it's perfectly acceptable for men to slur sexual advances at them from passing cars.

I spoke at length with Laura about her experiences working with adolescent girls. 'I think these things are different for everyone, and no two girls experience their teen years in exactly the same way,' she told me. 'But sadly, for many of the teenage girls I hear from through Everyday Sexism it seems that harassment, discrimination and even assault are worryingly common rites of passage. The majority of girls I speak to on school visits have experienced men commenting on them in the street, using very sexualised and often aggressive language, following them, asking them for sexual favours and even touching them against their wishes from a terrifyingly young age. It often starts around the age of nine or ten, and many girls report that it is worse when they are in their school uniform, suggesting that they are *deliberately* targeted because of their age. They also report sexism as a rite of passage at school, with everything from being called a slut or slag, being told to get back in the kitchen, being rated out of ten, being pressured for nude pictures, to being harassed and even assaulted all common experiences reported to us as occurring in UK schools.

* Don't get me wrong though – I was heckled and spat at as a feminine gay man on many an occasion. I wasn't able to 'pass' as straight.

'We also hear from lots of girls who are experiencing these issues combined with and intersecting with other forms of prejudice – from an Asian young woman being asked if she is a "mail-order bride" to a disabled girl being mocked for the way she looks in her wheelchair, to trans or non-binary young people experiencing bullying for not conforming to the gendered "lad" or "girly" norms and gender stereotypes expected of them. There doesn't seem to be any way to win – those who don't conform face abuse, and those who do suddenly find themselves labelled sluts or whores.'

I ask if harassment (online or on-street) is inevitable for teenage girls? 'It certainly seems to be overwhelmingly common.' God, that's depressing. 'The most recent stats we have suggest around 85 per cent of teenage girls experience street harassment and over 70 per cent of young people hear girls being described as sluts or slags regularly at school. Almost one third of 16–18-year-old girls report experiencing "unwanted sexual touching" (sexual assault) while at school. And the vast majority of girls I have spoken to report some form of online harassment, ranging from "get your tits out" type comments to graphic rape threats and abuse about self-harm.'

Although I have been catcalled and harassed as an adult trans woman (and also as a gay man – unwanted touching, I'd say, is endemic on the gay scene), I never experienced that sort of fuckery at the key developmental stage of puberty – when everything feels unsettled to begin with. I ask Bates what impact harassment is having on teenage girls.

'I think it often feels truly awful and that the implications are enormous. What some people don't understand is that each of these incidents sits alongside thousands of others, making up a daily landscape of inequality, prejudice and pressure. So, one comment taken out of context might not seem like the end of the world, but when you look at the bigger picture, particularly given that there's no escape from this 24/7 now thanks to social media, you have an almost unbearable bombardment of expectations, pressures, stereotypes, harassment and abuse. In particular, there are very real mental health implications, with recent statistics suggesting really alarming rises in the number of young women screening positive for PTSD, anxiety, depression or self-harm. It also manifests itself in girls often experiencing a huge loss of confidence, doubts about their own academic and social abilities, reduced future career aspirations – literally shrinking themselves down and making themselves smaller and less noticeable, whether that means contributing less and less in class or restricting their calorie intake more and more to make themselves smaller. I see lots of cases where eating disorders and self-harm seem to be linked to harassment and sexist abuse.'

With harassment so widespread, it's a sobering thought that young women are getting the message that this is *normal* behaviour from men. What baffles me is *where* are men getting the message that this is acceptable? Let's not forget I had access to the inner circle of mandom for thirty years. During that time, I did *not* think it was OK to grope or harass women. Why? Was it that I wasn't sexually attracted to women? Was it that I strongly identified as one? Was it that my mum and dad raised me right? Was it that my feminine appearance and traits 'blocked' me from truly experiencing masculine 'banter'? (Something which I actively loathed and that felt entirely alien anyway.)

Whatever the answer, *some* men and boys are getting (and sharing) the message that harassing girls and women is *harmless* and *normal*. It is neither of these things. An even darker alternative is that young men know full well harassment is wrong, but do it anyway.

'In my experience,' says Bates, 'this [message] isn't coming from any one explicit place, but rather it is so vastly ingrained across society, from billboards to adverts to music videos to films to video games to online memes to pornography to the pavement to the playground, that young people simply pick it up and think it is normal. Put together all those different influences and you can easily piece together the message that women are bitches and hoes, that men have to be tough and aggressive, that boys don't cry, that domesticity is for girls, that women's looks are their sole value, that thinness, white skin and big breasts are all that matters, that sexual violence is either arousing or funny, that harassment is normal, and much more.

'A major part of the problem is the absence of any clear message challenging these norms, or even giving young people of all genders the opportunity simply to think about them and explore them, and to learn about simple concepts like healthy relationships and sexual consent, which might help to offset some of the more negative messaging. One clear, age-appropriate way to achieve this would be through compulsory sex and relationships education on these issues, yet in spite of years of campaigning the government continues to reject this option.'

At the time of writing, a select committee into sexual harassment in schools led by Maria Miller MP has found that a widespread 'lad culture' pervades, and girls routinely experience abuse dressed up as banter. Miller reported boys spur each other on and collude in harassment. This is not me saying teenage boys are inherently evil, it's me saying illegal behaviour, that wouldn't be tolerated in any workplace, is normalised in schools.

This again suggests that young men are *learning* this behaviour from somewhere. Is it from their fathers? The media? Pornography? The internet? Who is telling boys that this is acceptable behaviour?

My first experience of this sort of harassment was shortly after I had my hair extensions put in (so I supposed 'passed' better), when a man walked past me and muttered 'legs'. He's right, of course, I *do* have legs, but a) what sort of dickhead thinks that's OK? and b) I *cannot* imagine what that shit's like for an eleven- or twelve-year-old girl. If nothing else, I was in my thirties and well-schooled in the fucking frosty glare. In fact, there is a certain satisfaction in receiving street harassment and telling them to fuck off in my most manly voice.*

But while street harassment is one part of a pyramid scheme of bullshit, both at home and globally, the domino effect of patriarchal values gets more and more damaging. There isn't really a good or nice place to do this next bit,

---

* Yes, I know I am putting my life on the line when I do this.

but we are absolutely going to talk about it. Women, all over the world, walk very different paths and have different cultural rites of passage. Something we've not talked about – but must – is female genital mutilation (FGM).

I think we *have* to talk about it, because it's a very observable gender distinction. This practice – still common-place in some African, Middle Eastern and Asian countries – sees girls and women having surgical changes made to their genitalia. The charity Forward UK estimates there are 60,000 girls in the UK alone who are at risk of FGM, despite it being illegal both here and in many of the African, Middle Eastern and Asian countries where it's most common.*

The World Health Organization clearly states there are no health benefits to female genital mutilation yet, for many girls globally, this is another rite of passage, and another tied to their reproductive value. Hark! I hear the distant cry of Internet Men suggesting that penis circumcision is also genital mutilation.

I agree that there are few health benefits to having the foreskin removed, and it is utterly ludicrous that it's done as standard in much of the USA and across Africa simply because 'it's the done thing'.† BUT, and it's an important distinction, the side effects of male circumcision *usually* don't include: urinary problems; infection; problems

---

* For context, Unicef (2015) estimate AT LEAST 200 million women and girls worldwide have been subjected to FGM.

† There is some evidence circumcision has reduced the spread of HIV in sub-Saharan Africa.

menstruating; sexual dysfunction; childbirth issues; and further surgery to reopen the sealed vagina.

From where I'm sat (and yes, I understand I am sitting slap bang in the middle of white western culture) FGM is the most horrific procedure a girl can go through on her journey into womanhood, and a reminder of what happens when we don't question gender norms. In Egypt and Somalia, the *norm* is that girls will have their genitalia cut.

The whole practice occurs *because* of gender. Expectations of what a woman should *be* or *do* are at the heart of FGM. There is a direct correlation between prevalence of FGM and the belief that it will improve a woman's 'marriage-ability'. Often the procedure is carried out to protect a girl's modesty; to ensure virginity or prevent infidelity. It is thought in some regions that the clitoris is unclean or even *male* and must be removed to protect a girl's virtue.

FGM is the tangible culmination of all the bullshit I've hinted at through this entire book: male privilege; slut shaming; sex versus gender; reproductive value; virginity; feminism. It's all in there. It's the most obvious way in which women suffer at the hands of Gender.

And no, it's not one of the ways in which trans women suffer.* The choice to seek out genital surgery is *not* the same because of that very important word – 'choice'. No culture, no societal pressure, no doctor is telling our parents that is 'the norm'. It's why I don't ask (and you shouldn't either) trans men or women about their surgeries. It's a

* It's worth noting here that in some Middle Eastern countries, enforced gender reassignment is/was a traditional punishment for homosexuality.

very big and difficult choice, and one I'll have to make in the coming years.

I have absolutely no doubt that the struggle is real and I avoided some of that struggle. This takes us back – again – to intersectionality. I also can't know what it's like to be a person of colour, have a disability, or suffer from a chronic illness. I can't know what it's like to experience Islamophobia or anti-Semitism. As I've said before, I am wary of getting into 'ranking' societal struggle or suffering, purely because I'm not sure that's a contest anyone should want to win.

But what I am aware of is that I won't ever be a cisgender woman.

I'm not a fucking idiot. There isn't a surgeon, high priestess, Botox merchant, online quiz, newspaper or judge that can *truly* give me what I feel I should have had all along.

Shit happens.

This is what Therapist Dean meant. Yes, in the eyes of the law I am now a woman. It says so on my passport, driver's licence and eventually I'll even get a new birth certificate. BUT I won't ever have the body or life I would have chosen. Trans people probably aren't supposed to vocalise that. Yes, I am proud to be trans, but yes, I'd rather have been born with a female body.

Who *does* get the exact life they would have chosen? These are the biological cards I got. What I'm *supposed* to say as a trans woman is how, if I had a do-over, I wouldn't change a thing. At the risk of alienating the entire trans community, that's not true for me. If Voldemort popped out of a wormhole or something (just go with it), would I sell him my soul to go back and be born with the body

I really want? Yeah, I probably would. Not gonna lie. I'm sorry.

But I'm also a realist. Voldemort probably isn't going to pop out of the wormhole, so I guess I have to make the best of what I got. I'm not even going to whine about it. That's not going to happen, so *instead*, I'm pretty happy to work with some options. And we already know the options: transition, or don't transition and feel entirely wrong for the next fifty years.

So I'm making the best of what I've got, fully aware of my limitations.

We all have limitations. We all learn to live with them.

Biology is limiting. Don't we all wish we were a little bit taller, thinner, had a different nose, smaller chin, perkier boobs or a bigger dick? Some of those things we can do nothing about. Plastic surgeons tell us they can make us happier, but they can't, not really. If you're unhappy with a big nose, you'll be unhappy with a small nose. Sometimes, though, they help. Yeah, you're still pretty fucked up, but at least you like your nose.

I've been through that one, remember. Of all my problems, my nose isn't one of them anymore. That's why I'm firmly in the 'if you think a change will help . . .' camp. Better to be proactive than stew and moan.

Of course, the biggest limitation biology has placed on me – and many thousands of other women – is the inability to 'birth live young', as farmers would say. I can't say I'm too bothered, to be honest. I don't *think* I ever want kids. I italicise the 'think' because I'm not so stupid as to say 'never'. Never say never.

I was a teacher for seven years. I see children as work. I find babies and baby chat really, crushingly boring. If I *was* to 'have kids' I think I'd rather foster teenagers and young adults. *They*, I think, are hilarious, smart and intelligent.

I have my tiny chihuahua, Prince, and I feel fiercely protective of him. He is sitting on my knee as I type this very sentence. Like many pet owners, we refer to me as his mother. I got Prince in 2014 because I felt it was weird that I'd never had any responsibility in my personal life. In fact, I had often shirked it professionally too. I decided it was time to grow up.

I went on Gumtree and searched Chihuahuas for sale. I wish I'd rescued now, but back then I didn't know too much about the process. I soon found a litter of puppies had recently been born in Peckham and were ready for homing. I travelled to one of the toughest council estates in South London and was able to see Prince's parents. Prince was tiny, a little ball about the size of my palm. His brother was much feistier, but I fell for the smaller, dopier one who just wanted cuddles. Once he was in my arms, there was no way I wasn't getting that dog.

It was a bit like preparing for a baby. I played Supermarket Sweep in Pets At Home, buying a basket, teeny tiny little clothes and harnesses, toys and food. I was starting from scratch. I bought three different books on raising and training Chihuahuas. I was a very responsible single parent. I set boundaries, I disciplined him, I cleaned up his shit. God, I was a nervous wreck. Puppies are *hard*. My friend, poet Laura Dockrill, was about six months ahead of me with her Pug, Pig, and, as I was ready to collapse, assured me it would get better after six months, and it did.

Having a little dog meant having to put some roots down. I'd have to make sacrifices to properly care for him. I quite deliberately took on the responsibility and I think it's done me good. I love him with all my heart and he loves me back. I didn't know how much I could love something until I got Prince. It is lovely.

When I talk to my child-rearing friends, they speak of an *urge* to have children and particularly a desire to give birth (for women) or pass on their genes (for men). 'I'm not raising someone else's kid,' said one male friend when I asked if he and his wife had considered adoption. I reacted with utter horror and he couldn't understand why I was so appalled.

I think I fundamentally lack either of those desires. Again, never say never, but I don't think any amount of oestrogen is going to change my mind. Perhaps it's because I'm single, I don't know.

Women who say they don't want children are almost unanimously met with a chorus of:

- 'You'll change your mind!'
- 'Wait until you hit thirty!'
- 'Just you wait until the right man comes along!'
- 'That's what they all say!'
- 'You'll hear that biological clock ticking eventually!'

Men do *not* hear those things – remember, people thought I was one. Having never been on WOMBWATCH I can only imagine how fucking infuriating that shit must be. Another weird privilege.

To get another view, I rounded up a whole bunch of mothers and women who have no intention of becoming mothers to examine this fundamental facet of womanhood.

'Initially, I didn't want children,' said one mother I spoke to. 'It was a rebellion against my mum, who had just given up work and everything to stay at home with children. I didn't wanna be that; I wanted to be the woman out of *Sex and the City*. But when I met my husband I loved him so much I started to wonder what it would be like if we made someone together.'

The speculation, the Wombwatch, continues even beyond the birth of a first child. 'It's not even just womb harassment,' said one mother I spoke to. 'Once you are having a baby, there's a million different forms of harassment. Pregnancy is something *everyone* thinks they know something about. Carrying a bump or having a child, you become public property. You get comments from complete strangers. Even once I had one, people felt they could comment on whether I was having *another*. People have said my choice to have one child is *cruel*.'

If motherhood is a rite of passage, I wonder if it's a competitive one. 'If you have one, people ask if you're going to have another,' said one mum. 'If you have two girls, they ask if you'll try for a boy. I'm "one and done", but a friend of mine who has three kids is always getting asked if she thinks she has too many.'

It became apparent while examining the female rites of passage that I hadn't perhaps realised how many of them are tied to reproduction. It seems to me that menstruating, becoming pregnant and giving birth are very much 'celebrated'. WELL DONE YOU HAVE REACHED PEAK WOMAN! And they should be, *if* that's what an individual woman wants. But what if it's not what you want? What if you *can't* have kids. Does this somehow speak of your 'success' as a woman?

'I had PCOS [polycystic ovary syndrome], so my body just wasn't working in the way a woman's should. I have too much testosterone so I don't ovulate naturally. When we thought about having children, I hadn't had a period in years, so we had some tests and my ovaries were covered in cysts. I took a drug called Clomid [clomifene] and responded well so we were able to conceive, but I don't think I would have been able to naturally.'

In an age of mummy bloggers, Mumsnet and Netmums, motherhood seems to be more central and defining to women than ever. There are women and there are mothers. 'My sense of self has changed massively,' said one of my mums. 'I feel like a completely different person. Since getting pregnant, I have grown up massively. My identity as a woman *has* changed and that's because now *other people* see me differently.

'No one ever asks a man if they're going to go back to work and that sort of thing. Those sorts of questions triggered me becoming a feminist – and also having a daughter. Why is it a woman's sole responsibility to raise children? I feel awake to how society treats women differently to men.'

I also spoke to a number of cisgender women who, for

various reasons, never had – or never plan to have – children. I've changed their names because they all agree there's a certain stigma, or judgement, that comes with their decision to not have kids. Former Australian Prime Minister Julia Gillard, for example, was accused of being 'wilfully barren'.

Nina – in her late twenties – wrote to me about her choice to not have children: 'I've ticked boxes throughout my life. I've ticked the school box, the university box, the house box, the husband box, the career box and then every box that gets you from A to B.

'Box-ticking, for the most part, is addictive, but it comes with a price. The price being a sense of achievement at the expense of a life. "Woah there," I'm sure you're exclaiming at this point. "Hold. The. Phone." And yes, there's a massive caveat in that if it's right for the person, then is it box-ticking? Aren't you just living? But when it came to the baby box I found myself drawing a line. A firm line that led to my questioning whether I wanted to box-tick at all, and whether box-ticking was ever truly for me in the first place.

'Children, babies, mini humans you're (hopefully) stuck with forever, or at least until you die before they do, were my sticking point. I didn't know this going in [to the marriage]. Actually, I didn't know this going out and I completely reserve the right to change my mind in the future, but for me and for then the answer was no.

'The impact of children felt too high a price to pay for the life I wanted to live at that point. The consequences and reverberations from that decision and that choice are ongoing and many.

'Children are in my life. My choice to not have children at that time does not mean I do not like children or potentially want children in the future. But children are a choice, and it took choosing to not have them to make me realise that.'

Christina, forty-seven, has a slightly different story to tell. 'I spent most of my life thinking I wanted children. In my twenties, I was totally convinced I wanted them . . . not because I was desperate to have kids, it was just what you did. I was in a relationship and I assumed that was where it was heading. But then that relationship ended and, during my thirties, it just didn't happen.

'At the time, I was devastated. All – well most – of my friends were having children and I very much felt like I was missing the window. So yeah . . . it just never happened.' I ask Christina if she regrets this. 'You know, I really thought I would, but now – and I mean this honestly – I'm so glad I didn't. I don't know if it's because I didn't have kids, but my life sort of started again once they weren't an option any more. I started a new relationship, I got out of a job that I *hated* and started a business. I suppose it was like, "If there's not going to be kids, what *else* is there?" I'm happier now than I've ever been, and I don't think kids would have made me any happier.'

It seems to me, whether women do or do not choose to have children, this choice will in some way define them in a way it would not define a father or child-free man. Biology is not destiny.

While we continue to make assumptions about gender, inequalities will exist. Perhaps we need to be more mindful

of rites of passage and what, societally, we're really celebrating. We must celebrate the value of women beyond
their reproductive capability.

I know I've missed out on a great number of key
'moments' of womanhood. I regret some of these, and
avoiding some is no doubt a blessing. The last few years
have been a crash course in 'living as a woman', but I have
always been acutely, painfully aware of gender. That's one
privilege I didn't have.

29.

THE FUTURE

AKA And then There was a Woman

And so, we're up to date. I'm living in Brighton, trying – against the odds frankly – to survive as a freelance writer and adjust to life as Juno. I'm writing, drinking aspirational cocktails I can't afford, dating, walking the dog. With each passing week, my body changes as the oestrogen takes hold. My shoulders are vanishing, I'm growing little boobs! It's SO WEIRD, but very exciting.

The novelty factor is almost certainly wearing thin. In just two short years, I've been through seismic personal change. This part of transition – the transformation – is well documented. What comes next is almost scarier.

Having changed outwardly, now comes the business of changing inwardly. Don't get me wrong, I have a whole load more changing to do, but I think once the biggies are out of the way, the dust settles. You live out the rest of your days as the person you were always meant to be.

I see this when I speak to Rebecca, or Nicole, or Paris, or Leng, or any trans person whose initial transition was more than about five years ago. Discussion of trans issues or gender is met with a polite sigh. It's become almost boring. Indeed, after a while, you have to *live* life, not endlessly discuss it. You're still trans, but somehow post-trans.

Eventually, people will forget my old name, forget what I used to look like. A lot of people have only ever known me as Juno and gasp in disbelief when they see old pictures.

Right at the start of this book, I asked YOU to reflect on your experiences of gender – where being a man or a woman has helped or hindered you. I asked the same question of my Twitter followers. From the thousand or so respondents, it's readily obvious that gender – being a man or a woman in this world of ours – impacts your life. There were positives – both men and women could identify the situations in which their gender had in some way benefited them. Men, especially white, heterosexual, cisgender men, were happy to acknowledge their 'privilege', which they had wisely 'checked'. Women were aware of a certain 'quality' that could be used to their advantage: 'I think I am seen as less threatening or pushy at work (I'm in sales) than a man might be. I perhaps get away with a bit more without being seen as an arsehole.' There was also an understanding of how 'toxic masculinity' threatens men's mental health more than women's: 'It's also easier and more acceptable for them to ask for help when they need it. If I'm depressed I can always find a girl's shoulder to cry on. When my husband is depressed he really only feels comfortable talking to me.'

But then I asked how respondents' gender had *negatively* impacted on their lives. It was a deluge:

- 'As a female in Spain, my opinion was often overlooked in favour of males saying the exact same thing. I work in the video games industry. I am often seen as a quota to fill, not as a person who has tons of experience and abilities.'
- 'I can't begin to list the number of times I have felt that, as a woman, I have been looked down on, not properly respected or dismissed – particularly professionally.'
- 'Being female negatively impacts me almost every day. As sad as that is to admit, I honestly feel that it's true. As I identify as female and I dress "stereotypically female", I attract a lot of unwanted attention from males who catcall and stare. Every time I walk home alone from work, just from the bus stop to my house, at night, I feel quite afraid and apprehensive purely because I'm female. I feel that if I were male, then perhaps I could walk home in the dark and not feel so scared.'
- 'Being passed over at work by male managers. Being dismissed and boxed into a category of "emotionally unstable female" alongside other strong, purposeful females. Having a male on a lower rung of the professional ladder take me aside to congratulate me for being strong enough, brave enough to have an opinion. Then being told, by the same guy, not to do it again: "Leave the hard decisions to the big boys."'
- 'Ah, where do I start? When I have to be careful not to make male colleagues feel threatened by my intelligence. When I was told, "you're one of the guys" by my boss, and it was meant as a compliment. When my female bosses trusted men's opinions over mine time and time again. The general fog of sexism I have to navigate. When

I feel afraid walking home at night. When I worry that it doesn't matter how much I succeed if I'm not beautiful.'

- 'Expressions like "man up" or "be a man" are frustrating and patronising, especially when I've had problems with anxiety. I think that men with mental health problems are dismissed much more easily than women with mental health problems. I'm gay and not feminine and some (straight) people struggle with that. People see my wedding ring and assume I have a wife and so I am coming out constantly. When I first came out to my parents, my mother said to my father "This is your fault for not taking him to the football like the other boys." As though playing football is part of what made them boys. If I don't play football and if I'm attracted to men, does that mean I'm not a man?'

- 'Professionally speaking, I have found that I am not listened to in a lot of work contexts, as a young woman. I can make a suggestion about a policy or procedure in a team environment and have it completely ignored. On multiple occasions, I have asked male colleagues to repeat the exact same suggestion in front of the team and it has been immediately agreed to, or responded to positively.'

- 'My thirty-something male boss tried turning every one of my colleagues against me while making my work life hell just because I wouldn't sleep with him.'

- 'Multiple instances of abuse and assault. Being publicly humiliated for my weight, for not looking like other beautiful women. Being treated like one of the boys in every social situation, a "non-option". I'm not beautiful enough to be called female.'

- 'Being a woman is tough for any number of reasons. Facing harassment on the street, discrimination at work, sexual assault. I recently had a senior work role taken away from me to give to a man. I was told it was to protect me from a more senior man, but in retrospect I realise it was to further the career of a more junior man. So not only did I lose the role, but now I am expected to train up the junior man.'
- 'I struggled when I tried to be an au pair, as boys are not considered good choices to take care of children or clean the house. The same thing happened when I was a teacher, maybe because it is a profession often associated with women.'
- 'I don't feel I'm taken seriously in uni when I say things in class. The guys who speak up are "intelligent" even if they've nothing of substance to say, but I'm "opinionated" and "a know-it-all". I've been sexually assaulted on a number of occasions because I'm seen as too small and defenceless and dainty and female to fight anyone off – and I've been personally blamed for being assaulted.'
- 'Never felt comfortable in my Man role as, although I did not realise it at the time, I had an inbuilt self-censor that did its utmost to keep me within society's acceptable man limits. It took a recent crisis to awaken my inner self, and I can now open up more to other people.'
- 'The clothes I would prefer to wear are not deemed gender acceptable. I apply make-up because I feel it's a required thing to do for my sex. I have taught myself feminine mannerisms over the years because to be considered more "masculine" is deemed wrong or out of

place. It's exhausting. I often question how I speak (pitch, etc.) and worry it's not feminine enough.'

- 'As soon as I went part-time after having my first child I stopped being promoted at work. My career has stagnated because I am a "mummy" (I hate that word). I work in an industry that is probably 70–80 per cent women but the vast majority of MDs and heads of department are men.'

Variations on those themes appeared time and time again. Reading through the responses, even copying and pasting them, was gruelling – a word that recurs throughout this book. It took an afternoon to go through the replies and by the end of it, I was exhausted. I just can't really see ANYONE enjoying the male and female ideals we've wound up with. Women exhausted from being patronised, harassed and overlooked; men weary from the weight of masculine expectation, tight-jawed from holding emotion back; trans and non-binary people ground down from justifying their place at the table, just trying to get through the day.

No one, just no one, is winning. I wish I had more answers, I wish I knew how we could reach up and snip Gender's puppet strings. Remember this, whoever you are, *however* you are, you are equally valid, equally justified and equally beautiful.

Nonetheless, I'm excited for the future. Perhaps the new wave of trans and non-binary people living among you *are* the way we demolish those stifling gender norms. I'm not suggesting we all immediately transition (duh); what I'm saying is every trans and non-binary person out there is living proof that gender is fallible. We all, to some degree, told Gender 'no', and so can you. We can all take the bits we like and shun the bits we don't. It isn't easy, it isn't easy at ALL, but you *can*. I did.

I think the future I'm stepping into is uncertain but full of possibility. But don't get me wrong; as a transgender woman in 2017, I am aware of the world I live in. It's scary out there and in some ways it's getting scarier.

Let's imagine I have a crystal ball. What do I see in our future?

THE END OF GENDER?

These kids today. When I visit schools with my YA novels, I'm overwhelmed by the open-mindedness of the students I meet. They're not *all* free-loving queers, but none of them seem to give much of a shit about the ones that are. Those who mock LGBTQ people are very quickly slapped down because nearly *everyone* now knows someone who is in the community. 'Don't talk shit about lesbians,' someone will say. 'My sister's a lesbian!'

If they haven't experienced it directly, no young person today has grown up bereft of LGBTQ role models. From Ellen to Tom Daley to Cara Delevingne to Tyler Oakley to Olly Alexander to Jazz Jennings, young people *know* we are a reality and the vast majority are pleasingly nonchalant about it.

Increasingly, the *questioning* portion of sexuality or gender awareness is becoming something everyone gives a bit of thought. I think this is healthy and should be encouraged. As we've seen from my dating experiences of late, younger people certainly veer towards experimentation. While the majority will always identify as straight and cisgender, I think *questioning* both of these things irons out inner conflict before it even occurs.

Not only is there less homophobia and transphobia/more acceptance of the LGBTQ community, but 'millennials' are creating their own tribes – first online and increasingly in the real world (who can even tell the difference anymore?). Pansexual, demisexual, asexual, genderqueer, genderfluid, and so many more. Perhaps the final destination is freedom from labels.

I don't think this means Gender will be exorcised once and for all. Sex and gender, although different, will always be inextricably linked and babies will still be heralded to the world as X or Y. Shops will continue to sell pink and blue. Expectations will continue to pervade every nook and cranny of an infant's life.

What we will see, however, is increasing awareness and suspicion of gender. Already parents, teachers, hospitals and children are part of a conversation about sexism. Whether they call it feminism or not, most girls are fully aware of bullshit and calling it out. Parenting has well and truly become a verb, something to succeed at. Succeeding at parenting has now gone beyond keeping a child alive and into nurturing a child's personal growth and well-being. Any good parent will tell you they 'want what's best for their child', and that involves treating a child as an individual. There is *nothing* individual about treating a child as a 'boy' or a 'girl'.

THE BACKLASH

But this isn't the future, this is now. 2016 was an utter clusterfuck of a year that culminated in someone off a reality TV show becoming President of the United States.

Everyone (except the people who actually voted Trump) offered hand-wringing and thinking on America's (narrow) decision to elect him. The same was also true of the UK's (narrow) decision to 'Brexit' the European Union.

Beyond those people we already discussed in the 'Alt-Right'/neo-Nazi camp, one popular theory is that 'normal, hardworking people' grew tired of the black, immigrant, transgender, homosexual, Muslim 'elite' chomping down on their slice of the pie. 'When is it Straight Pride?' 'What day is International Men's Day?' 'Where are *our* rights?' cried people who have all the rights already.

Scapegoating is nothing new. Right-wing politicians and right-wing press found an ember of dissatisfaction and fanned it until it caught fire. So much easier to blame a minority group than it is to blame decades of systematic corruption, inequality, financial waste, a failing education system, arms deals, toxic debt and unnecessary military action.

Worse still, Brexit and Trump have somehow now validated both right-wing thinking and right-wing press. It's open season for assholes – it's like a fisting party at a leather club. Since Brexit, there's been an increase in hate crimes *or* the reporting of hate crimes, or both – either is significant because if people are reporting 'low-level' hate crimes (spitting or verbal abuse rather than violence), it reflects that minority groups won't take it lying down anymore.

If Brexit and Trump signified *anything*, it's that left-wing, liberal or moderate voters have got to get the fuck off Facebook or Twitter and go out into the real world. Simply existing in the world as a minority is activism. Every trans man or woman happy to venture out in daylight; every LGB person willing to hold hands with their partner; every Muslim woman who chooses to wear her hijab; millions of women marching against Trump . . . We are all making a statement. We won't fuck off quietly into the night because it's *our society too*. It always was, we were just hidden away or subjugated. We aren't after your slice of the pie, we want our own slice, thank you very much. If all the fucking pie wasn't going to the 1 per cent we'd have plenty to go around.

For too long, we lurked in underground, nocturnal bars or clubs, hidden from view. Throughout my childhood, the Pakistani community of Bradford was 'contained' away from the whites in ghettos. Trans people either lived in the wrong gender, lived 'stealth', or faced ridicule. Times are a-changing; every shop assistant who serves us, every taxi driver who gives us a lift, every old person we help, every human we experience, goes away from that encounter knowing we aren't a dangerous 'swarm' (thanks, *Daily Mail*), we're just humans doing the best we can.

Also, it's somewhat a generational thing, and – not being funny – a lot of those people will be dead soon. Sorry 'bout it.

Things likely will get worse before they get better, but I'm a big believer in the truth always working its way out. *Some* people voted for Trump because they are blatant racists and bigots, but many *think* they're not. Eventually – and I hope sooner rather than later – those people who did vote for Trump or Brexit will see that the current economic and political climate was *not* the fault of minority groups. I have *faith* that people are smart enough to recognise that.

The promises the public have been sold by political and media charlatans are fool's gold. My gender isn't going to change that. We – LGBT people, POC, Muslims, women, students – are not 'the elite'. Far from it. I'd have thought it'd be obvious, but we need systems that work for all, not just the very rich – for they are the only people in society who *aren't* suffering right now.

This book is called *The Gender Games*, in part, after the popular novel *The Hunger Games*. Haymitch was right; we must always keep sight of who the true enemy is. Transgender awareness has galloped forward in the last ten years, peaking perhaps with Caitlyn Jenner's *Vanity Fair* cover. It was inevitable our 'moment in the sun' would be followed by a backlash – it always is.

The same backlash happened to the gay community in the 1990s. After fears about AIDS died down and people largely understood you weren't going to die from sharing a mug with a gay person, the right-wing press instead started to link gay men to paedophilia. This was manifest in Section 28, furore around the age of consent, same-sex marriage and gay adoption. You know what?

As a community, we fought and won ALL THOSE BATTLES.*

And now the trans community has some fights on its hands too. We are *now*, twenty years on, fighting for legal recognition, access to healthcare, bathroom rights and employment rights. We're not there yet, but history, I believe, is on our side. I hope the rest of the LGB community will stand by us. It's encouraging that Stonewall is on our side, because I feel it might get ugly.

More importantly, I need *you*, dear reader, alongside me as a champion. Being a woman, or being from a minority group, is inherently political. That might make you bristle, but it's true. You might not vote, or watch the news, or read a paper, but it's *still* true. I think the politicians who would vote against transgender bathroom rights would *also* vote against abortion rights, access to free contraception or equal pay for women.

'I'm not that familiar with the term "Identity Politics" as such,' says DJ and author Gemma Cairney on what, for many, is a millennial hobby. 'But I do think there's such a thing as identity and I can see how it's political. I believe some people have a stronger understanding of how they depict their identity than others, and I think there is no "right" or "wrong" when it comes to discussing what it means to us as individuals. We are, however, living in changing, raw and nuanced times – conversation among

* And the battles are still being won. At present in the US, some gay and trans rights are being rolled back by the Senate. Scary times. We will keep fighting.

all cultures and people with different experiences and backgrounds is something I believe in wholly.'

For me, pretending there isn't a problem isn't going to make the problem go away. For most of us, droning on about privilege and power is, weirdly, a form of privilege, but I think conversations need to be had about who gets what treatment in our society.

Cairney tells me, 'Exploration [of identity] through kindness, empathy and discussion is a good thing in the quest for equality – though it's important not to let rage in.' I agree. We must be equally mindful of despair.

And if you're a man reading this book, I salute you. I'll be honest, I didn't write it with you in mind – but crikey, I need your help too. You might not know it, or even feel it, and you didn't ask for it, but I truly believe you had a birthright to walk on this land just a little bit easier than we did. So now I ask you to fight on our behalf.

Much is made of allying online, but it's so true. Women and minority groups need to get on each other's shoulders, and then, just maybe, we'll start to reach that glass ceiling holding us all down.

THE END OF 'TRANSGENDER'?

A very insightful question was asked of me by a fifteen-year-old girl from an East London school. 'If you hate gender that much, why do you even bother calling yourself a woman?'

Good point, well made.

1. I don't think we're free of labels yet. As a society, we use them and I feel more aligned to 'woman' than I do to 'man'.

2. I sometimes wonder, when faced with transphobia, if it's partly because I've so blithely (not to mention quickly) shifted from what we consider male to what we consider female. Trans people are a living reminder that something we steadfastly believe to be carved in stone (gender) is actually a very moveable feast. I slightly feel like I *have* defeated gender. Gender told me I was a boy and would *always* be a boy. Well I showed you, you fucker.

3. I am actually doing what I want. I was *pressured* into having a beard and muscles and expensive suits. Now, the hair, the make-up, the shoes, the jewellery . . . It's exactly what I want and so that's easier and more fun. My body, while still changing, feels increasingly like the body I was always meant to have. No better or worse, but more *accurate* somehow. I like these things.

Personally, I didn't embark on this voyage because I was especially craving the labels 'female' or 'woman' – although I am aware they are hugely important legally, culturally and societally. I'm just quite a lot happier living my life this way. Life is hard enough; if there's a change that makes it more bearable, grab it with both hands, I say.

Of course, many others *are* rejecting the traditional concept of transgender being a move from A to B. Actor Krishna Istha tells me: 'Why did I chose to shun binary notions of gender? Because it didn't make sense to me to have to like only certain things, and to not be able to wear a certain thing. I've always actively shunned binary notions of gender, was consistently called a tomboy even when I was a kid and didn't spend a second even thinking about what it all meant. Who decided what was for girls and what was for boys?'

They (Istha's preferred pronoun) tell me, 'I think gender is both an identity and a (false) biological legacy. And by that, I mean gender is often imposed on us due to our anatomy at birth. Some people choose to embrace it, some people shun it, and some people embrace parts of it and shun other parts.

'To me gender is an identity to some extent, in the way I relate to others and my community. It was important for me to claim the identity of "genderqueer" and "trans" to be able to communicate and create a sense of community for myself. It is a part of my identity, just like being Indian is, or like my sexuality is. It creates a whole picture of me and how I navigate the world.'

Few media franchises have inspired gender rebellion like *RuPaul's Drag Race*. Increasingly, thanks to Netflix, it has been elevated beyond cult viewing, and gender performance is becoming mainstream. 'I've always felt like I've fallen somewhere in the middle on the gender spectrum,' 2016 *RuPaul's Drag Race* All Star, Alaska, tells me. 'When I strip away all the trappings of the character that is Alaska Thunderfuck, I'm really what we all are when we take off our clothes – an amorphous squishy blob with a heart and a soul and a spirit and feelings. I feel very lucky I get to live and work in a space where the strict rules of gender are loosened and bent and broken – if even just for a night.'

THE END OF GAY?

An effect of the mainstreaming of transgenderism (oh come on, if one of the *Kardashians* is doing it, if there's trans models in H&M ads, it's mainstream) may well be a slight shift in numbers within the lesbian and gay community.

It seems likely that I was not the only child of the 1970s, 1980s or 1990s to confuse messages about gender with messages about sexual attraction. Chaz Bono, Paris Lees, Evan Urquhart, Carmen Carrera and untold scores more identified as gay or lesbian before eventually figuring out they were actually supposed to be men or women. Not all trans people were gay or lesbian prior to transition, but many were. Of course, that inversely means some trans people become gay or lesbian *after* they've transitioned.

It's a really a case of heightened awareness, both on the frontline of playgrounds and schools and also in the media. It's that train line metaphor. In the 1990s I had no idea that the Identity Express had a stop called Transville. Had I known, I would have never got off the train at Gay Town. Nowadays, few people aren't aware of Transville's exist-ence, so yeah, I think we'll see a whole bunch of kids stay on the train all the way to the end of the line and *simul-taneously* see many more gay or lesbian people hop back on the train and make the journey too.

CLEARLY I'm not saying *all* gay men and women are secretly trans. That would be crazy. After all, it was the realisation that NOT all gay men want to be women that initiated my therapy sessions. Of the first hundred femme gay men to grace *RuPaul's Drag Race*, only 6 per cent (to date) have gone on to transition. I actually think it's really important that 'camp' men and 'butch' women are allowed to carry on subverting those gender norms. *Orange is the New Black* star Lea DeLaria suggests, 'Butch dykes, even within our own community, are pariahs,' and that many face continued speculation about when (and not if) they'll transition. The same is also true of 'femme' gay men. Gendered behaviour and clothes shouldn't have to define an individual's gender identity. And, as we know, being transgender runs so, so much deeper than being a Kylie fan or wanting a beard.

I think we'll also see a generational difference in 'uptake' of trans services. I had a very definite choice to make: go for it, or 'make do' as a gay man. I chose to go for it, but I think a good number of gay men and women are now, quite naturally, re-questioning their identities in the wake of better information, but will decide to 'make do' for a number of reasons: family, relationships, age, career and simply 'can't be arsed'.

There is no doubt in my mind that uptake will be higher among children and teens, because access to hormone blockers delivers 'better results', bodily speaking, for their later transition. I've spoken to many young trans people on the cusp of puberty and they are chomping at the bit to get on the hormone blockers that will hold their bodies in 'genderless' stasis. If I was ten years old now, I would have sold my soul for a 'magic pill'. As adults who've already gone through puberty, we know there is no such pill.

Since starting my transition, I'm told – at least once a day – that I'm Brave™. I personally think I'd have been braver had I been six foot three and eighteen stone and *still* started my transition. I knew from my Cherry Filth days I'd probably 'pass' some day. I don't think you're any less Brave™ if you choose to 'make do'. Whether a person transitions or not, it's an ongoing process of accepting oneself and learning to live with the 'inner' you. Changing exterior things is no guarantee of happiness. It never is.

EPILOGUE
THE FINAL WORD

AKA Voiceover Carrie, Typing in Her Window

So it seems like my life will exist in two halves. I'm halfway through. If the first half was about figuring my life out, the second half, hopefully, will be about living it.

I think that's quite exciting! The glass is half full, not half empty! I'm so fired up by all the things I still want to do. Now that I'm who I was always meant to be, my accomplishments, professionally and personally, feel more like they belong to me. I feel active in my success, less disassociated. All that running around, chasing boys, book deals, status . . . I was looking for *me* the whole time. It's the most fundamental, but frustratingly amorphous, advice we give each other: 'be yourself'. Easier fucking said than done.

Of course, I still have goals. I've already said I now feel able to contemplate a meaningful relationship with a man. I'm no less picky, mind you, so don't hold your breath on that front. Professionally, I'm increasingly keen to write for TV and film and continue to boost my experience as a presenter or 'pundit'. God, if ever we needed the continued presence of diverse voices in the media, it's now.

I don't feel the same better-apply-to-*Big-Brother* urgency I once did. I'm not so much interested in fame, it's more that I like the work. I now don't feel like an imposter if I call myself a journalist. If those media things happen, they happen. I already feel like I won, so everything else is a bonus now. I don't think I have to prove anything to anyone. As long as I can carry on writing, I'm happy.

My friend Niall recently visited from Sydney – the same Niall I'd surveyed the horror of the XXL darkroom with. He hadn't been able to afford flights over for two and half years so had missed the whole 'Juno' incarnation thus far. Obviously he'd seen pictures on Instagram and Facebook, and we'd talked on Skype, but we hadn't been in the same room since I'd started the transition.

We had had afternoon tea at the Ham Yard Hotel in Soho. We caught up and he noted, 'You seem so much happier now.' I hadn't really thought about it, but he was right. All that time fighting against myself, the inner struggle. It's gone. I suppose I am happier, but the word I would use is 'content'. I am contented.

Has it all been worth it? Yes. It's worth every sideways glance, Twitter spat, injection and tablet. In the words of *Gender Outlaw* author Kate Bornstein, who I'd urge you *all* to read: 'Do whatever it takes to make your life worth living.' And that's advice for us all. What are you waiting for?

Fans of *Buffy the Vampire Slayer* will be familiar with the 'cookie dough' metaphor. Before I felt raw, malleable, unfinished. Now it feels like I'm baked, or at least bak*ing*. I spent so many long years *imagining* life as a girl.

Now I'm alive.

GLOSSARY

ASEXUAL Sexual identity describing someone with characteristically low sex drive or little interest in sex. Can also describe lack of sexual orientation.

BISEXUAL Sexual identity describing someone attracted to both genders.

CISGENDER A person whose gender identity matches the one they were assigned at birth.

DEMISEXUAL Sexual identity describing someone who rarely or infrequently experiences sexual attraction. Aka 'gray' or 'grey'.

GENDERQUEER/GENDER NON-BINARY Term to describe a person who identifies as neither man nor woman and exists outside of defined, binary notions of gender. 'Gender fluidity' refers to gender identity changing over an individual's lifetime.

INTERSECTIONALITY Term coined by Kimberlé Crenshaw to describe how the impact of multiple identities cannot be examined in isolation. Gender, skin colour, religion, class and disabilities will ALL impact on a person's life and status.

PANSEXUAL Sexual identity describing someone who is

attracted to people regardless of their gender orientation. Thought to be more inclusive than the binary 'bisexual'.

QUEER Umbrella term for any person not identifying as straight or cisgender.

SAPIOSEXUAL A person who finds intellect sexually arousing.

TRANSGENDER An umbrella term describing any individual who moves between traditional notions of gender. This can include 'trans' people, transsexuals, cross-dressers, drag kings and queens.

TRANSSEXUAL A term sometimes used to describe a transgender person who is medically altering one or more elements of their biological sex. Less commonly used than 'transgender'.

ACKNOWLEDGEMENTS

Thank you with all my heart to . . .
Kate Adair
Anthony Anaxagorou
Attitude magazine
Bola Ayonrinde
Natasha Bardon
Laura Bates
Adam Bennett
Holly Bourne
Kate Brunt
Matt Cain
Gemma Cairney
Dr Owen Carter
Niall Caverly
Kim Curran
Kat Dare
Angela Dawson
Ian Dawson
Janet Dawson
Joanne Dawson
Sarah Lea Donlan

Jo Elvin
Shon Faye
Fox Fisher
Emma Gannon
Darren Garrett
Nicole Gibson
Glamour magazine
Salena Godden
Bryony Gordon
Gavin Gunter
Dr Olivia Hewitt
Kate Hewson
Lisa Highton
Ayla Holdom
Sali Hughes
Mr Christopher Inglefield
Krishna Ishta
Kristian Johns
Owen Jones
Keri Kennedy
Isis King
Asifa Lahore
Lauren Laverne
Stuart Lee
Paris Lees
Beth Lintin
Dr Stuart Lorimer
Louis MacGillivray
Phyllis Martin
Ruby Mitchell

Jack Monroe
Leng Montgomery
Caitlin Moran
Patrick Ness
Dawn O' Porter
Lauren Oakey
Hanne Gaby Odiele
Samantha Powick
Non Pratt
Prince
Katie Roberts
Joe Romaine
Rebecca Root
Rory Smith
Sophia Spring
Nicola Strachan
Patrick Strudwick
Sallyanne Sweeney
Chardine Taylor-Stone
The Pool
Alaska Thunderfuck
Matthew Todd
Erik Tomlin
Mary-Kate Trevaskis
Dr Firhaas Tukmachi
Kerry Turner
Hannah Witton

ABOUT THE AUTHOR

JUNO DAWSON is the multi-award-winning author of dark teen thrillers. Her first non-fiction book, *Being a Boy*, tackled puberty, sex and relationships in a frank and funny fashion, and a follow-up for young LGBT people, *This Book is Gay*, came out in 2014. Juno is a regular contributor to *Attitude*, *Glamour*, *GT* and the *Guardian* and has contributed to news items concerning sexuality, identity, literature and education on BBC *Woman's Hour*, *Front Row*, *This Morning* and *Newsnight*. She writes full time and lives in Brighton.

Stories . . . voices . . . places . . . lives

We hope you enjoyed *The Gender Games*.
If you'd like to know more about this book
or any other title on our list, please go to
www.tworoadsbooks.com

For news on forthcoming Two Roads titles,
please sign up for our newsletter.

enquiries@tworoadsbooks.com

TwoRoadsBooks